Teaching Mathematics with ICT

Adrian Oldknow and Ron Taylor

CONTINUUM
London and New York

Continuum

The Tower Building
11 York Road
London SE1 7NX

370 Lexington Avenue
New York
NY 10017–6503

First published 2000

British Library Cataloguing-in-Publication Data

A catalogue record for this book is available from the British Library.

ISBN 0-8264-4806-2

Designed and typeset by Ben Cracknell Studios
Printed and bound in Great Britain by the Cromwell Press, Trowbridge, Wilts

Integrating Information and Communication Technology in Education

Series Editor: Michelle Selinger

Teaching Mathematics with ICT

Related titles

Julia Anghileri: *Teaching Number Sense*
Duncan Grey: *The Internet in School*
Avril Loveless: *The Role of IT*
Anthony Orton: *Pattern in the Teaching and Learning of Mathematics*
Brian Robbins: *Inclusive Mathematics 5–11*

Contents

Acknowledgements

Eugene Billam of Asher Research for assistance with TrueBasic; The British Educational and Communication Technology Agency; Microsoft Corporation for excerpts from Microsoft® Encarta® images reprinted by permission of Microsoft Corporation; Scala/Art Resource NY for reproduction of Leonardo's *Vitruvian Man*; The Teacher Training Agency for excerpts from *ICT Needs Identification* materials; Texas Instruments for their support with software and equipment.

We also wish to thank: Sam Crane, Regents Park School, Southampton; Alison Clarke-Jeavons, Admiral Lord Nelson School, Portsmouth; Peter Ransom, David Sadler and Ian Rimmer, The Mountbatten School, Romsey; Steve Downes, Gordon Jackson and Mark Pinsent, the City of Portsmouth Girls' School; Stella Rowlands and Theresa Rowlatt, Henry Beaufort School, Winchester; Jenny Thimbleby and Nicola Pennel, Hounsdown School, Hampshire.

Introduction

The relationships between mathematics, teaching and computers are long-standing and complex. The actual practice of mathematics has changed its nature considerably because of the availability of powerful computers, both in the workplace and on researchers' desks. But those very computers themselves are only powerful because of the variety of clever mathematical applications on which their operation relies. These include coding, data compression, fractals, cryptography and computational geometry. Experiments in the applications of computer technology to teaching have been widespread over the last 30 years or so. The advent of fast and widespread communications such as e-mail, the internet and video-conferencing are radically changing our access to data and information. The fierce competition and the size of the market for computer-based consumer products has ensured that prices have fallen to a point where it is now quite normal (in some areas of some countries, at least) for students' bedrooms to be better equipped than their school classrooms. So it is not surprising that many countries are now taking stock of their educational response to this 'Information Age'.

We shall need to emphasize here, and throughout the book, that mathematics is rather different from many subjects in its relationship to ICT-supported pedagogy. We take the view that at least one major rationale for including the compulsory study of mathematics in the secondary school is that it is widely applied in the world outside school – and that this implies that students will need to be able to use ICT tools both to solve mathematical problems and to communicate their results to others. Many of the techniques associated with school mathematics were developed to solve important problems at times when tools such as electronic calculators and computers were not available. The very existence of these computational tools is now having a profound effect on the way mathematics is being developed and applied in the world outside education. New skills of modelling, estimating, validating, hypothesizing and finding information are becoming more important than many traditional ones, such as accuracy of recall. Formal changes in education necessarily take longer to bring about than changes in practice in industry or commerce. An important issue for mathematics teachers is to ensure that their students are well prepared for their future lives and careers by gaining necessary skills, whether or not the curriculum and examination system explicitly encourage them.

The widespread presence of ICT in the mathematics classroom will not necessarily have any impact in bringing into question the current relevance of any particularly long-standing aspect of the mathematics curriculum. To take an extreme example we could imagine some very effective multimedia software that provides a self-learning guide to using obsolete tools such as a slide-rule, or a table of logarithms, for multiplication. The point here is that the use of the technology as a teaching aid will not, by itself, bring into question whether the content and skills being taught are actually relevant at all in our current technological society. Indeed, those responsible for the development of mathematics curricula may be unaware of the obsolescence, or significantly diminished importance, of some of its content. There are also aspects of content, such as matrices and complex numbers at advanced level, that are increasingly important in other subjects such as geography or engineering. These may be have been ruled out of current curricula on the grounds of difficulty in teaching and learning proficiency of basic techniques. However, ICT tools can obviate the need for proficiency with such techniques: many models of graphing calculators can, for example, manipulate both matrix and complex expressions. So ICT can enable students to concentrate on more interesting and important aspects of content. Despite the inertia of the formal curriculum, mathematics teachers need to be able to examine more critically the basis on which the knowledge, understanding and skills of the curriculum are founded.

A less obvious issue, but one which is arguably at least as important, is that citizens in a technological society need to have an informed view of just what computers can, and cannot, do. All too often we hear phrases like 'the computer won't let us do that', as if it was an animate (and stubborn) object. An increasing number of subjects, such as geography, chemistry and economics, make use of computer simulations. We know, and our students need to know, that these are not infallible but just someone's mathematical model of a situation that needs to be treated with a healthy amount of scepticism! So modelling and validation are now important aspects of mathematics that students should experience during their secondary school education.

Of course, most teachers do not have a great deal of control over the curriculum they teach. So they need to be able to apply ICT in ways that enhance the teaching and learning of the current established curriculum while also seeking to bring out some of the important relationships between mathematics and computer technology referred to above. The role of ICT in the teaching and learning process is not just constrained to uses such as an 'electronic blackboard' to assist in a teacher's exposition, or for 'hands-on' use by pupils working at a task, important as both those applications are. The technology may aid the teacher in the preparation for a lesson, e.g. in gathering data, or preparing materials. It may also have a role to play in the assessment of students' learning. So this is truly a book aimed to support the full *integration* of ICT into secondary school mathematics teaching.

We are acutely aware of widespread differences in the resourcing of mathematics departments. We have at times stared in wonder at demonstrations of fancy uses of the latest state-of-the-art technology and have come away with the frustration of knowing that such equipment would be out of our reach for the foreseeable future. So we have taken great care to be as realistic as possible about the kinds of resources that our readers may be able to get their hands on. We have tried to concentrate on generic ideas which can be realized using a variety of different forms of ICT including, wherever possible, cheaper hand-held devices such as graphing calculators and personal computers. We have been fortunate to be able to work with both Texas Instruments (TI) and with the UK's Mathematical Association (MA) to try to ensure that as many examples of resources as possible can be found on the accompanying CD-ROM and/or the TI and MA websites.

We have tried to make this book as accessible and relevant as possible to mathematics teachers from different countries and cultures. Of course, the very term 'secondary school' has different interpretations, but we are using it to include the teaching of pupils aged from about 11–18 years, with a concentration on those in the 11–16 range. From time to time we will refer to the current context either in the UK, or in England alone. This is because there are a number of interesting national initiatives in the use of ICT in education which provide some useful frameworks for the integration of ICT into subject teaching. It might be convenient to summarize the current UK situation at this point.

EDUCATIONAL ICT DEVELOPMENT IN THE UK

The major elements are training, resources and support.

Training

The New Opportunities Fund (NOF) has been created to channel funding from the government's National Lottery proceeds towards projects in public spending departments such as Health and Education. £230 million is being spent in 1999/2003 on training the vast majority of teachers and librarians currently working in maintained schools in the UK in the effective use of ICT. The government's Teacher Training Agency (TTA) has produced regulations that make it clear that the training must be subject focused, should take place with minimum disruption to teaching and should be tailored to the individual teacher's needs.

Resources

The government's British Educational and Communications Technology Agency (BECTa) is working with professional agencies and publishers to review the need for further software development. Those in the Department for Education and Employment (DfEE) responsible for government websites such as the National Grid for Learning (NGfL) and its Virtual Teacher Centre (VTC), are working together with the professional associations, such as the Mathematical Association (MA), to improve access to subject-based content.

Support

Financial support for new developments in schools is channelled to Local Education Authorities (LEAs) and schools in England via the Department for Education and Employment's (DfEE) Standards Fund. (There are similar mechanisms in other parts of the UK.) Details of this are contained in a large, and very complex, document called Circular 16/99. Within the details of its 31 different forms of individual grants is section B25, which is rather confusingly entitled 'National Grid for Learning'. In fact this provides for a very wide range of ICT purchases related to the curriculum, not just those needed to connect to the Internet. These include hardware, and purchases may include 'class sets of portable computing devices; whole class teaching aids such as projection equipment; digital cameras, scanners and digitisers and other equipment which can be used to help create educational resources'. At least 15% of the money must be spent on software. The budget for England is £150 million in 2000/2001, and is set to rise for 2001/2002.

At the time of writing the NOF-funded ICT training for all UK teachers is taking place, and the National Curriculum for the use of ICT in subject teaching has become compulsory in all courses of Initial Teacher Training in England. In both cases the TTA has produced a large amount of materials to support this training. We have written a book that draws upon our own experiences and beliefs, and should apply to any country's mathematics curriculum. We have taken care to ensure that it meets the requirements of the current UK training programmes and have included, within two 'bridging' sections, extracts from the relevant TTA materials. So, against this context, we conclude with an introduction to the structure of the book.

Chapter 1 is for you to work at privately! It is there to help you get a feel not only for the hardware, software and other ICT tools, but also to get some experience in using them to tackle some interesting bits of mathematics. Very often in working on courses with teachers we use the maxim: 'start from the mathematics'! Of course you will want to be thinking also about the role of such tools in teaching as well. By the end of this chapter you should be in a strong position to know:

(a) *what* ICT there is to use.

As a bridge into the next chapter we will take at look at the different styles of ICT use exemplified in the four mathematics case studies that the Teacher Training Agency (TTA) distributed to schools on its Needs Identification CD-ROM in preparation for the NOF-funded training. We also look at the TTA's review of ICT tools for mathematics.

Chapter 2 is where we break the curriculum down into bite-size chunks and look for ways in which ICT tools can support teaching and learning of specific pieces of mathematics content, such as number or algebra. However there are many dangers in creating false divisions between parts of mathematics, and in treating mathematics apart from other subjects, so we also try to inject examples of more synthetic, and cross-subject, approaches. By the end of this chapter you should be in a strong position to know:

(b) *which* aspects of school mathematics are amenable to its use.

As a bridge into the next chapter we will examine some of the teaching issues raised about ICT use in the case studies on the TTA Needs Identification CD-ROM, and review the TTA's expected outcomes for the ICT training.

Chapter 3 builds on the practical experience from Chapters 1 and 2 in developing a more analytical structure for the planning, implementation and evaluation of ICT use in teaching and learning. By the end of this chapter you should be in a strong position to know:

(c) *how* to select and plan for its effective pedagogic use.

We ask you to review your progress and to draw up an action plan for your future continued professional development (CPD) in the use of ICT in your teaching.

Chapter 4 looks outwards to what others have said, and researched, about the links between mathematics, ICT and education.

This is intended to help you answer the additional question:

(d) *why* should we aim to integrate ICT into mathematics teaching?

The range of references in this chapter should be particularly helpful if you intend to undertake any academic work, such as an MA module, as part of your CPD.

Chapter 5 attempts to take a peek into the future, and to look at how ICT, mathematics and mathematical pedagogy may develop in the next generation. At least this should raise the question:

(e) *where* is it going?

Even if does not actually provide any very reliable answers!

Finally we conclude with an appendix to assist you in obtaining copies of the programs and files referred to in the text.

A note of warning! The pace of change in ICT developments is very fast, so while we have taken considerable care to ensure that the material is up to date at the time of writing, it may well be that some of the websites to which we refer will change their content or even disappear. Similarly versions of software which we have used for illustrations may develop and not appear exactly in the form we show. This is the inevitable price of change, but we hope it will not detract too much from the worth of the book.

We are aware that different readers will have different experiences and different needs. So you may well want to skip sections on aspects with which you are familiar, or leave sections for later which you think less relevant to your current needs.

✎ *We have tried to give you plenty of opportunities for practical work to complement the text and we highlight these in this way.*

We have certainly had a great deal of challenge, fun and sense of reward in putting this book together. We very much hope that you have a fair share of each in reading through, and working at, the book. We wish you all the best in your future attempts to apply educational ICT in bringing the subject of mathematics to life for your students.

Adrian Oldknow and Ron Taylor
February 2000

To our friend and inspiration:
Warwick Evans

Chapter 1

What resources are, and will be available?

This chapter is for you to work at privately! It is here to help you get a feel not only for the available hardware, software and other ICT tools, but also to get some experience in using them to tackle some interesting bits of mathematics. Very often in working on courses with teachers we use the maxim: 'start from the mathematics!' Of course you will want to be thinking also about the role of such tools in teaching as well. By the end of this chapter you should be in a strong position to know *what* ICT there is to use. As a bridge into the next chapter we will take at look at the different styles of ICT use exemplified in the four mathematics case studies that the Teacher Training Agency (TTA) distributed to schools on its Needs Identification CD-ROM in preparation for the NOF-funded training.

Nowadays we tend to think of computers as a few boxes on (or under) the desk or a thin box on the knee of the person opposite in the train. This reflects the move from the 1960s onwards to concentrate on personal computer use. So companies purchased desktop PCs (Personal Computers) to improve the productivity of their employees, and now households purchase similar hardware for the entertainment (and/or education) of family members. But when you purchase a PC you are buying far more than the combination of silicon chips, circuit boards, video displays etc. which make up the hardware elements of the system. Like a body without a nervous system, a PC cannot be used without the system's computer programs (the system software – called the operating system), which make it responsive to hardware elements such as the keyboard and the mouse, and allow it to communicate with peripheral hardware such as disks, CD-ROMs, printers and telephone lines. But again, like a body without a brain, the PC is relatively useless without computer programs to help us carry out the tasks we would like to use it for (the applications software). So for the purposes of this chapter we will include hardware and system software in the next section, and applications software in the subsequent section.

Returning to our company employee using a PC at her/his desk, the application software is likely to include familiar names for items, such as a wordprocessor, a spreadsheet, a database, and support for sending and receiving messages (e-mail). This kind of software is often now called generic software (and given a name such as an office suite). By 'generic' we really mean multipurpose. Such software can also play an important part in helping teachers to carry out their job more effectively, e.g. by better record keeping. The household PC is likely to have software for playing games, for getting information from a CD-ROM (such as an encyclopaedia) and for connecting to the Internet. Each of these may well have educational applications, but they are aimed at the individual user and may not easily relate to the actual curriculum in schools.

So we can already distinguish two classes of applications software: those that can make the individual learner and teacher more efficient, and those that can contribute to individuals' learning. In the context of the school, though, we need to consider a third context, that of helping the teacher teach a class more effectively. This will require consideration both of the available specialist and pedagogical software in a given subject such as mathematics, and also the kinds of hardware that are available, and appropriate, for use when teaching a whole class, or a group, of students.

Thus the aim of this chapter is to ensure that, as far as possible, you are aware of the current range of hardware and software to support teachers and learners inside and outside the classroom so that you can make informed choices when planning your use of ICT. We have tried to do this in as non-technical a manner as possible, making few assumptions about your previous experience. We hope that you will not feel patronized by this, and will skip over any sections with which you are already quite familiar.

The Teacher Training Agency has widely circulated its publication *The Use of Information and Communications Technology in Subject Teaching: Identification of Training Needs: Secondary Mathematics*. This sets out the expected outcomes of ICT training for secondary school mathematics teachers in terms of nine points to do with 'effective teaching and assessment methods – section A', and a further nine points to do with 'teachers' knowledge and understanding of, and competence with, information and communication technology – section B'. This chapter is particularly concerned with supporting you in achieving aim B13: *Teachers should know those features of ICT which can be used, separately or together, to support teaching and learning.*

1a   ICT HARDWARE FOR EDUCATION

Currently the term IT (Information Technology) is being increasingly replaced by the acronym ICT (Information and Communication Technology). In each case it is to emphasize that PCs, and other computers, are just one – albeit very important – element in the range of electronic devices that is revolutionizing our society. In the introduction we referred to the directive from the UK Department for Education and Employment (DfEE circular 16/99) that explains how a source of funding may be used to support ICT in 2000/2001:

> *Schools may purchase ICT equipment (this may include class sets of portable computing devices; whole class teaching aids such as projection equipment; digital cameras, scanners and digitizers and other equipment which can be used to help create educational resources)*

We will now take a closer look at what these, and other, items of equipment can do.

Stand-alone PCs

Of course, systems vary, but the central element of a PC usually consists of a rather drab box, with the on/off button, one or two slots for disks, and a couple of small lights on the front. On the back are a variety of sockets for connection to the other components. Inside the box is the microprocessor (which used to be called the CPU: central processing unit), with a name such as *Pentium II*. This sends out instructions to the other parts of the PC at a frequency measured in Hertz (Hz), which is the rate of 1 cycle per second. Current PCs usually have 'clock rates' measured in hundreds of megaHertz, which means getting towards 1 billion clock-ticks per second! Instructions, and unchanging data, needed by the microprocessor are stored in Read Only Memory (ROM). This is memory that does not change, and is not volatile – that is to say that when you switch the machine off it does not become forgotten. The changing bits of data are stored in Random Access Memory (RAM), which now usually come in multiples of 16 Megabytes (Mb). A byte is a measure of information that depends on how the PC stores information, but it can hold the equivalent of between one and four printing characters, like a letter or a digit. So a modern PC with 64Mb RAM can hold the equivalent of about 160,000 printed pages in its 'memory'. RAM is volatile, and its contents are lost when the PC is switched off.

The other key element of the central box is usually hidden within it. This is the hard disk or hard drive, which is non-volatile, and which can hold a massive amount of data, but which cannot be retrieved quite as quickly as from RAM. The capacity of hard disks is measured in gigabytes (Gb), which are a billion bytes. Again a modern PC may have about 100 times as much hard disk space as RAM, and one use of the hard disk is to extend the available RAM by creating what is known as 'virtual memory'. Some systems will copy the contents of RAM onto the hard drive when you close down the computer (the 'suspend' mode) so that you can restart from where you left off. As we shall see later, there may actually be more than one hard disk, but the principal one is also usually referred to as the 'C: drive'. The hard drive of a PC will come with some software already installed on it. The essential software is called an Operating System (OS). There will usually be other software, especially generic software such as a wordprocessor, already installed. Software included within the price of a PC is referred to as 'bundled software'.

The main sockets at the back are for the connection of the power supply, the monitor, the keyboard and the mouse. The keyboard is more or less that of the old-fashioned typewriter, using the familiar QWERTY system. As well as the usual shift-key and shift-lock, for moving between lower and upper case symbols, there are special keys called 'Ctrl' (for Control) and 'Alt' (for Alternate). In manuals you will sometimes see shorthand being used where, e.g. Ctrl-C (or ^C) means 'while holding down the Ctrl key press the C key, and then release both.' Similarly Alt-C means using both the Alt and C keys. Some keyboards contain some light bulbs (actually Light Emitting Diodes – LEDs) to show whether any of the keyboard locks (shift, alphabetic, numeric) are currently selected. There is also an additional row of usually 12 keys, called function keys, denoted by symbols like F7, which have special meanings in different circumstances.

The PC's display unit is called a 'monitor', although sometimes the older phrase 'Visual Display Unit' (VDU) is used. Nowadays these are almost always colour displays, usually with a resolution considerably finer than that of a conventional domestic TV. The size of monitor is usually given in inches, so that a 15in. monitor will have a maximum diagonal distance from corner to corner of the box of 15in., with a rather smaller diagonal distance across the actual display. The 'aspect ratio' is the ratio between the horizontal and vertical measurements of the screen, usually 4:3, so that a 15in. monitor has a display a bit less than 12in. wide and 9in. high. The 'resolution' of the screen is measured in 'pixels', which are the smallest picture drawing elements (like atoms). A high resolution monitor may have 1240 pixels horizontally and 1024 vertically, sixteen-times more detail than the 320×256 screen of a typical (not digital) TV set. Of course a high resolution picture in many colour tones will require a large amount of RAM to store it and this needs to be accessed very quickly. Hence the importance of having large and fast video RAM. The screen may be divided into a number of regions, called 'windows'. The screen will usually show a small moveable image (an icon) which looks like an arrow-head. This 'pointer' can be moved around the screen using the 'mouse'. This has a small ball on its underside, which is usually dragged in contact with a 'mouse mat'. On the top it may have one, two or three buttons and/or perhaps a wheel. When you have moved the mouse pointer over a part of the display you are interested in there are three key techniques available. The first is to make just a single click on the left-hand button, which normally highlights the image under the cursor. The second is to hold the left-hand button down while dragging the mouse across its mat, which normally drags the image across the screen. The third is to click the left-hand button twice in rapid succession. This double click normally causes an action to take place linked with the icon.

All but the oldest PCs now have operating systems based on the components of Windows, Icons, Mouse and Pointer, or WIMP for short. Perhaps the best known

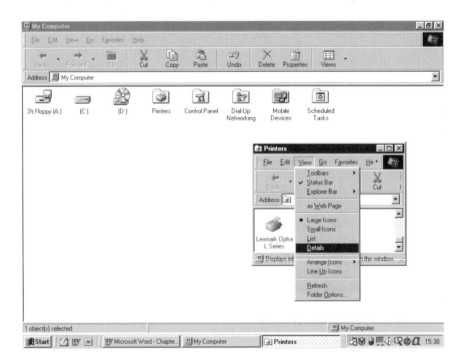

current such operating system is the family of *Microsoft Windows* products. The picture on p. 4 shows a typical screen. Here the very top line of the screen shows we are in the 'My Computer' window. Below this is a 'menu bar' and below this are a number of 'buttons' with icons attached. Then there is an 'address bar', and below this we have the actual contents window with eight icons. The fourth of these is called a 'folder' which has information about the printers that the system has been set up to use. Double-clicking on this folder icon opens up a second window called 'Printers'.

The highlighting in the top line of the Printers window shows that it is the one now being used (the 'active' window). Clicking on the <u>V</u>iew option in the menu bar causes a 'menu' to be 'dropped down'. Now the mouse can be used to select an item from the menu, such as <u>D</u>etails. At the very foot of the main display screen there are some important icons. The group on the right tell you about the system, such as the current time. The buttons in the middle refer to currently open windows, and can be clicked to make one of them the active window. The 'Start' button in the bottom-left corner is used to install and run software, to alter system settings, and to shut the PC down.

Now we return to the slots in the front of the PC's main box. One or more of these is for use with a 3.25in. diskette, which typically holds about 1.44Mb of data. This is shown on the first icon in the 'My Computer' window, and is also given the identification as the 'A: drive'. Some PCs may have two similar slots for diskettes to facilitate copying data from disk to disk. In that case the second will be called the 'B: drive'. The second icon in the window is the internal hard disk drive called the 'C: drive'. The third icon refers to another slot in the front of the box, called the 'D: drive', which is a retractable tray that can hold a Compact Disk (CD). Most PCs include the hardware inside to make sounds (an 'audio card') and connect to external speakers, so that you should be able to play a music CD on your PC. However, CDs can be used to store all sorts of data: audio, video, image, text, programs, etc. Until recently they were prohibitively expensive to re-record, and this was emphasized by calling them CD-ROMs (for 'read only memory'). More recently other forms of drive are also being added to the main box including Digital Video Disks (DVD) and 'ZIP-drives', which are mainly used to back-up (i.e. make secure copies of) data.

We have now dealt with most of the components that are usually to be found on any PC. Returning to the sockets on the back of the main PC box there is usually a 'parallel port' for attaching a printer cable, and one or more 'serial ports' for attaching other devices such as a joystick. If the PC is to be connected to the telephone network for access to e-mail and the internet it will need to have a 'modem'. This is a device to code and uncode computer signals into forms suitable for sending via telephone cables. It may be internal (i.e. the hardware is inside the computer box), or external. An external modem is connected to the serial port of the computer, and to a telephone point. An internal modem just requires a connection from the telephone point to the back of the computer. The speed of a modem is given in kilobits per second (kbps). A printing character is usually represented by an 8-bit binary number – so a 115.2 kbps modem can transfer data at a maximum rate of around 14,000 characters per second – equivalent to about four A4 pages of printing – or one medium-sized high resolution picture! This is why documents containing many images can take a very long time to transfer. The actual transfer rate also depends upon the kind of connection being used. Using a conventional telephone line, 4,000 characters per second is about the fastest currently attainable.

Most manuals assume everything works perfectly. However, from time to time, you may find your PC failing to respond, or behaving in an unfamiliar way. There is a combination of keys which will usually retrieve the situation: press the Ctrl, Alt and Del (Delete) buttons simultaneously (Ctrl+Alt+Del). Often this will enable the PC to start up from the beginning. This is known as a 're-boot'. You will normally 'close down' your computer by clicking in the 'Start' Icon at the bottom left-hand corner of the screen.

Now we have established the common ground for most PCs we will take a look at a number of variants now available.

Networked PCs

Each PC on a network is called a 'workstation' or 'terminal'. Normally it is an ordinary PC with some extra hardware and cabling to allow it to connect to a network. Thus it could be used as a stand-alone PC when not connected. Sometimes (usually with older systems) the terminals do not have any external disk drives, and (rarely) they may not even have an internal hard drive. At the heart of each network is a special PC (or more powerful computer) called a 'file server'. This will have access to a variety of large central storage devices on which the Network Manager will have installed all the software. Often there will be more than one network. For example there may be one or more networks within a school, called Local Area Networks (LANs), but also the school offices may be connected to a network linking a group of local schools and a central office.

In addition to the usual operating system software it should be possible now to access a range of software, information sources and video clips held centrally on the file server using an 'in-school intranet'. The network may also be connected to the telephone system so that workstations can access the internet. Workstations may be dedicated to a particular person and kept on someone's desk, or they may be 'open access' and available to any authorized user, such as in a library. Groups of workstations may be held together in a dedicated room, sometimes called an 'IT suite', for work with classes. In any of these cases the normal etiquette is to 'log on' when you sit down at a work-station by entering your name and password, and to 'log off' when you finish your session.

Laptop computers

Nowadays these often have a very similar specification to desktop PCs, and cost a relatively small amount more. Nearly all modern laptops have clear flat colour displays inside their lids. Most have an alternative to a mouse attached to the keypad. This might be a touch-sensitive pad, or a 'tracker ball'. They can be powered by mains electricity, or by special rechargeable batteries. These batteries will power the laptop usually for between two and five hours. When using batteries it is very important to follow the makers' instructions about keeping batteries in good condition. A nice feature of working with a laptop is that usually the operating system offers a 'suspend mode' where the computer can be 'sent to sleep' at any point and will 'wake up' ready to go from the same place in an application. While there is less room to add additional hardware than on a PC, there are usually one or two small slots to take 'PCMCIA' cards, e.g. for connecting to mobile phones or modems. Some laptops do not contain built-in diskette or CD-ROM drives to reduce weight, but can be connected to an external drive, or to a 'host' PC. Nearly all laptops have sockets for connection to external PC monitors. Some laptops also have video sockets for connection to the video input of a TV monitor.

Notebook (and sub-notebook) computers

Designed to be very lightweight these will usually fit into a pocket. Mostly they have a monochrome display screen. Newer versions have an operating system similar to that for PCs, such as Microsoft's Windows CE. The start-up screen usually displays a number of icons for built-in applications such as diary, address book, spreadsheets and wordprocessor. These are usually selected using a number of dedicated buttons on the keypad ('hot keys'). They can be linked directly to a printer, or with a PC, where the information is exchanged via a cable. They usually work from conventional batteries as used in radios and flashlights. Instead of using diskettes many will accept removable memory cards known as 'flash-ROM cards'.

Palm-top computers

Smaller still than notebooks, these computers usually have a touch-sensitive screen so that menu choices can be made by tapping directly on a given area using a small stylus. Many also have software which can identify handwriting and replace handwritten text with printed versions.

Personal organizers

Cheaper than palm-tops or notebooks, these usually contain some dedicated 'personal productivity' applications such as a diary, notepad or address book.

Graphing calculators

Of particular importance for mathematics, and for numerate subjects such as geography and science, these are a blend of calculator and computer technology. Their keyboards normally resemble a calculator keypad where each key may have, say, three different functions. For example on the TI-83, the 0 key can be used to enter the digit 0, but in combination with the 'alpha' key it will produce the letter 'V', and in combination with the '2nd' key it will produce the symbol '<'. The display screen is usually a monochrome LCD with a limited resolution of around 120 by 90 pixels. Graphing calculators (GCs) are powered by ordinary batteries but also have a hearing-aid style battery as back-up. Values, data and programs stored in RAM (typically 32 Kb or more) are thus retained even the GC is switched off. Modern GCs may also contain large amounts of 'flash-ROM', which can be used to store applications software, archive data, etc. (effectively the GC's hard-disk drive).

The built-in software will carry out all the normal mathematical, scientific, statistical and financial calculations. In addition the software enables a wide variety of graphs to be drawn and analysed. Some versions will also perform symbolic manipulation. Instead of a mouse, four cursor keys are used to move around the screen. Nearly all models have the capacity to exchange data with similar GCs, with PCs, and with compatible products such as data-loggers. Nearly all models have teachers' versions with large LCD display screens for use with an overhead projector (OHP). Versions are now appearing which will also connect to a TV for large display.

> *Note:* UK usage usually refers to 'graphic calculators', or to 'graphical calculators', whereas we think the US usage of 'graphing calculators' is rather more accurate. Better still would be to use something like PCT for Personal Computing Technology!

Whole-class displays

If you are working with a whole class, whether or not they all have access to ICT tools themselves, you may well want to be able to draw everyone's attention to the same display. Just as there are a number of ways of deploying ICT tools in the classroom, so there is a range of means of providing whole-class displays.

- *Large colour monitors*: these can be up to 26in., but are usually very bulky and quite expensive. Flat screen technology is only just becoming available and will remain very expensive in the short term, but in the future we can expect these to become far more common.
- *Data projectors*: these connect directly to the VGA output of a PC and contain a high-powered bulb which throws a colour image onto a screen or wall. They can be permanently mounted, or there are portable versions. Prices are coming down fast but currently they cost around twice as much as a PC. They accept a variety of input sources such as PC, audio and video.
- *Interactive whiteboards*: these are still relatively expensive and relatively rare. The computer's output is displayed on the surface of the board, which the teacher can also write on using large pens. The whiteboard is 'intelligent' in that you can interact with projected application software by tapping directly onto portions of the board corresponding to buttons, icons, etc. for the software. Currently they cost around five times that of a PC.
- *OHP displays*: there are display pads which connect to a PC and which produce a VGA monochrome or colour image on a transparent screen which lies on top of a conventional OHP. Unless the room is slightly darkened, and the OHP has a high power bulb, these displays can be hard to read, and are becoming obsolete. However the more robust LCD displays for use with graphing calculators are far less expensive and seem to work well in normal light.
- *TV interfaces*: a number of commercial companies make adapters to connect the VGA output from a PC or laptop to the Video input of a conventional TV or VHS recorder. These, used in conjunction with one or more large TV sets, can provide a low-cost solution to providing whole-class displays (see, for example: http://www.lindy.com).
- *Graphing calculators*: as mentioned above, the output from most models of GCs, and associated data-capture devices, can be displayed via OHP, TV or data projector.

Data capture devices

- *Motion detectors*: these emit ultra-sound signals which are reflected by the nearest object. By timing the gap between sending and receiving a signal, the detector can calculate the distance to the nearest object. Estate agents now use similar devices to measure dimensions of rooms in houses. Sending out signals at frequent intervals, the detector can track the movement of an object by storing data on time and distance. Such data can be captured remotely (such as with pupils on a running track) and later transferred to a computer or graphing calculator for analysis and display. For example, the TI Calculator Based Ranger (CBR) costs about the same as a graphing calculator and has a range of between 0.5m and 6m.
- *Sensors*: the motion detector is a special kind of sensor: for measuring distance. There is a wide range of sensors designed mainly for scientific experiments, which can measure, e.g., temperature, light intensity, voltage, sound intensity, force, pressure, acceleration, acidity, heart rate, amounts of CO_2 etc. Such sensors (or probes) are used in conjunction with a box, called an 'interface', which allows them to be set up by, and to download data to, computers and graphing calculators. For example, the TI Calculator Based Laboratory (CBL) costs about twice as much as a graphing calculator and has probes for temperature, light intensity and voltage.
- *Digital cameras*: these are now quite common in high street stores. They are cameras which are designed for single images, like a conventional camera, which store them usually on an internal flash-ROM or diskette. These images can be downloaded to a PC where they can be edited, saved in one of the conventional formats for exchanging pictures (such as JPEG) and/or inserted into documents. There are also digital video cameras, like a conventional camcorder, which also have large amounts of local storage. They can transfer data to PCs which can be edited to produce, say, video clips in a standard format (such as AVI).
- *Scanners*: these are devices to produce digital images of source objects, such as text, photographs, handwritten documents, etc. The technology is that used in fax machines, and so the sheer volume of sales has led to rapid falls in prices. The accompanying software often includes tools to enable typed text to be scanned and turned into meaningful text, rather than just a graphic image. This process is called Optical Character Recognition (OCR). Some can also be 'taught' to recognize, and convert, handwriting. It is also possible to use some fax machines as scanners.

Printers

These have improved dramatically in recent years, and prices have also fallen. The best quality is usually obtained with a laser printer, but colour versions are still very expensive. Colour inkjet printers are now very common and can print with a quality comparable with a laser printer (but usually slower). Ribbon-based (dot matrix) printers, which were the most common ones ten years ago, are now virtually obsolete. Consumables (laser toner, inkjet cartridges, coated paper, etc.) can be quite expensive.

Special kinds of paper, e.g. for photographs, overhead transparencies (OHT), labels, etc. are available, but can also be quite expensive.

The educational context

Now we have considered the main forms of ICT hardware we can attempt to place them in an educational context. This will very much depend upon the extent to which a school already has ICT resources and what it sees as their main purpose. We will consider four separate contexts:

1. a teacher using ICT to help plan, prepare and manage teaching;
2. individual pupils using ICT outside normal lessons;
3. a group of pupils using ICT within a lesson;
4. a teacher using ICT with a whole class.

Using ICT to plan, prepare and manage teaching
In order to plan, prepare and manage your teaching you will need to have access to a PC or laptop. This might be a workstation on a school network, possibly in a computer lab, open-access area, library or staff work room. It could be a laptop or stand-alone PC you use in the mathematics office, or at home. You will need to have access to the sorts of application software and hardware for mathematics education relevant to the part of the curriculum in which you plan to work (e.g. graph-plotter, spreadsheet, graphing calculator, data-logger, etc.), other forms of resources (reference books, text books, task-sheets, instruments, etc.). You may need to be able to access the internet to retrieve other resources and/or information.

You will need suitable generic software to enable you to prepare your lesson plans, task-sheets, assessment records, evaluations, etc. You may need to be able to scan in information from other sources, such as a book. You will also need to be able to produce printed output either in place, using a connected printer, or by saving your work to diskette so that you can obtain hard copy using another work station, etc.

Individual pupils using ICT outside normal lessons
You may want to plan that students follow up work, write up reports, prepare for new work, etc. You will need to consider what kinds of access they may have outside the lesson, either in school, at a public library or centre or at home. Thus you will need to know what facilities exist within school, such as open-access areas, use of school networks outside teaching times, availability within the school library, etc., and what software is available. You can also ask pupils to tell you what access they have to computers locally or within their own homes. You will then need to consider what sorts of software they may have already, and how they may obtain access from other sources. It may be that hand-held technology, such as graphing calculators, would be an alternative. Again you will need to know which pupils have access to such technology. It may be that the school has provision to lend graphing calculators to students to take off-site.

A group of pupils using ICT within a lesson

You may be able to arrange access to just one or two PCs in your classroom – perhaps workstations to a network, or PCs on trolleys, or laptops – or maybe you have access to just a few graphing calculators. One way to deploy them is to use them with a group of students. This may be because, say, different groups are working at different aspects of a topic, or that you plan to give each group ICT access in turn.

A teacher using ICT with a whole class

If the school has one or more computer suites, it may be possible to book a computer room for one or more lessons. In this case students will usually have access to a workstation (perhaps shared) for the whole lesson. If the school is well equipped it may be that one or more of the mathematics classrooms has several workstations. Alternatively, it may be that there are sufficient lap-tops available (or other suitable portable devices such as graphing calculators) to share between the class. Another important form of organization that you need to consider is the use of a single PC, laptop or graphing calculator together with a whole class display.

It is now time to consider what sorts of mathematics software are available.

1b   SOFTWARE FOR MATHEMATICS EDUCATION

Because there are so many types of software currently available it is useful to consider how any piece of software addresses three particularly important sets of questions for mathematics teachers:

- **Pedagogical**: can it be used to help teach content, to develop concepts, to increase knowledge, to improve understanding, to practise and reinforce skills?
- **Mathematical**: can it be used to compute results, to produce tables, to draw graphs, to solve problems, to manipulate expressions, to compute statistics?
- **Organizational**: can it help me to produce materials more efficiently, to keep records, to manage time, to communicate with others, to find resources?

In 1997 the DfEE/NCET published a review of software for curriculum subjects. The section 'Review of software for mathematics – Key Stages 3 and 4' concentrated on the following type of software for mathematics:

- **small software**: i.e. programs aimed at specific, highly-focused, curriculum content
- **programming languages**: e.g. *Logo, Basic*
- **generic software**: particularly spreadsheets, but also databases
- **content-free, subject specific**: e.g. graph plotting software (GPS)
                                         computer algebra systems (CAS)
                                         dynamic geometry software (DGS)
                                         data handling software (DHS)
- **courseware**: i.e. structured curriculum materials with integral use of software
- **graphic calculators** (GC) (or graphing calculators)
- **CD-ROM and the internet** as sources of data.

We shall devote this part of the chapter to taking a detailed look at examples from each category. Of course the available titles, and their features, change constantly so we can only reflect the current position. In order to make this more than a paper exercise we have, with the help of Texas Instruments, provided you with some sample software on the accompanying CD-ROM. Further sources of free, trial or demonstration software can be found on the Mathematical Association's website: http://www.m-a.org.uk . We shall give more information about useful websites for mathematics towards the end of this section.

There are also other types of software related to mathematics testing which are outside the scope of this section. These include Integrated Learning System (ILS), item-banks of examination questions and revision tests for public examinations.

Small software: i.e. programs aimed at specific, highly-focused, curriculum content

Again these come in a variety of forms. Perhaps the most frequently used examples are in the form of games or challenges where the interaction by an individual, or a group of pupils, with the computer, involves them in practising and applying some particular mathematical skill or knowledge. There are many advantages of using ICT in such a context. Here are just a few:

- the computer responds to pupils in a non-judgemental way;
- it can motivate and hold attention through the use of moving images, sounds, etc.;
- pupils can respond in their own time;
- pupils can refine their strategies as the result of feedback;
- the teacher is freed from having to check answers;
- pupils and the teacher can co-operate together in working at problems posed by the computer.

To illustrate the kind of software available we have produced some simple examples of small programs – see the Appendix. We must stress that these are not 'professional versions' written by programmers (and so may 'crash' if used in ways that were not anticipated!), but they are 'home-made' samples provided in order to discuss some of the different features of small programs. We have also provided some similar programs for the TI-83 graphic calculator. The programs are:

GLASS
BEARINGS
TRANSFORM

Load and run the program GLASS. This is a simple version of computer-aided design (CAD) software written some years ago for a leading UK manufacturer of high-quality drinking glasses. The idea is for the designer to specify a few points on the screen through which a smooth curve will be 'faired' to give the impression of the profile of the right-hand side of the glass. In reality the points would be specified in an analogue fashion using a pointing device such as light-pen, tracker-ball or mouse. For the educational context, students have to define the points by giving their co-ordinates with reference to a grid. Try entering five or six points to start with. When all the points have been defined, the software first draws a smooth profile curve through the points, and then produces the (crude) impression of the glass by revolving the profile through 60°, 120° and 180° towards the viewer and drawing some cross

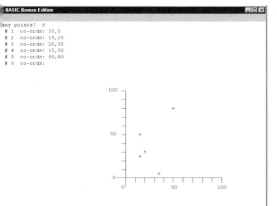

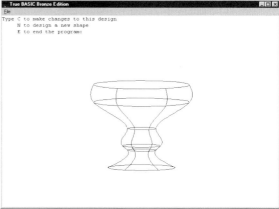

sections (ellipses). You can then modify the design by changing, adding and/or removing the points used to define the original profile. The object of this program is to achieve a pleasant shape. In order to do this you have to learn how to control the shape by the manipulation of the control points. In order to communicate their position you have to apply, and practise, your knowledge of co-ordinates in the first quadrant. Thus, from a mathematical viewpoint, it is an example of 'small software' in that it exercises students' facility with a standard piece of the geometry curriculum. There are many other commercial examples of small software that address this piece of mathematics, such as games involving the location of 'buried treasure' on a pirates' island or a 'missing elephant' in Manhattan!

Now load and run the program called BEARINGS. This is a much more 'closed' piece of software than GLASS. The computer screen just shows a vertical line segment *ON* representing North (000°), and generates another segment *OP* at some random angle to it. The object of the 'game' is for the viewer to try to estimate the bearing of *P* from *N* in degrees using the conventional notation. When you input your estimate *x* for the bearing, the computer displays another segment *OQ* where the bearing of *Q* from *N* is *x*°. Now the display screen provides visual feedback, which allows you to see whether you have made an under- or over-estimate. You continue, using trial-and-improvement, until your input is within say 5° of the exact value.

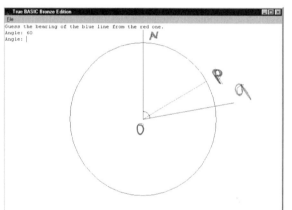
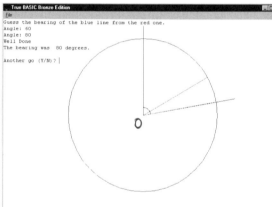

Finally load and run the program called TRANSFORM. This is a *TrueBasic*™ version of the program developed in section 5.5 of *Microcomputers in Geometry*, A. Oldknow, Ellis Horwood 1987. It has been written explicitly to illustrate two different approaches in the exploration of transformation geometry. You can use it to define your own starting shape (the 'object') and then to perform a sequence of transformations on it, producing its 'images' using a combination of translations, rotations, reflections and enlargements. Alternatively you can let the computer define a starting shape and a randomly chosen target shape so that you have the challenge of finding a single transformation, or chain of transformations, to map the object onto the target. So, for example, you could apply the program using the first approach as an 'electronic blackboard', projected for interactive whole-class teaching either from a PC or with a graphing calculator. You could also use it this way in the second mode, or students could work 'hands-on' with multiple screens.

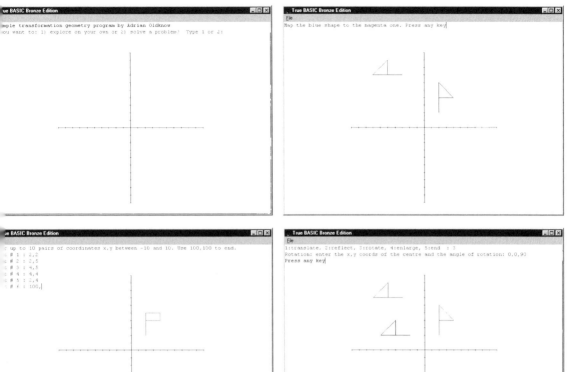

Programming languages: e.g. *Logo*, *Basic*

The capacity of modern computers, including graphing calculators, is now such that many of the applications that previously required teachers to write blocks of code in a programming language can now be performed within the command structure of suitable software. For example, the simulation of the sums of scores from a number of rolls of two dice, which might have been carried out by a short *Basic* program, can now be easily carried out using the data lists on a graphing calculator. Similarly the creation of a regular polygon, which is a common task using *Logo*, can be performed by a number of constructions and transformations using dynamic geometry software, which also affords the opportunity to develop procedures. There are aspects of the mathematics curriculum where the writing of short programs by pupils using *Logo*, *Basic* or the programming language of a graphing calculator may well be appropriate. Fortunately there are now versions of *Logo* (*MSW Logo*™) and *Basic* (*TrueBASIC*™) that are available to schools at no cost via the Internet (see the set of links on the Mathematical Association's website: http://www.m-a.org.uk).

Here we will illustrate some programs in *MSW Logo*™, in *TrueBASIC*™ and in the programming language of the TI-83 graphing calculator. If you are not very familiar with graphing calculators we suggest you skip that section and return to it later when you have had some experience of its other facilities.

Logo

When you start *MSW Logo*™ the screen shows two windows. The bottom part, known as the Commander, is where you enter instructions. Most *Logo* commands can be abbreviated, and they can be strung together using spaces to separate them. With the cursor in the bottom line of the Commander enter the string:

CS FD 100 RT 90 FD 50

and press the Enter key (i.e. the large key on the right of the keyboard, next to '@'). Your commands are transferred into the 'history' area of the Commander. If there are no errors then you should see the graphic image change on the *MSW Logo*™ Screen Window. The triangular arrowhead shows the current position and heading of the cursor and it is known as the 'screen turtle', or just 'turtle', from the earlier use of *Logo* with floor robots called 'turtles'.

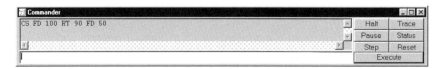

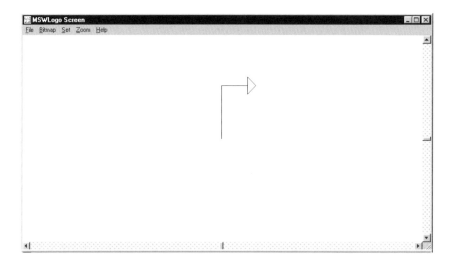

There were just four commands:

CS	ClearScreen
FD 100	Forward 100 units
RT 90	Right Turn 90 degrees
FD 50	Forward 50 units

The power of *Logo* is in the 'extensibility' of the language, which means you teach it new words, by defining procedures. To illustrate this, type EDIT "HEX in the command line.

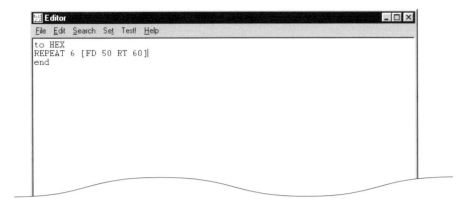

This opens up another window: the Editor window. Put the cursor before the 'end' statement and press Enter. Then type the line: REPEAT 6 [FD 50 RT 60]. Open the File menu and select the first option: Save & Exit. This has defined the new word HEX which uses a REPEAT loop. This draws six sides by going forward 50 units and then turning right through an (external) angle of 60 degrees. Enter: CS HEX in the command line to draw a hexagon.

```
to HEX
REPEAT 6 [FD 50 RT 60]
end
```

Suppose we want to 'tile' the screen with hexagons. We could start by trying to draw a band of them across the screen. The mathematical challenge is to find where to position the cursor after drawing one hexagon so that the next one joins on cleanly.

We can define another procedure using:

EDIT "SLIDE

```
to SLIDE
PU RT 90 FD 100*COS (30) LT
90 PD
end
```

Here we use the commands PU and PD for PenUp and PenDown, so that we do not leave a trace across the last hexagon. We have also used some trigonometry to calculate the required displacement. You can test the program by keying, e.g., CS HEX SLIDE HEX.

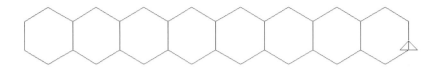

Finally we shall put the ideas together by using EDIT 'HEXBAND' and entering the program to draw eight hexagons side by side. First, though, we have to clear the screen and move the cursor to the left-hand side of the screen.

```
to HEXBAND
CS PU LT 90 FD 350 RT 90 PD
REPEAT 8 [HEX SLIDE]
end
```

 Can you now define a procedure, maybe called HEXTILE, which puts say 4 HEXBANDS cleanly above each other?

Although *Logo* is usually used for graphical output, it can be used to print numbers, words, etc. like other programming languages. The procedure ITER illustrates the point. Here "x means 'the variable named x', while :x means 'the value stored in the variable named x'. PR is the shorthand for Print. This little program is using an iteration to find successive approximations to the golden ratio ϕ, which is a solution to the equation:

$$\phi = 1 + 1/\phi$$

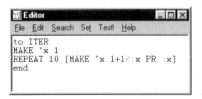

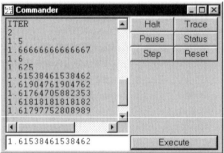

Note: If students have met any *Logo* programming in primary schools they may have learned to call these 'quote x' and 'dots x'.

Basic

When you run *TrueBASIC*™ you have an Edit window in which you enter your programs. Like other versions of *Basic*, you can use line numbers if you wish, but in most cases they are unnecessary. Each program has to start with a PROGRAM line and finish with an END. In the first program we are just going to give the *Basic* version of the golden ratio iteration program for which we gave the *Logo* version above. When you select Run from the editor's Run menu (provided there are no errors) the output appears in another window.

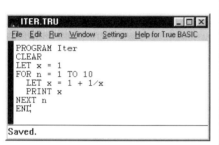
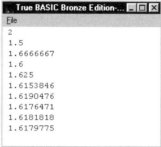

Of course the output can be graphic as well as numeric. One of the problems, though, is that the graphic window can be re-sized, so we need to take care with the aspect ratio of the window. The program HEX uses two procedures. The procedure 'screen' adjusts the co-ordinate system for the graphic window. The procedure 'Hex' draws a hexagon using three numbers: the co-ordinates of its centre and the radius of the circle in which it lies. So the output is a hexagon whose centre is at (1,2) inscribed in a circle of radius 3.

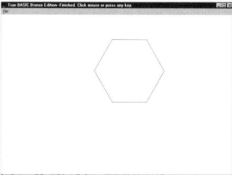

 Can you adapt the program to draw a vertical band of small hexagons? How about tiling the display window?

The PLOT command is very versatile. PLOT x,y will plot the point (x,y).

PLOT x1,y1;x2,y2   or   PLOT x1,y1;
                                      PLOT x2,y2

Both result in the line from (x1,y1) to (x2,y2). We shall use this technique to develop a versatile graph drawing program.

```
GRAPH.TRU                              _□×
File  Edit  Run  Window  Settings  Help for True BASIC

PROGRAM graph
DEF f(x) = 1 + 1/x
READ xmin, xmax, ymin, ymax
DATA -3, 3, -3, 3
SET WINDOW xmin, xmax, ymin, ymax
SET COLOR "red"
PLOT xmin,0 ; xmax,0
PLOT 0,ymin ; 0,ymax
LET y1 = f(xmin)
SET COLOR "blue"
PLOT xmin,y1;
FOR x = xmin TO xmax STEP (xmax-xmin)/100
   LET y2 = f(x)
   IF ABS(y2-y1)>10 THEN PLOT
   PLOT x,y2;
   LET y1 = y2
NEXT x
PLOT
SET COLOR "green"
PLOT xmin,xmin;xmax,xmax
END

Run successfully.
```

 Edit the second and fourth lines of the program to draw graphs of different functions using different axes.

Programming graphing calculators

Below we give more details about the use of graphing calculators using the Texas Instruments TI-83 as an example. Each of our examples can be tackled on most GCs without using any programming at all. But here we give a brief idea of the similarities and differences between a GC programming language and others such as *Logo* and *Basic*. First we will enter and run the ITER program. Press the 'PRGM' key to see a menu of the programs already stored on the calculator. If it is a new one there will be no names! Move the cursor right twice to highlight 'NEW' and press 'ENTER'. You are now in the program editor where you first type the name of your program. Just press the keys corresponding to the letters in green above them, e.g. 'x²' gives 'I', '4' gives 'T', 'SIN' gives 'E' and 'x' gives 'R'. Press 'ENTER' again to start writing the program.

```
EXEC EDIT NEW
1█Create New
```

```
PROGRAM
Name=ITER
```

The first line is entered using the following four keys: '1', 'STO→', 'X,T,θ,*n*' and 'ENTER'. This stores the value 1 into the variable X. In order to enter the next instruction, for the counted loop, press the 'PRGM' key and select item 4 from the 'CTL' menu. When you press 'ENTER' this pastes the phrase 'For(' on the next line. Use 'ALPHA' and 'LOG' to get the letter 'N' and then complete the line 'For(N,1,10)' before pressing 'ENTER'. If you want to indent the body of the FOR-loop to help clarify the loop structure you can include extra colons using 'ALPHA' and '•'. Hence enter the line '1+1/X→X' and press 'ENTER'. To enter the command to display the result, press 'PRGM' and cursor right to select 'I/O' (for Input and Output), and choose item 3: 'Disp'. For the command to 'End' the counted loop use 'PRGM' and select item 7 from the 'CTL' menu.

In order to run the program first use '2nd' and 'MODE' to 'QUIT' the editor. Press 'PRGM' and select the line containing the program name 'ITER' which you want to execute. Press 'ENTER' to paste the name into the normal screen, and then 'ENTER' again to run it. If you want to change the program then press 'PRGM', cursor right over 'EDIT' and down to select the name of the program to edit. Now there is so much software built in to the TI-83 that there are much more convenient ways, say, of performing an iteration, plotting a hexagon, or of drawing a graph of a function like $f(x) = 1 + 1/x$.

  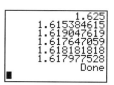

However, in order to give a feeling for the range of programming commands we will show a possible version of the HEX program – this one draws a hexagon within a circle of radius R, centre (P,Q). Note that variable names can only use single characters. Note that 'ClrDraw' and 'Line' are found on the 'DRAW' menu ('2nd' 'PRGM'), that 'Degree' is found on the 'MODE' menu, and 'ZDecimal' on the 'ZOOM' menu.

  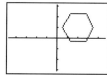

Generic software: particularly spreadsheets, but also databases

Most networks and PCs come with a set of basic software already installed. This is often in the form of an integrated package, such as *MS Works*™, or a suite of software incorporating any or all of: a wordprocessor, spreadsheet, database, graphics package, Internet browser, e-mail system, presentation software (such as Microsoft's *Office 2000*™). As IT is a subject on the curriculum in most schools, often mathematics departments are expected to demonstrate uses of spreadsheets. But there is a snag. Essentially spreadsheets have been developed from accountants' tools, and their graphical output usually derives from presentations of sales figures. Their developers are, in the main, large software houses that may not be particularly responsive to the needs of education in general, and of mathematics in particular. Also features may vary considerably between different versions of the same software. The notation used for functions is usually very different from mathematical convention. Standard mathematical graphs and diagrams (such as box-plots in statistics) may be awkward or impossible to produce.

Spreadsheets

So, while there are good uses for spreadsheets in mathematics, we need to remember that ICT requirements for school mathematics cannot be met through spreadsheets, or other generic software, alone. That said, we shall take a look at some examples of problems tackled using the spreadsheet feature of the *TI Interactive!* ™ software from the CD-ROM.

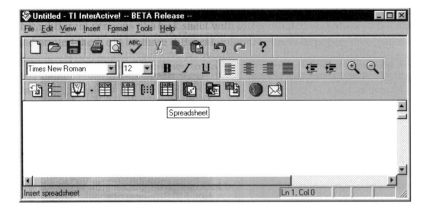

First we shall show the equivalent of the ITER program. We need to open the spreadsheet application. The seventh icon on the bottom tool bar shows a tiny portion of a spreadsheet. Click on this to open Interactive's Data Editor. We enter the starting value into a cell, e.g. with the cursor over the cell A1, type '1' and press the Enter key. Now, in cell A2, we want to give a formula involving the cell above: so put the cursor on cell A2 and press '=' to start a formula. Enter '1+1/' and then either type 'A1' or move the cursor up to the A1 cell. When you press the Enter key the cell shows the result, i.e. '2', but the 'edit line' above shows the formula: '1+1/A1'.

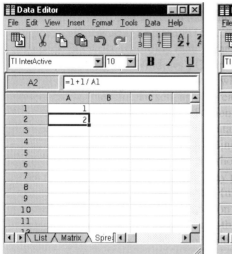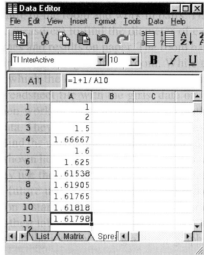

The box around cell A2 has a small 'blob' on its bottom right-hand corner. Position the mouse over the blob and press and hold down the left mouse button. Slowly pull the mouse towards you to 'drag' the box into one covering all the cells A2 down to A11. Then release the left mouse button. You will find that you now have a set of successive iterations. If you place the cursor say over A6 you will see the formula '=1+1/A5' has been entered into the edit line. If you now go to cell A1 and type a different starting value, e.g. 2, then when you press Enter, all the values in the cells A2:A11 will be recomputed. This is the key feature of any spreadsheet.

In the next example a set of heights of 11 students are entered in cells A1:A11. Use the mouse to click on the top of the column, i.e. the box marked A. This highlights the whole A column. From the Edit menu select copy. Then use the mouse to highlight the B columns and use Edit Paste to make B1:B11 an exact copy of A1:A11. Still with the B column highlighted, go to the upper toolbar and choose the 9th icon i.e. the blue A over the red Z. This is the icon to sort in ascending order. When you click on the 'Sort ascending' icon column B should immediately change to be in ascending order of height. Now it is easy to pick out, for example, the minimum, median and maximum values of the heights. To calculate the mean, just go to an empty cell, such as B13, press '=' for a formula, and click on the $f(x)$ icon to see a list of the vast range of available functions. Select the one called 'AVERAGE(' – of course you can also type this in directly – and then enter 'B1:B11)' to complete the formula.

 Can you now compute the value of the range (max–min) in, say, cell B12?

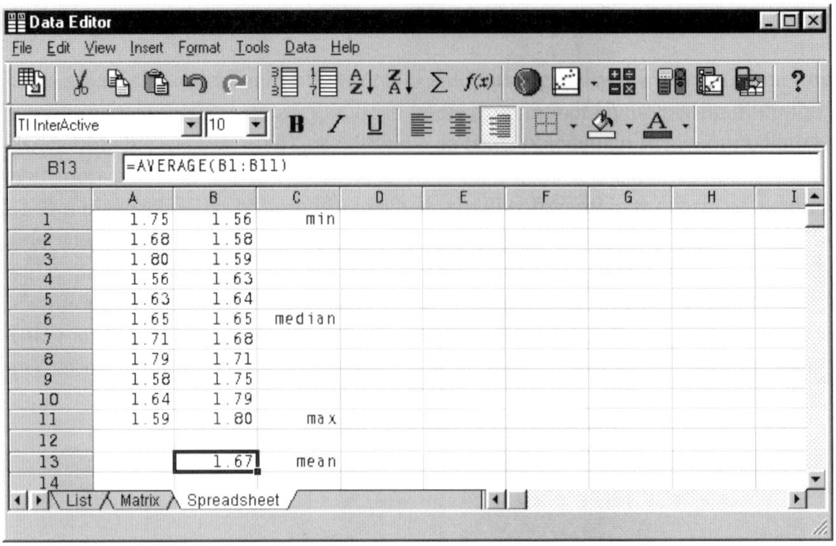

```
Data Editor                                                    _ □ ×
File  Edit  View  Insert  Format  Tools  Data  Help

[toolbar icons]

TI InterActive          ▼ 10  ▼  B  I  U  ≡ ≡ ≡  ⊞ · ✎ · A ·

   B13          =AVERAGE(B1:B11)

        A       B       C       D     E     F     G     H     I
  1    1.75    1.56    min
  2    1.68    1.58
  3    1.80    1.59
  4    1.56    1.63
  5    1.63    1.64
  6    1.65    1.65    median
  7    1.71    1.68
  8    1.79    1.71
  9    1.58    1.75
 10    1.64    1.79
 11    1.59    1.80    max
 12
 13            1.67    mean
 14
◄ ►  List  Matrix  Spreadsheet            ◄  ►
```

Content-free, subject specific, software

Such software has an increasingly important part to play in the context of secondary school mathematics. Many graph-plotting packages now have additional facilities, such as the ability to plot data, to perform geometric transformations, etc. Computer algebra software has other desirable features, such as graphing, and the handling of exact arithmetic for large numbers. Dynamic geometry software has the ability to perform calculations on measurements, and hence can be used as an analytic and modelling tool. At the time of the DfEE/NCET document there were few accessible tools for data-handling suitable for secondary school use, but now more of these are coming on-stream, albeit at prices rather higher than the other types of software in this category. A new species of software for mathematical communication and computation is now becoming available which incorporates features of a mathematical wordprocessor, web browser and spreadsheet with computation, graphing and statistical features similar to those found on a graphic calculator. Once again we have provided sample software on the CD-ROM which illustrates features of the main types of such software.

Graph-plotting software (GPS)

Here we use the graphing features of the demonstration version of *TI Interactive!* ™. From the bottom toolbar select the third icon, with a picture of a graph. This will take you into the Function Editor, where you can define the functions to be graphed, together with their colour, style etc. Here we enter $1+1/x$ for $y1(x)$ and x for $y2(x)$. The graphs are plotted on axes in the Grapher Window. The default uses scales from -10 to 10 for each axis, but these can easily be edited, e.g. to -3 to 3. If you pull down the Calculate menu you will see that Intersection is one option. This opens up the Calculate Intersection Window.

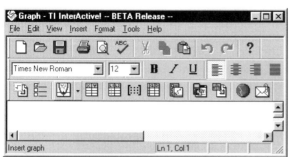

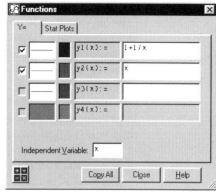

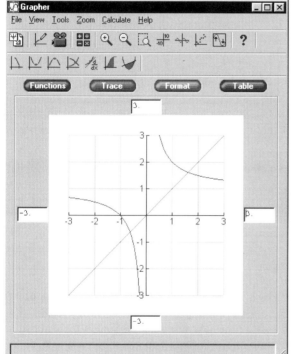

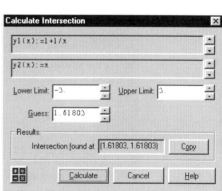

You can enter an initial value, such as 1.5, in the Guess box, and then press Calculate to make the computer use its own iterative method to find the intersection of y1(*x*) and y2(*x*). So, once again, we have computed a value for the golden ratio ϕ.

Experiment with the Grapher to draw graphs of functions defined parametrically, or by polar co-ordinates.

Computer algebra systems (CAS)

There is a demonstration version of the versatile *Derive*™ software developed by D. Stoutemeyer and A. Rich of the University of Hawaii. *TI Interactive!* also has quite a few features to support symbolic manipulation. We shall illustrate both, starting with *Derive*.

In the Author menu select Expression to open up the Expression editor window. Enter the equation to be solved for Golden Ratio: i.e. what number is 1 more than its reciprocal? So type 'x=1+1/x' and click on OK.

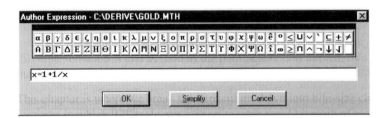

So now we have a different situation from our previous examples, where the variable *x* always had a numeric variable. In a Computer Algebra System (also known as a Symbol Manipulator) variables need not be assigned values, just as in algebra textbooks! We shall now work through the steps to obtain the complete picture below.

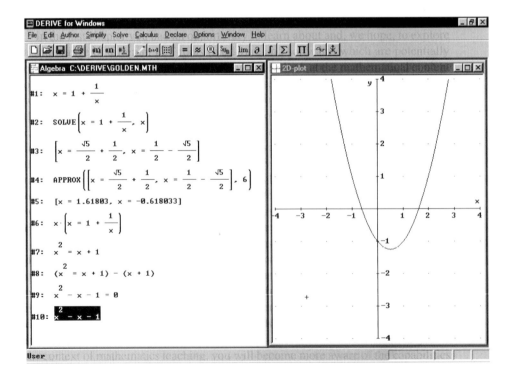

With expression #1 highlighted, click on the Solve menu and select Algebraically. This opens another dialog box. Click on OK to accept the expression and variable offered.

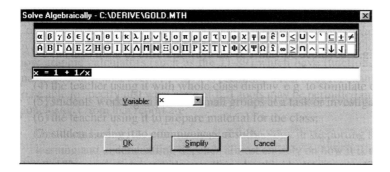

Note that this yields the expression: SOLVE(x=1+1/x,x) rather than the solution. If we had clicked on the Simplify button instead of on OK we would avoid this intermediate step. For now click on the Simplify menu and select Basic to see the symbolic solution, in terms of square roots. To evaluate these numerically click on Simplify Approximate. Here you can change the number of decimal places to be displayed. Clicking on OK gives an intermediate expression, which will again need to use Simplify Basic, or you can click on the Approximate button to get the result directly.

Now use Author and enter 'x * #1' or 'x #1' to multiply expression #1 throughout by x. Simplify this, and then use Author again, entering '#8 - (x+1)' to subtract x+1 from both sides of the simplified equation in expression #8. So we now have a quadratic function in a conventional form. To plot the function use Edit and Copy Expressions, then Author and Edit Paste to put the quadratic equation in the editor. Delete the final '=0' and click on OK.

Click on the 2-D graph icon (the last but one on the tool bar) to open up a set of axes. At the top right-hand corner of the graph window click on the middle of the three icons, and then resize the graph window by dragging on the sides of its frame. Finally use the fourth icon on the Graph toolbar to draw the graph of the selected function from the Algebra screen. Now you should get a parabola whose positive root corresponds with Golden Ratio.

Now we shall see how to follow a similar approach using the symbolic manipulation facilities of *TI Interactive*!

The first icon on the lower toolbar produces a Mathematics Box and the Mathematics Palette. The Algebra menu contains functions for symbolic manipulation. Select 'solve(' and complete the equation 'x=1+1/x,x)', i.e. solve x = 1+1/x for x. Opening further such boxes you can approximate the result, using 'ANS', and also manipulate the equations as with *Derive*. Then, from the Grapher, you can plot the graph of the resulting quadratic function and locate its roots, e.g. by Tracing.

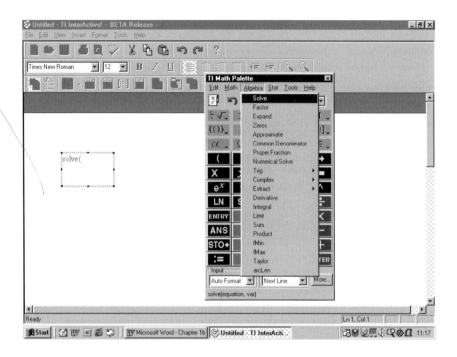

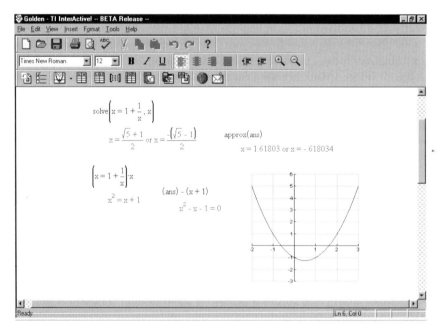

Dynamic geometry software (DGS)

Here we use the demonstration version of *Cabri Géomètre*™. This software was developed at the University of Grenoble as a specific aid to geometry teaching.

However the software is very flexible and versatile, and can be used in many aspects of mathematics as well as in areas such as design, technology, etc. We shall use it to explore a particular problem. You know that if you have three coins, maybe all of different sizes, that you can push them together so that they touch each other in pairs. Can we solve the reverse problem? Given three points, can we always find circles with those points as centres, such that each pair of circles touches each other?

We start by fixing three points A,B,C. The toolbar shows eleven icons. The left-hand one, the arrow, is the usual mode where the mouse just moves a pointer across the screen. If you click on the second icon you get a menu to do with Points. Select the first of these: Point. Now use the cursor to position the pointer over the place you want one of the points, and then click the button to place it there. Repeat to put two other points on the screen. Now click either on the first icon (called the pointer) or anywhere in the grey area of the toolbar. The next step is to join the points by segments. Go to the third icon and select Segment from the menu. Position the cursor over one of the points (you will see a message saying 'this point') and click, then position it over the other end-point and click to make a segment. Repeat this for the other two sides of the triangle. Now we shall make a variable point on one of the sides. Open the Point menu again, but this time select the second option: Point on object. Move the pointer to somewhere on one of the segments (such as point P in the diagram), and click. Select the Pointer tool again and check that you can slide this point freely along, but not off, the segment.

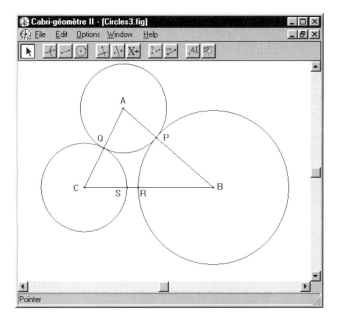

Now we can construct the circles whose centres are the end-points of this segment (A,B) and which pass through the variable point (P). Open the menu for the fourth icon and select Circle. Click on a centre-point (A) and then on a radius point (P). Repeat for the other circle. Return to the Pointer tool and check that, as you slide P, both dependent circles change size. Now we can find their points of intersection with the other two sides (AC, BC) of the triangle. Select the Points menu again, but this time the third option: Point at Intersection. Move the cursor to each intersection and click to define a point (*Q,R*). Finally we create a circle whose centre is the third vertex (*C*) and which passes through one of the intersection points (*Q*). Create the intersection point (*S*) of this third circle and the remaining segment (*BC*). If you like you can put labels on the point using the tenth icon and selecting Label from the menu. As you click on each point you can enter a label in a little dialogue box.

Now we have seen some of the mechanics of drawing we can use the results for geometry. First drag *P* on *AB* until the intersections *S* and *R* are as close as possible. Now we can try to make some conjectures from the picture. For example we know that tangents at *P* and *Q* to the circles are perpendicular to the lines of centres *AB* and *BC*.

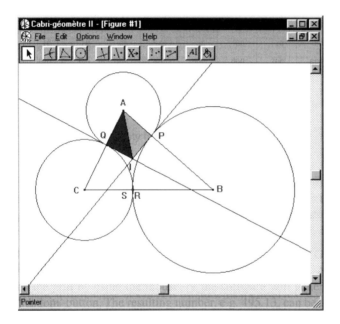

Use the fifth icon to open up the main construction menu and select Perpendicular. Click first on *P*, then anywhere on *AB* to construct the perpendicular to *AB* through *P*. Repeat for the perpendicular to *AC* through *Q*. Create the intersection point and label it *I*. Also create the segment *AI*. Use the third icon and select the Triangle menu item. Click in turn on *A,P* and *I*. Repeat for *A,Q* and *I*. From the last icon menu choose Fill, select a colour from the palette and click on triangle *API*, repeat to fill *AQI* with a different colour. What can you deduce about these triangles? You can also use the measurement tool (ninth icon) to select Distance and Length, and the click in turn on segments *IP* and *IQ* to check whether they are equal in this case. The point *I*, which is equidistant from sides *AB, AC* must also be equidistant from *BC* in the 'ideal' case. So this gives us another way of characterizing points *P,Q,R*: they are where the incircle, centre *I*, touches the sides *AB, BC, CA*.

Double click on the point *P* and select Edit Cut. Everything dependent on *P* will now be removed. Construct the angle bisectors of *BAC* and *ABC* (use the Construction tool and click in turn on the three points defining the angle). Create and label their intersection point *I*. Use the Hide/Show menu item of the last icon to hide the angle bisectors. Now create the perpendiculars from I to each of the three sides. Then create and label their intersections with the sides. Hide the perpendiculars and create the circle centre I through P, and each of the three circles centres A, B and C.

> *Note:* This neat result, linking the three touching circles to the in-centre was, of course, known to the Ancient Greeks. Many more interesting results and ideas for explanation can be found in the books by Coxeter and by Wells.

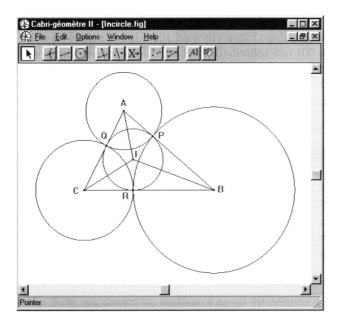

✎ *Can you set up a diagram with a circle and a chord to illustrate circle properties, such as the centre lies on its perpendicular bisector, angles subtended in the same segment are equal, angles subtended in opposite segments add up to 180°, etc.?*

✎ *Can you set up a diagram to show each of the major centres of the same triangle* ABC: *the in-centre* I, *the circum-centre* O, *the centroid* G *and the ortho-centre* H? *As you deform the triangle can you find any invariant properties connecting* I, O, G *and* H?

✎ *Experiment with some of the other icons, such as the fifth one for working with transformations. For translations you may need to create some vectors, using the third icon, and for rotations you may need to enter some numbers using the tenth icon.*

> ✎ *Can you show that successive reflections in different mirror lines are equivalent to a single transformation? What is it?*

Data-handling software (DHS)

Here we use the statistical features of the demonstration version of *TI Interactive!* ™. First we use the List icon on the toolbar (the fifth icon) to go into the Data Editor. We will study the familiar 'handshake' problem. That is when there are four people A,B,C,D in a room, six handshakes are needed to introduce everyone to each other: {AB, AC, AD, BC, BD, CD}. How many handshakes are needed for *n* people? These are the 'triangle numbers'.

In list L1 we enter the numbers {2,3,4,5,6,7} as the numbers of people in a room. In list L2 we enter the corresponding number of handshakes require: {1,3,6,10,15,21,28}, the so-called triangle numbers. On the middle toolbar select the graph-drawing (the fourteenth) icon. This brings up the Functions Window showing the entry screen for Stat Plots. The little picture with three spots is the icon for a scattergram. Enter L1 for the independent variable and L2 for the dependent variable.

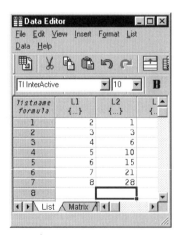
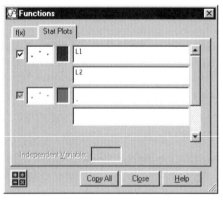

Clicking on Copy All puts the data onto the axes in the Grapher. From the Zoom menu select Statistics. You can edit the minima and maxima for the axes if you like.

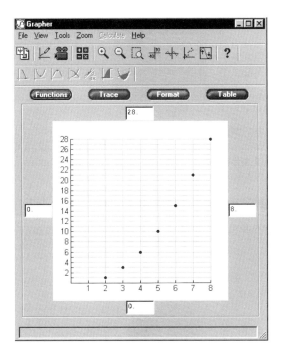

Close the Grapher and other windows to return to the Data Editor. Click on the seventeenth icon on the middle toolbar (Statistical Regression) to enter the Statistical Regression Calculation window. Select Quadratic regression as the Calculation type, and L1, L2 as the X List and Y List. Enter 1 for the frequency, and y1 as the Regression Equation. When you click on Calculate you will see that computed equation is $0.5\,x^2 - 0.5\,x$, which is stored as y1(x).

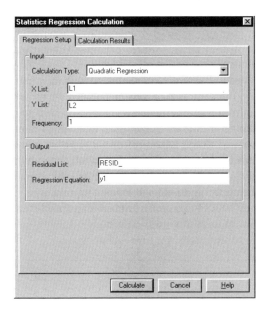

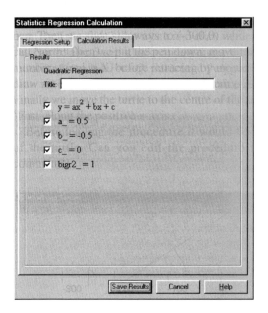

Returning to the Grapher we can go to the Functions window and select the f(x) tab. Then enter y1(x) as the equation to be superimposed on the scattergram. Of course we need to remember that our original data was discrete (you can only have a whole number of people!) whereas our new function is continuous and so can be evaluated, e.g. for $n = 3.7$ which doesn't make much sense in the context of our original problem!

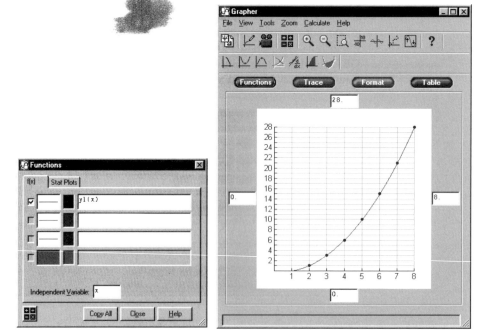

Mathematical communication tools (MCT)

Here we use the full features of the demonstration version of *TI Interactive!*™. Using the example of the handshake problem we can create a document giving our report on the problem. This report can be printed, or e-mailed via the built-in web browser.

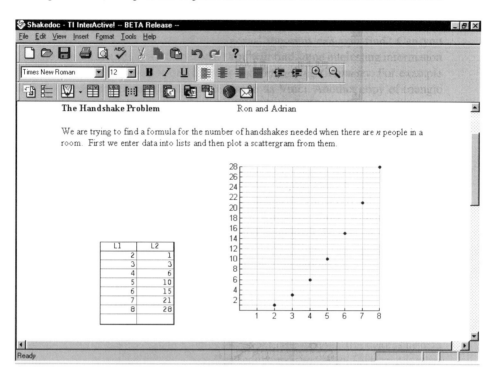

Courseware: i.e. structured curriculum materials with integral use of software

This form of software is far more prevalent in the USA than elsewhere, mainly because of the costs involved and the economies of scale required. There have been some attempts to produce integrated courseware for mathematics in the UK, but mostly for students post-16. Some of these have left a lot to be desired. For obvious reasons we cannot provide examples of such materials here as part of the accompanying CD-ROM. A recent government report on software for mathematics made the following points for potential future developers:

To be successful such software should satisfy three main principles:

- It must be an integral part of accompanying published materials.
- It must support the teacher by adding new features which cannot be provided other than through ICT.
- It must be supported by materials which help teachers to make good pedagogical use of the ICT elements.

So it is important that mathematics teachers can cast a critical eye over any such allegedly integrated schemes to evaluate just how useful the ICT contributions are.

Graphing calculators (GC)

In the time since the publication of the DfEE/NCET document on software for mathematics there have been rapid developments in hand-held technology. These include the development of 'flash-ROM' which enables both system and application software to be downloaded from the Internet. The development of compatible cheap and easy-to-use data-loggers – particularly motion detectors – makes the acquisition of real data very practicable even in a conventional classroom. Together with the low-cost displays for whole-class teaching, such tools have a place in several subjects in the curriculum and can be vehicles for encouraging co-operation between teachers across subjects. (See for example our BECTa book: Oldknow and Taylor (1998) *Data-capture and Modelling in Mathematics and Science*)

Ideally you will have a graphic calculator (preferably a TI-83) to hand in order to try the following activities. However many of them can also be performed using *TI Interactive!*™ First we show how to solve $x = 1 + 1/x$ graphically in order to illustrate the general technique. Press 'MODE' and make sure that 'Func' is highlighted in the fourth line. If it is not, then move the cursor to the left to highlight it and press 'ENTER'. Use '2nd' and 'MODE' to 'QUIT'. Now find the blue 'Y=' key immediately below the screen. Press this and enter the functions 1+1/x into Y1 and x into Y2. If any of the 'Plot' areas on the top line are highlighted, then move the cursor over them and press 'ENTER', repeating until all are cleared.

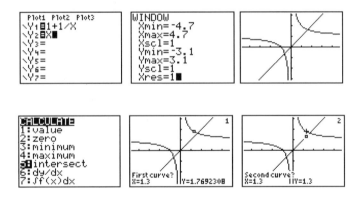

Either press 'WINDOW' and set the values as in the screen-shot, or else press 'ZOOM' and select '4:ZDecimal'. Finally press 'GRAPH' to see the pair of graphs. Now use '2nd TRACE' for the 'CALC' menu. Select '5:Intersect'. You will now have to use the cursor keys to select which functions to use (even though there are only two of them!), and a starting point for the built-in numerical algorithm to find the intersection.

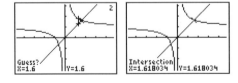

As promised earlier we can now show an easier way to draw a hexagon using the TI-83's graphing facilities. From the 'MODE' screen you need to select both Parametric graphing, and degrees. In the 'Y=' editor enter the parametric equations for a circle of desired centre and radius. In the 'WINDOW' screen make sure that the parameter T goes from 0 to 360 in steps of 60 degrees. You might want to change the screen's appearance. Use '2nd' 'ZOOM' for the 'FORMAT' screen where you can hide axes, put in grid points etc. Try making other polygons, or hexagons, that touch.

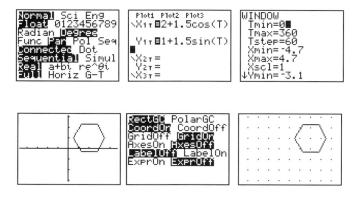

✎ *Try making some polar graphs, e.g. try some variations on*
   $r = 2 + cos(5\theta)$.

Now we can see how the graphing calculator also contains powerful software for statistics. First we can attack the handshake problem. Press 'STAT', select '5:SetUpEditor' and press 'ENTER' twice. Then 'STAT' and '1:Edit' to go into the statistics editor. Type in the number of people in the list L1, and the number of handshakes in the list L2. Then press 'STAT' and move the cursor right to select 'CALC', and choose '5:Quadreg'. The expression 'QuadReg' appears on the home screen. You must tell it which two data sets to use. So enter 'L1,L2' and press 'ENTER'. 'L1' is found from '2nd' and '1'.

We can show the fit graphically by pressing '2nd' and 'Y=' to get to 'STAT PLOT'. Select '1:Plot1..'. Highlight 'On' and the symbol for scattergram. Enter the lists 'L1' and 'L2', and highlight the square symbol. Then choose a suitable 'WINDOW' and press 'GRAPH'. You should see the scattergram with the superimposed quadratic model. Remember, though, that the data here is discrete, yet the fitted function is continuous! In the 'MATH', 'PRB' menu there are functions for permutations and combinations. If you go back to 'STAT' 'Edit' you can place the cursor over the symbol 'L3' at the top of the third column. Press 'ENTER' to go into the entry line. We shall now enter a formula, similarly as in a spreadsheet, for column L3 in terms of column L1. First find the inverted commas symbol ' by using 'ALPHA' and '+'. We can the enter the formula "L1 nCr 2', where 'nCr' comes from the 'MATH' 'PRB' menu. When you press 'ENTER' the whole list L3 is now computed in terms of L1.

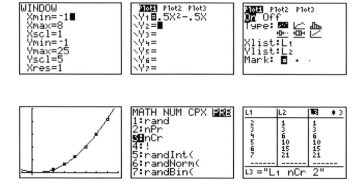

Finally we use the ideas of lists and statistics plots to explore the box-plots of rolls of simulated dice. From the 'MATH', 'PRB' menu chose '5:ranInt(' and enter the line: randInt(1,6,50) STO→ L1 to place 50 simulated rolls of a six-sided die into list L1. Repeat for L2. Then we can add lists L1 and L2 together, term-by-term, and store the result in list L3. From the 'STAT PLOT' screen we can define each of the three plots to be a box-plot of the data in lists L1, L2 and L3 respectively.

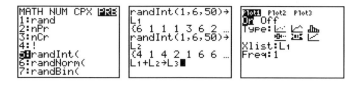

You will need to clear any functions in the 'Y=' editor and choose a suitable WINDOW, e.g. with x from -1 to 13 and any scale for y, e.g. 0 to 4. Pressing 'GRAPH' should now show the three box-plots for comparison. You can trace these to see the medians, quartiles etc. To see statistics about any one of the three lists use STAT CALC and 1:1-Var Stats followed by the name of the list, e.g. L1.

Data-loggers (e.g. CBR™ and CBL™)

The use of a very portable motion detector, such as Texas Instruments' Calculator Based Ranger (CBR™), provides a simple means of getting real data, gathered first hand, for analysis in mathematics classes. The CBR™ can be set up for use either controlled by a GC or a PC. Here we give examples of its use both with the TI-83 and with *TI Interactive!*™

With the TI-83 you need to download the link software from the CBL. Attach the black link cable to the TI-83 using with the socket below the keyboard (press very well in!). Attach the other end to the round socket on the right-hand side of the CBR. On the TI-83 press '2nd' and 'X,T,θ,*n*' keys to get the 'LINK' menu. Cursor right over 'RECEIVE'. On the CBR open the lid and press the grey key marked '82/83'. The TI-83 will then show 'Receiving' and later 'Done'. Press 'PRGM' and you should see 'RANGER' added to the list of programs stored on your calculator.

Use 'EXEC' and cursor down to 'RANGER', then press 'ENTER' twice. From the Main Menu select 1:SETUP/SAMPLE, and then adjust the settings as below. For example to cycle through the possibilities for 'BEGIN ON' just place the cursor on that line and press 'ENTER' repeatedly to see the options available. When you have set it up, cursor to the top line of the screen next to 'START NOW' and press 'ENTER'. Now you can take your TI-83 and CBR for a walk. Point the CBR at a wall, press 'ENTER' on the TI-83, and walk back and forwards until the CBR stops ticking (15 secs).

  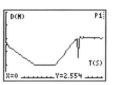

As you walk, the distance–time graph is shown at the same time. Can you interpret the graph above? Can you explain the little 'spike' around 15 secs? Press 'ENTER' to get to the next menu. If you go back to the main menu and change the settings to read 'REALTIME: NO' then you can sample over longer or shorter periods. Then you can also change the representation to velocity–time or acceleration–time graph.

TI-Interactive! also provides facilities to capture data directly from the CBR. When you install *Interactive* you specify which serial port of the computer (COM1, COM2 etc.) you will use, and which connection cable (grey or black). Plug the connector cable into the serial port of your computer, and into the little round socket on the left-hand side of the CBR. The last three icons on *Interactive*'s tool bar are for connection to compatible graphical calculators and data loggers. The sixteenth icon shows a CBL and CBR. Clicking on this opens up the Quick Data window. Select 'Motion' and adjust the number of samples, and the collection interval. When you are set, then click on Run. Now, as you move in front of the CBR so the data is logged in the CBR and also transferred to the computer.

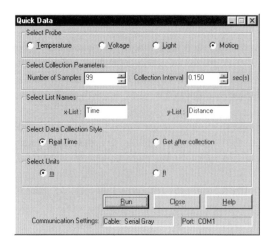

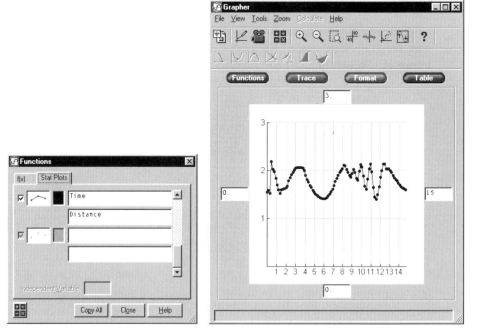

You can edit the settings in the Functions window for the Stat Plots, e.g. changing a scattergram to an xy-plot etc. Again you can edit the minima and maxima for the axes in the Grapher window. When you return to the Data Editor window you will see that new columns, headed Time and Distance have been added.

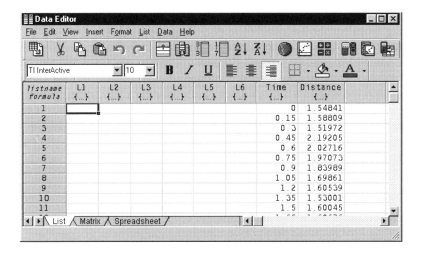

The CBR™ is a special purpose device for sensing distances. A more versatile device, such as TI's Calculator Based Laboratory (CBL™), can accept a wide range of sensors, e.g. for light intensity, sound, temperature, voltage, pressure, etc. Here we give examples of its use both with the TI-83 and with *TI Interactive!* ™. If you have a TI-83 Plus graphing calculator then this comes with an Application called CBL/CBR. Press the blue APPS button and select it. Select '2:DATA LOGGER' and use it to set up the Temperature probe. Plug the black cable into TI-83+ and CBL and the Temperature probe into Channel 1 on the CBL. Turn the CBL on and follow instructions on the TI-83 screen.

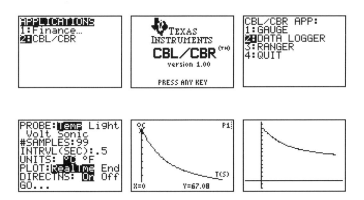

In this experiment we shall place the temperature probe in a mug of warm water for a minute or so to heat up. Then when we select GO from the CBL/CBR program we can remove the sensor from the liquid and let it cool in air. The resulting decay data should be captured and graphed.

When you have got the data captured you can leave the program by pressing 'ENTER' to return to the menu and then selecting 'Quit'. If you look at 'STAT PLOT' you will see it is set for an xy-line graph of data in lists TTEMP and TEMP. You can now manipulate these lists, change the data display, window etc.

If you do not have a calculator with a built-in CBL/CBR Application (such as a TI-83) you can download the Vernier Physics program for the CBL which is contained on the CD-ROM using the TI GraphLink software. Run the PHYSICS program and set up for a single temperature probe in Channel 1. Then specify TIME GRAPH for data collection, and set the sample interval and number of samples. If you want a real-time graph you will have to feed in information for the y-axis scales. Now the program will just gather, store, transfer and display data as before. When you leave the program the time data is stored in list L1 and the temperatures in list L2. In *TI Interactive!* the Quick Data window from the Data Editor window allows you to set up the CBL as well as the CBR.

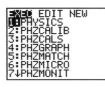  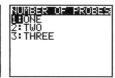

 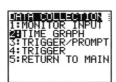 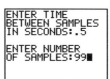

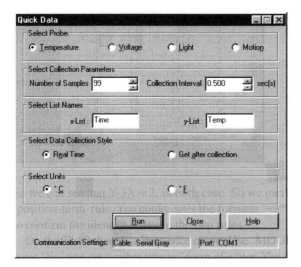

 You can collect data at very short time intervals. Can you set up the light probe to show the flicker rate of a neon tube?

CD-ROM and the Internet as sources of data.

Secondary sources of real-data are very important in providing realistic contexts for, e.g. the analysis and display of data in mathematics. As mathematics teachers we need to recognize both the availability and potential of such data sources, but also to be cautious about their reliability. Again this provides opportunities for co-operation with colleagues teaching other subjects.

Data-sets

Here we consider the use of one of the data sets provided (see the Appendix) for use with *TI Interactive!* ™ and with the TI-83 graphing calculator. This gives data on the planets in our solar system which appeared in the NCET IT Maths Pack. We will explore the relationship between the Distance from the sun (column F) and the Period of the orbit (column E). Copy column F, open the List editor and paste it into list L1. Similarly copy column G to list L2.

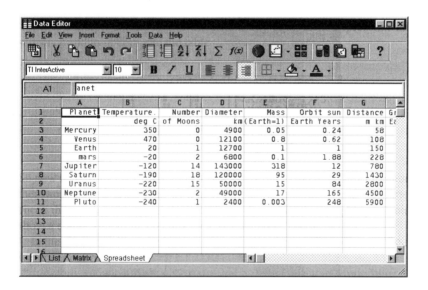

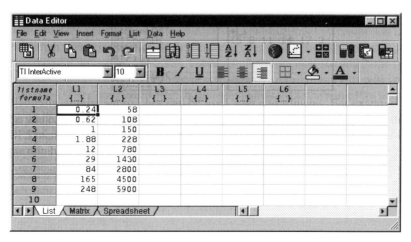

Now use the Statistics Regression tool and select Power Regression of L2 on L1. You should find Kepler's third law, i.e. that the square of a planet's period is proportional to the cube of its distance from the sun! Of course you can arrange to transfer the whole data set, or just parts of it, to students' graphing calculators for further analysis at home, or in class, if required.

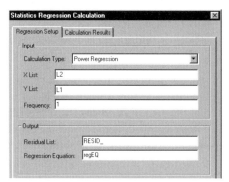
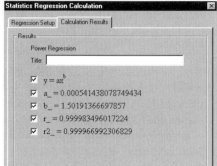

Websites

To explore the world of the internet your computer needs a device called a modem, and a connection to the telephone. You also need an internet service provider who will supply a telephone number and a password. Assuming you can connect to the internet we will now use the Web browser of *TI Interactive!* ™ to explore just a few websites. Click on the Globe symbol, the eleventh icon on the main toolbar. This launches the Browser and automatically brings up the *TI Interactive!* home page on TI's website in the USA.

You can see that there is a box with the internet address you have just used:

`http://www.ti.com/calc/interactive`

This is the standard form of address (called URLs) on the internet. If you know the URL of a good site you can just type it into the address window. You will find quite a lot of useful material on the website of the UK Mathematical Association. Its address is:

`http://www.m-a.org.uk`

✎ *See if you can navigate your way to it, and find its index page.*

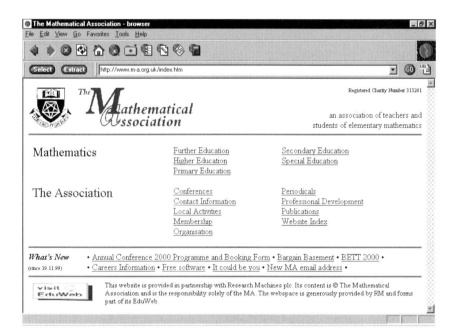

The site has a link to 'Free software' – click on this link to get to the next page.

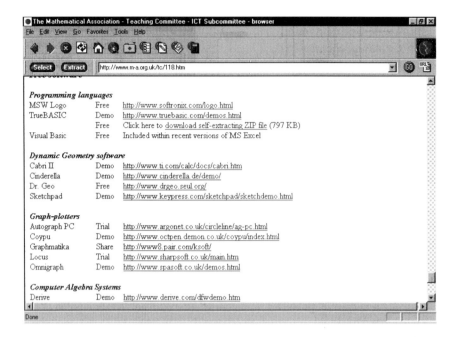

This is how you can download trial and free versions of software, such as *MSW Logo*™ and *TrueBasic*™. Now we will explore the Virtual Teacher Centre (VTC) on the UK government's National Grid for Learning. We will enter via the website of the government's British Educational Communications and Technology agency (BECTa).

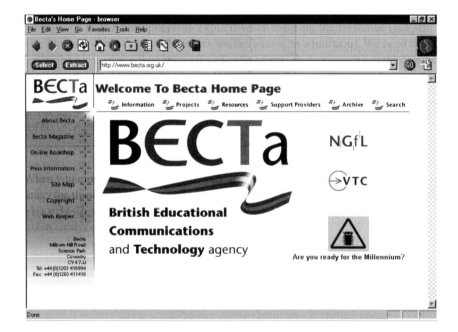

Use the address: http://www.becta.org.uk and click on the VTC symbol. This takes you into the 'front page' of the VTC site at http://vtc.ngfl.gov.uk. See if you can follow the links for resource materials on secondary school mathematics until you end up at pages to do with a 'Pupil's Entitlement'.

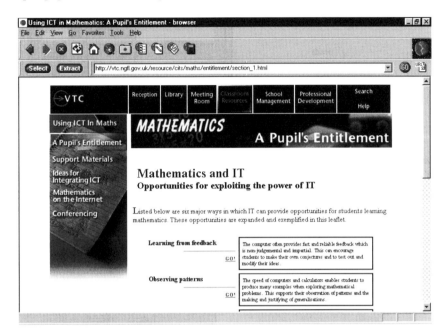

Here you can see an electronic version of a booklet which was published free by NCET. The internet is one way of preserving documents from going out of print.

If you go to the TI Calculator home page: http://www.ti.com/calc you can find information about support in your own country. This includes how to borrow equipment, such as graphing calculators via the 'loan programme', who to contact for support, how to get further training, e.g. via the T-cubed (Teachers Teaching with Technology) programme, etc.

If you click on the globe icon (sixth) on the Browser toolbar you will enter a search dialogue. Here we can see if there are any websites with planetary data by asking for sites which include each of the keywords: statistics, planets and period.

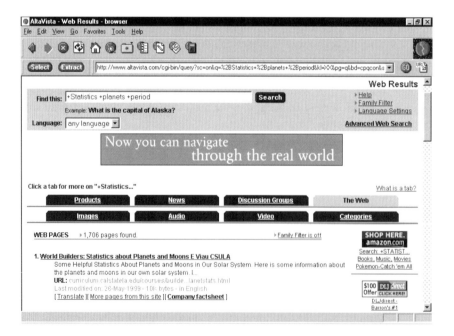

Sure enough, the first site offered does indeed include the sort of table we used above.

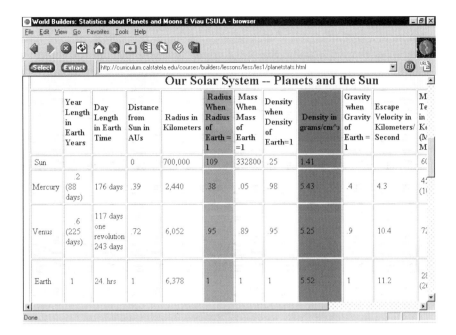

Note: there are many such opportunities to use data in mathematics lessons which are related to other subjects in the curriculum, such as science, geography, design technology, etc. There are case studies on the TTA Needs Identification CD-ROM, such as in science, which make good starting points.

Summary

We have tried to give you a practical introduction to the features of many of the main types of ICT tools which have potential benefits for mathematics teachers. Once you have started to get familiar with the features of such tools, you should then review their potential to offer you pedagogical, mathematical and/or organizational support.

Problems and activities (you choose the tool!)

- *Fibonacci sequence, golden ratio, pentagons and pentagrams: find out as many links between them as you can and use ICT tools to explore them. For example, given that the ratio between the lengths of the sides and diagonals in a pentagon is golden ratio* φ, *can you find a way to construct a pentagon using 'straight edge and compasses' only? Can you locate interesting information about Fibonacci and golden ratio on the internet?*

- *Investigate the intersections of* $y = x$ *with* $y = k^x$ *for different values of* $k > 0$. *For what value of* k *is the line tangent to the curve, and at what point does this occur? Investigate the iteration given by* $x_0 = 1$, $x_{n+1} = k^{x_n}$ *for* $n = 0,1,2,....$ *What is the largest value of* k *for which this sequence does not diverge?*

- *Read about ways of testing for prime numbers, and for generating sequences of prime numbers and implement them as algorithms using ICT tools.*

BRIDGE ONE

In preparation for the ICT training for serving teachers in the UK, the government's Teacher Training Agency has produced a series of books to help teachers of different subjects to identify their training needs. At the time of writing these books can also be downloaded from the TTA's website: http://www.teach-tta.gov.uk/ict. Here we refer to the book *The Use of Information Technology in Subject Teaching: Identification of Training Needs: Secondary Mathematics*, published by the TTA in March 1999. For convenience we reproduce here Section 1 of this book:

Overview of the use of ICT in teaching secondary mathematics

There are many possible uses of ICT in teaching and, as with all materials and methodologies, some have a greater potential to contribute to the teaching of different subjects. This section highlights the aspects of mathematics teaching where ICT has the potential to make a significant contribution to teaching and learning.

When making decisions about the use of ICT in subject teaching, there are three key principles which you may find useful to apply:

  i. decisions about when, when not, and how to use ICT in lessons should be based on whether the use of ICT supports good practice in teaching the subject. If it does not, it should not be used.
  ii. in planning and in teaching, decisions about when, when not, and how to use ICT in a particular lesson or sequence of lessons must be directly related to the teaching and learning objectives in hand.
  iii. the use of ICT should either allow the teacher or the pupil to achieve something that could not be achieved without it; or allow the teacher to teach or the pupils to learn something more effectively and efficiently than they could otherwise; or both.

These principles are important, whether:

- ICT is to be used by *all the pupils*, individually, in groups or as a whole class;
- ICT is to be used by *some pupils only*, e.g. for support or extension work;
- ICT is to be used by *the teacher*, e.g. where the teacher uses the ability of a spreadsheet to calculate the results of varying factors and to demonstrate the results in graphical form to the full class with the help of a large screen or display; where the teacher downloads lesson plans from the NGfL, or where the teacher downloads selected resources from the internet in advance of the lesson so that pupils can browse through them.

Practical considerations may also play a part in decisions about whether or not ICT should be used. These will include the nature of the available resources: e.g. teaching objectives that could be met very effectively if a suite of computers were available in the classroom might not be attainable if there is just one stand-alone computer.

Using ICT in secondary mathematics lessons

ICT has the potential to make a significant *contribution to pupils' learning in mathematics* by helping them to:

- *practise and consolidate number skills*, e.g. by using software to revise or practise skills and to give rapid assessment feedback;
- *develop skills in mathematical modelling through the exploration, interpretation and explanation of data*, e.g. by choosing appropriate graphical representations for displaying information from a data-set; by experimenting with forms of equations in trying to produce graphs which are good fits for data-plots; by using a motion sensor to produce distance–time graphs corresponding to pupils' own movements;
- *experiment with, make hypotheses from, and discuss or explain relationships and behaviour in shape and space and their links with algebra*, e.g. by using software to automate geometric constructions, to carry out specified geometric transformations, to perform operations on co-ordinates, to draw loci;
- *develop logical thinking and modify strategies and assumptions through immediate feedback*, e.g. by planning a procedure in a sequence of instructions in a programming language, or a sequence of geometrical constructions in geometry software or a set of manipulations in a spreadsheet;
- *make connections within and across areas of mathematics*, e.g. to relate a symbolic function, a set of values computed from it, and a graph generated by it to a mathematical or physical situation, such as the pressure and volume of a gas, which it models;
- *work with realistic, and large, sets of data*, e.g. in using box and whisker diagrams to compare the spreads of different data sets; to carry out experiments using large random samples generated through simulation;
- *explore, describe and explain patterns and relationships in sequences and tables of numbers*, e.g. by entering a formula in algebraic notation to generate values in an attempt to match a given set of numbers;
- *learn, and memorize, by manipulating graphic images*, e.g. the way the graph of a function such as $y = x^2$ is transformed by the addition of, or multiplication by a constant: $y = a. \; x^2$, $y = x^2 + a$, $y = (x+a)^2$, ... etc.

ICT also has the potential to offer valuable support to the *teacher of secondary mathematics* by:

- *helping them to prepare teaching materials*, e.g. downloading materials for classroom use from the internet, such as mathematical problems for pupils to solve with accompanying teachers' notes, software for computers and graphic calculators, reviews of published resources;
- *providing a flexible and time-saving resource that can be used in different ways and at different times without repetition of the teacher's input*, e.g. by enlarging fonts, adding diagrams or illustrations, adapting parameters used in problems;
- *providing a means by which subject and pedagogic knowledge can be improved and kept up to date*, e.g. accessing the Virtual Teacher Centre in the NGfL to

obtain practical advice, to exchange ideas with peers and `experts' outside the school;
* *aiding record keeping and reporting*, e.g. storing and regularly updating formative records which can form the basis of a subsequent report.

Having read this chapter you should now be able to identify which type or types of software would be likely to be helpful in each of the above aspects. In the next chapter we get down to detail in looking at applications of the resources met in this chapter to the content of the secondary school mathematics curriculum. Before starting this, now would be a good time (if you haven't already done so), to set out what you think are your main needs at the moment in improving your ability to deploy ICT effectively. The TTA subject Needs Identification books contain a four-page form to help with this and the CD-ROM also contains an electronic version of it. For convenience we reproduce the form below.

Individual Training Needs

1.   Planning

In planning to use ICT to achieve subject teaching objectives, you might consider the following aspects of the TTA's Expected Outcomes as possible training needs:

    a. understanding and considering the advantages and disadvantages of using ICT;

    b. planning to use ICT so as to provide access to the curriculum for those pupils who might otherwise have difficulties because of their special educational needs;

    c. preparing for lessons using ICT by selecting and preparing appropriate sources of information, relevant software and the appropriate technology, and deciding on the most effective organisation of the classroom and pupils.

2.   Teaching

In using ICT effectively in your teaching, you might consider the following aspects of the Expected Outcomes as possible training needs:

    a. extending pupils' learning in the subject through the use of ICT;

b. intervening and posing questions to stimulate, direct, monitor and assess the learning of pupils who are using ICT;

c. employing the use of ICT with other resources and methods to achieve your teaching objectives.

3. Assessing and evaluating

In assessing pupils' progress in the subject and evaluating the effectiveness of using ICT, you might consider the following aspects of the Expected Outcomes as possible training needs:

a. enabling pupils to demonstrate their knowledge, understanding and skills in the subject while using ICT;

b. ensuring that pupils' learning in the subject is not masked by the technology being used;

c. judging how the use of ICT can alter expectations of pupils' attainment;

d. judging the effectiveness of using ICT in achieving teaching objectives.

4. Personal, professional use of ICT

In the context of the subject(s) that you teach, and to increase professional efficiency and reduce administrative burdens, you might consider the following aspects of the Expected Outcomes as possible training needs:

a. using generic and/or subject-specific hardware and software, e.g. databases, internet, presentation tools, scanners, printers etc;

b. using ICT to aid record-keeping, analysis of data, target-setting, reporting, transfer of information etc;

c. accessing and using resources, including from the NGFL and the Virtual Teacher Centre;

d. accessing research and inspection evidence.

Can you identify any of these fourteen points as ones you already feel reasonably confident with?

Can you identify, say, four of the remaining points you would class as immediate priorities?

Can you identify, say, another four of those points which are left as longer-term goals?

THE TTA CASE STUDIES

Finally we suggest you review each of the four secondary mathematics case studies on the TTA Needs Identification CD-ROM to see, e.g.:

- which ICT tools the teacher has chosen to use;
- how the choice of ICT has affected the organization of the lesson;
- what preparation was required to use the ICT.

In case access to the CD-ROMs is difficult or impossible here is a brief summary of the case studies.

Case study 1: Geometry

This example uses a Year 7 mixed ability class, ages 11–12, in an urban comprehensive school. The lesson is one in a series on angles and parallel lines paving the way for a proof that the angle sum of a triangle is 180°. The class is working in a computer suite which has enough networked Windows PCs for each pupil. However, the teacher has decided to organize the class to work in pairs to facilitate pupil–pupil discussion. The chosen ICT tool is dynamic geometry software (DGS), which the class has used before and for which the school has a site licence. The teacher has access to a dedicated PC linked to a video projector for whole class display. She is concerned that students develop good habits of record keeping when using ICT and she insists that they record their findings both on paper, and using the text facility of the DGS. As well as giving an oral and visual introduction to the lesson, the teacher has prepared differentiated printed materials. She used a wordprocessor to produce three different versions of a task sheet with differentiated outcomes and vocabulary, and printed these out on three different coloured sheets of paper.

✎ *How could you use Cabri in such a way to first help teach the angle sum of a triangle, and then develop this into a general rule for regular polygons?*

✎ *Could you approach this using any other ICT tools? How would this affect the approach?*

Case study 2: Data handling

This lesson takes place in a girls' inner city comprehensive school. The teacher introduces the lesson to an average ability Year 8 class, ages 12–13, without using ICT. The pupils sit around tables in the centre of the room and work in pairs. They using practical measuring apparatus (tape measures) to find the diameter of each other's neck and wrist, recording their names and results on paper. The room has a set of sixteen networked Windows PCs around the edges of the room. While the teacher discusses with the class ways in which the data might be displayed and analysed, the ICT technician sets up a spreadsheet file with the girls' data on the public area of the network. The girls then work in pairs using the PCs with a spreadsheet to extract statistics from the data. They calculate the means of the neck sizes and wrist sizes. They sort the data to find the maximum, minimum and median of each. They calculate the range, and are shown how to find quartiles and the inter-quartile range as a measure of spread. They use the graphing features to produce a scattergram. They save their results for future use. The teacher has her laptop connected to a large screen TV/monitor on a stand, using a VGA/TV convertor. The lesson finishes with the girls back at their tables interacting with the teacher who uses the whole-class display to bring out the ideas of fitting a linear graph to the data.

 Could you use graphing calculators for this lesson instead? What would be the benefits and/or disadvantages?

Can you plan a lesson using, e.g. spreadsheets and/or graphing calculators to involve practical measurements of the diameter d *and circumference* c *of a variety of circular objects to lead into the linear relationship:* c = π d.

[Note: from a geometric viewpoint this approach is unnecessary if the idea of similarity is well understood – but it does also help to bring out ideas about inaccuracies in measurements and the reliability of approximations.]

Case study 3: Number

Here a small class of lower ability Year 9 students, ages 13–14, from an inner city comprehensive school are participating in a lesson on numeracy involving multiplying and dividing by 10, 100, 1000, etc. The lesson takes place in an ICT room which has twenty networked PCs. The teacher starts the lesson with work on the whiteboard. The ICT tool the teacher has chosen is a piece of 'small software' in the form of a number game. The teacher demonstrates the software using a laptop computer with a colour display pad for the OHP. This requires the room to be darkened for a while. Then the students work in pairs using the same software on the PCs. The teacher pairs weaker and more able pupils together. Finally the lesson finishes with consolidation work around the whole class display.

 Can you locate resources, e.g. from catalogues of published software which could help teach aspects of number in this way?

 Could you use other ICT tools, e.g. graphing calculators, spreadsheets or True Basic to make your own version of the kind of game used in this example?

Case study 4: Algebra

The lesson takes place in a semi-rural comprehensive school with a top set of Year 10 pupils, ages 14–15. The lesson is about using algebra to model the areas of polygonal shapes, to graph them and to find the maximum value subject to some constraints. This case study also appears in printed form in the TTA book *Identification of Training Needs: Secondary Mathematics*. The chosen ICT tool is the TI-83 graphing calculator, and the lesson takes place in an ordinary mathematics classroom which is not equipped with PCs. The teacher introduces the lesson using a TI-83 with Viewscreen and OHP, projected onto a white-board. The pupils then carry out tasks in pairs using GCs, and recording results on paper. The lesson concludes with the teacher running through the problem and inviting students to come to the front to share their results by keying appropriate formulae into the teacher's display model of the GC.

 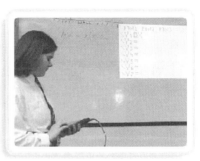

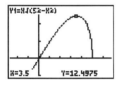 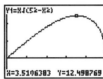 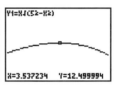

The problem starts with a 10m length of rope, a long wall and one post. The pupils find the maximum area of an isosceles triangle with two equal sides of length 5. The extension is to use two posts, first to create a rectangle, and then a trapezium.

✎ *Can you solve the triangle, rectangle and trapezium problems using a GC?*

✎ *Can you solve them using other ICT tools?*

✎ *If you were to use this, or a similar, problem in a lesson which ICT tools (if any) would you choose? Explain your reasons!*

Chapter 2

ICT and the school curriculum

This chapter is where we break the curriculum down into bite-size chunks and look for ways in which ICT tools can support teaching and learning of specific pieces of mathematics content, such as number or algebra. However there are many dangers in creating false divisions between parts of mathematics, and in treating mathematics apart from other subjects, so we also try to inject examples of more synthetic, and cross-subject, approaches. By the end of this chapter you should be in a strong position to know *which* aspects of school mathematics are amenable to its use. As a bridge into the next chapter we will examine some of the teaching issues raised about ICT use in the case studies on the TTA Needs Identification CD-ROM.

In the last chapter you had an opportunity to learn about and, we hope, to explore a wide range of different ICT tools (hardware and software) which are potentially of interest to mathematics teachers. Now we take a look at the mathematical content of the school curriculum and start to identify a selection of material and approaches where ICT can be an integral part of the teaching and learning process. Of course there is variety in both the content and style of presentation in the mathematics curriculum between different countries. For example now within the UK there are four different curricula for England, Scotland, Wales and Northern Ireland. Similarly there is variety between the amount of mandatory ICT use which teachers are obliged to provide for their students. For example, in England there has been a recent revision of the primary school mathematics curriculum (the National Numeracy Strategy) in which pupils of ages 9–11 are expected to be taught to be confident, competent and critical users of electronic calculators before they enter secondary schools.

Our style here is one of 'theme and variations' where we take an aspect, such as place value in arithmetic, and suggest a number of different ways this can be supported depending on the ICT available. Where possible we provide references to point to relevant examples of teachers writing about their own experiences. Our aim is to stimulate your imagination (and, we hope, whet your appetite) so that you will come up with ideas of your own to fit in with your personal teaching style and strategies. We also aim, that by working at applications which are realistic to you in the context of mathematics teaching, you will become more aware of the capabilities of suitable ICT tools and proficient in their use.

In considering the content we can identify some different roles for the ICT, e.g. as:

- (1) a generator of problems, e.g. using random numbers;
- (2) a checker of results, e.g. in comparing a student's input with computed results;
- (3) a provider of context, e.g. in the form of a game.

We can also think of different ways the ICT may be deployed, e.g. by:

- (4) the teacher using it with whole class display, e.g. to stimulate discussion;
- (5) students working in pairs or small groups at a task or investigation;
- (6) the teacher using it to prepare material for the class;
- (7) students using it to communicate results.

Beware! There are very many ideas contained in this chapter so you will probably just want to select a few at first reading, and maybe come back for more when those have been digested.

2a NUMBER AND ALGEBRA

Number

As a starting point we now take a direct quotation from the National Curriculum for Key Stages 3 and 4, i.e. pupils aged 11–16, in mathematics for England from September 2000:

Integers: *Pupils should be taught to use their previous understanding of integers and place value to deal with arbitrarily large positive numbers and round them to a given power of 10; understand and use negative numbers, both as positions and translations on a number line; order integers; use the concepts and vocabulary of factor (divisor), multiple, common factor, highest common factor, least common multiple, prime number and prime factor decomposition;* (This can be downloaded from http://www.nc.uk.net/)

Place value

If we start with the idea of rounding an integer to a given power of 10 then we can consider illustrating some of the different approaches in the bullet points (1)–(7) above. For example a very simple way of combining (1) and (4) is to use a graphical calculator to generate a random integer with, e.g. five digits, and to display it using the panel for the overhead projector.

Then the class can be asked to write down what they think the answer is to the nearest 10, 100, 1000 and 10000. The advantage here is that the teacher is just as unprepared for the actual problem as the students. So, psychologically, it may appear to be the class and the teacher working together to crack the problems posed by the machine. Of course we can get the calculator to display the set of answers.

But this probably is not something many of us would be too happy to try to explain to students, or even to ourselves! Here we have used one of the LIST operations to create a list of four elements where X takes the values 1, 2, 3 and 4. For instance, when X = 2 the value is 100*round(A/100,0) . This means A is divided by 100 to give 483.97, and this is rounded to zero decimal places to give 484 before being multiplied by 100, giving 48400.

The layout of a spreadsheet might be more attractive, and it can help show informative intermediate steps. Suppose we enter a number, such as 48397, in cell A1. How can we show the steps taken to round to each successive power of 10? Clearly we can enter the possible powers as 1, 2, 3, 4, e.g. in cells A3:A6 . In cell B3 we can enter the formula '=10^A3' to show the corresponding power of 10. In cell C3 we could enter '=INT(A1/B3)' which would give the correct result for this case. However if we tried to drag the formula down the next few rows this would be updated to '=A2/B4' in cell C4, '=A3/B5' in cell C5 and so on. We need a way of making sure that reference to cell A1 does not get changed. This is called an *absolute reference*, and uses the dollar symbol: '=A$1/B3' and '=$A$1/B3' are examples.

In the first case the $ in front of the 1 means that the 1 won't change, in the second it means neither the A, nor the 1, will change. In D3 we can enter '=B3*C3'. So this shows us the value truncated to the given power of 10. In E3 we can enter '=$A$1-D3' to show the discarded digits. We need to test whether these are more than half-way to the next value so we use an IF statement in F3 i.e. '=IF(E3>0.5*B3,B3,0)' . This means that if the number in the E column, the discard, is greater than half that in the B column then we record the corresponding power of 10, otherwise just a zero. Finally we add this adjustment to give the result in G3 by '=D3+F3'. We could have made one complex command to do all this, but here we have chosen to go in 'bite-size' chunks!

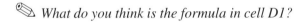

```
Data Editor                                                    _ □ X
File  Edit  View  Insert  Format  List  Data  Help

TI InterActive          ▼ 10  ▼   B  I  U  ≡ ≡ ≡  ⊞ ▼ ♦ ▼ A ▼

     F3          =IF(E3>B3/2,B3,0)

              A        B        C        D        E        F        G      ▲
    1       48397
    2
    3         1       10     4839    48390        7       10    48400
    4         2      100      483    48300       97      100    48400
    5         3     1000       48    48000      397        0    48000
    6         4    10000        4    40000     8397    10000    50000
    7
    8
  ◄ ► List ⋀ Matrix ⋀ Spreadsheet        ◄ ►              ►
```

Now you can highlight cells B3:G3 and drag them down to fill the block B3:G6 . If you change the value in cell A1 the table is automatically recomputed, but if the number has more than five digits you will also need to extend the table downwards.

We can use the same vehicle to illustrate points (2) and (5). Here the teacher has designed the layout of a simple spreadsheet into which students enter their own answers and check whether they are correct or not. Such a pre-designed sheet is often called a 'template'. The questions are set up in columns A and B, i.e. round the number in column A to the power of 10 in column B. Students over-type the 0 in the C column with their answer. Unless this is the correct one, column D displays the text 'No'. When a correct value is entered this changes to a 'Yes'.

✎ *What do you think is the formula in cell D1?*

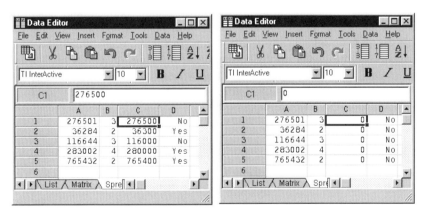

Our version of the formula for D1 is: '=IF(C1=10^B1*INT(A1/10^B1+0.5), 'Yes','No')

Of course you could make the sheet more attractive, include instructions, and/or compute a test score, but for the moment we are just aiming to show some of the principles. It may well be, too, that you can find published examples of 'small software' which embed this kind of approach in a more attractive environment.

One such example comes from the *Numbers* program which is part of the *Developing Number* software pack produced by the Association of Teachers of Mathematics (ATM).

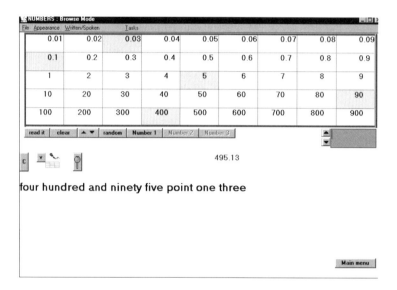

Here the teacher can use it to set up a grid (known as a Gattegno chart) giving a specified number of digits either side of the decimal point. A number can be entered on the grid by using the mouse, or the software will generate a number using the 'random' button. The resulting number, e.g. 495.13, can be copied to the area below the screen, one digit at a time, by selecting the 'Number 1' button. This number can then be shown in words, and also read out aloud (assuming you have audio output) by the software. The teacher can use the mouse to point to any digit of the number and the corresponding cell on the grid changes from yellow to red. Such flexible software can be also be used to set a variety of differentiated tasks for individual students.

A *Logo* number line microworld

We may also want to be able to show decimals on a number line. Here we will develop the idea of a *Logo* microworld. First we will produce a procedure which draws a number line from 0 to 1 marked in tenths and hundredths. If we plan to make use of colour, then it might be an idea to store some names. *Logo* has the commands SETPC (for SETPENCOLOR) and SETFC (for SETFLOODCOLOR). These are followed by a list of three numbers giving the amounts of red, green and blue to use on a scale from 0–255. Thus [255 0 0] is the information required to define 'red'. So in *Logo* we could use the instruction: MAKE "red [255 0 0] and later use the stored variable with SETPC :red . The utility procedure called Palette sets the useful colour names.

```
Editor                                                    _ □ ×
File  Edit  Search  Set  Test!  Help
To palette
 MAKE "red [255 0 0] MAKE "green [0 255 0]
 MAKE "blue [0 0 255] MAKE "magenta [255 0 255]
 MAKE "white [255 255 255] MAKE "black [0 0 0]
End
```

The procedure NumLine01 basically uses *Logo*'s screen co-ordinate system to draw a line between (-350,0) and (350,0) divided into 100 sections. There are three loops. The first draws 100 little green divisions at every 0.01 between 0 and 1. The second draws slightly longer magenta ones at 0.05, 0.15, etc. up to 0.95. The third draws and labels slightly longer black ones at every 0.1 from 0 to 1, and draws the number interval [0,1].

```
Editor                                                                    _ □ ×
File  Edit  Search  Set  Test!  Help
To NumLine01
 Palette
 MAKE "unit 7 MAKE "X 0
 PU SETX -350 SETH 90 PD SETPC :green
 REPEAT 100 [PU FD :unit PD SETH 0 BK 5 FD 5 SETH 90]
 PU SETX -350 SETPC :magenta PU SETH 90 FD 5*:unit
 REPEAT 10 [PD SETH 0 BK 9 FD 9 SETH 90 PU FD 10*:unit]
 PU SETX -350 SETH 0 SETPC :black PD BK 10 LABEL :X FD 10
 REPEAT 10 [MAKE "X :X+0.1 SETH 90 FD 10*:unit SETH 0 BK 10 LABEL :X FD 10]
 PU SETX -350 SETH 90 PD HT
End
```

For convenience we have a little procedure called Reset which just clears the screen and runs the NumLine01 procedure.

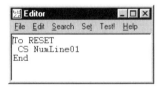

```
Editor                        _ □ ×
File  Edit  Search  Set  Test!  Help
To RESET
 CS NumLine01
End
```

In order to show points on the number line we have the equivalent of a 'mapping pin'. This procedure, called Blob, takes two arguments. The first is the decimal *x* between 0 and 1 to be represented, the second is the colour of the 'pin's' head. It draws a blue pin with a circular red top which is filled in with the colour specified by the second argument :c. This uses the *Logo* primitive CIRCLE :r to draw a circle whose centre is the turtle's current position and whose radius is :r. The command FILL floods the area from the turtle to the nearest boundary in the colour set with SETFC.

We now define a utility called Mark with the single argument :x which uses Blob to 'stick a pin' in the line at the decimal number *x* between 0 and 1.

The next tool is called Pick which uses *Logo*'s random number generator to pick a pseudo random integer between 0 and 100. This is used to call Blob, with the fill colour as white.

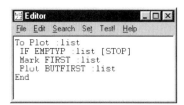

The final tool is one to let you plot a list of decimal numbers. It uses some list processing and recursion to strip each number from the list and stick the appropriate red pin to the line.

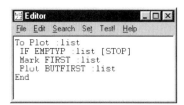

If we now issue the commands: RESET, Mark 0.92 and Pick we can illustrate some of the possible uses for our decimal number line.

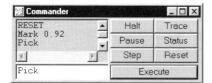

The screen below shows the result. The filled pin is at 0.92, whereas the hollow pin is at the computer's random choice. If you entered: Mark 0.49 you would see the pin's head become filled in with red as feedback for a correct identification.

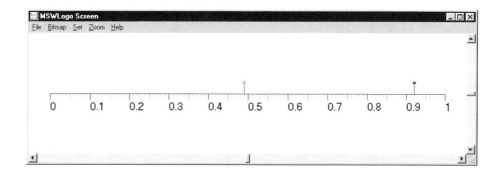

For example, you could enter the list: MAKE 'test [0.57 0.32 0.78 0.05] before showing the output to a class, and then use: RESET Plot :test to display your own values for the class to identify.

Directed numbers

Now we turn to negative numbers. The hint in the English national curriculum is to use a geometric model. So maybe we can make good use of *Logo* or dynamic geometry (*Cabri*).

In most versions of *Logo* we have the commands FD and BK which can both be used with positive or negative numbers. Thus BK 200 is equivalent to FD -200. So we can use these commands to perform 'shift operators'. In order to deal with position it would be helpful if we could have a co-ordinate system. Again this is provided in most versions of *Logo* using variations on a SET command. When you clear the screen with CS, the turtle is at the centre, co-ordinates (0,0) and heading up the y-axis. To move to the point (-200,0) you can use either the full form: SETXY -200 0 or the shorter: SETX -200 . These change the position, but not the heading, of the turtle.

So to set up a number line for a little 'directed numbers microworld' we can define the following procedure, using, e.g. EDIT 'Numline in *MSW Logo*™.

The variable X keeps track of our *x*-co-ordinate. We clear the screen and lift up the pen. Then we slide sideways to (-300,0) while still facing 'up-screen', which we'll call North! Then we put the pen down, move forward 10, then back 20, then write the number stored in X, before retracing by moving forward 10. Now we can repeatedly draw six sections of the number line from (-300,0) to (300,0) each 100 units long. Finally we move the turtle to the centre of the screen and change its heading to point 'East' along the positive *x*-axis.

Before leaving the procedure it would be sensible to show the final position of the turtle. Can you edit the procedure to insert a final 'PD' (pen down) command?

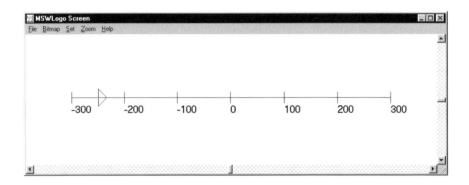

The turtle can be moved to the position shown by, e.g. FD -250, BK 250 or SETX -250 . Now you have a test-bed where directed number represents position using SETX, or a shift using FD. What you do with such a tool is entirely up to you! But it should be quite easy to show, for example that BK -*x* is the same as FD *x*, for any *x*.

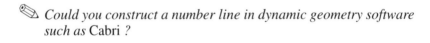

Could you construct a number line in dynamic geometry software such as Cabri *?*

One possible result is shown below.

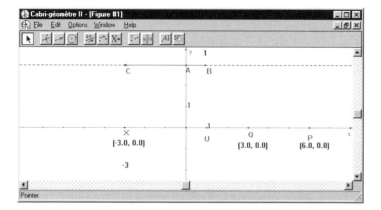

A more convenient approach might be to use some pre-prepared small software package. One example is an application developed for the TI-73 graphing calculator, and hence which can be used with an OHP for whole class teaching. With the development of 'flash ROM' for graphing calculators, it is now possible to download such larger programs, called applications or Apps for short, which extend the functions of the calculator. The TI-73 NUMLINE App gives the user versatile control over a number of different representations for number lines. The following screens show examples of its use for negative numbers as translations.

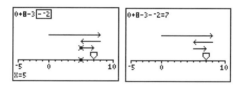

This software can also be used for exploring equivalent forms, and for ordering, using fractions, percentages and/or decimals as shown in the following screens.

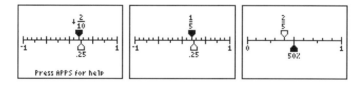

1/7 = 0.142857 142857 . . . has a block of 6 recurring digits . . .

✏️ *Can you suggest which ICT tools might help you to set up an exploration into the number of digits in the block for recurring decimals?*

Standard form

A simple starting point for work on standard form is provided by carrying out an iterative process on a graphing calculator and seeing when it changes the output. First we start with 1 on the display, and then continually use: ANS * 2 to make a doubling pattern. You can also divide by 2 to generate negative exponents.

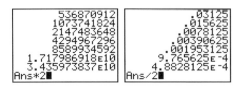

A good opportunity for developing pupils' knowledge and understanding of place value, including standard form, is provided by access to data-sets, such as the Planet's data in Chapter 1, where the units of measurement are very large or very small. Constructing a data base on chemical elements could be an activity which prompts the use of standard form.

Factors

Now we can turn to ideas for: '*use the concepts and vocabulary of factor (divisor), multiple, common factor, highest common factor, least common multiple, prime number and prime factor decomposition;*'
    Obviously we can use a calculator to help splitting an integer into its prime factors. For example the following screens show how we can use a blend of machine and mental calculation in finding the prime factors of 1998.

With *TI Interactive!* you can open up a Math Box (first icon), and then, from the Algebra menu you can choose Factor.

```
factor(1998)
                2.3³.37
```

The *I.T. Maths Pack* was published by the National Council for Educational Technology (NCET) in 1994 and is distributed via the Association of Teachers of Mathematics (ATM), and the Mathematical Association (MA). One of the four books is called *Number and Algebra with Computers and Calculators*. This refers to a number of interesting articles and resources. Accompanying it is a number of activity sheets. One of these is called *A database of numbers*. Here the suggestion is that students should build up their own computer data-base of properties of numbers such as:

> Is it even?
> Is it a square number?
> Is it prime?
> Is it a triangle number?
> What are its divisors?

So here we have an example of the seventh kind of ICT use, where students use ICT to gather, store and communicate results. For an interesting collection of number facts see *The Penguin Dictionary of Curious and Interesting Numbers* by David Wells, Penguin 1986.

A popular way of displaying patterns in multiples is to set up a grid and to highlight, for example, all multiples of a given number. This is quite easy to set up in a spreadsheet, such as the Data Editor of *TI Interactive!*.

✎ *Can you think which formulae could be used to generate, e.g. a 10×10 number grid?*

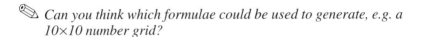

Now we can enter a particular integer into, e.g. cell A1. Then we can produce a replica of the grid with only the multiples of A1 being shown. The formula in A14 is:

=IF(A3/$A$1=INT(A3/$A$1),A3,'*')

If you copy this to the block of cells A14:J23 then the pattern will be shown. There are a variety of number games based upon this sort of grid. For example you could edit the formula above so that multiples of A1 are shown by one symbol, e.g. an asterisk, and others are shown by a dot. Now you could copy a subset of the grid, e.g. B15:H21 and paste it into a new sheet and print it out. So this way you could use a spreadsheet to produce resource materials, illustrating the sixth of our examples of ICT use. Students then have to work out which multiples are being shown by the asterisks and suggest possible numbers for them depending upon where they think the grid was taken from.

A set of grids generated this way could also be stored on a school's internal network (Intranet) for access by students and/or teachers as required.

A simple way to generate powers is using the ANS key on a graphing calculator. For example, to produce the powers of 3 just type '1' and 'ENTER' and then repeatedly use '3*ANS', where 'ANS' is found from '2nd' and '(-)'.

A different approach to this little foray into integers is to look at different ways of implementing Euclid's algorithm for the highest common factor of two integers. This is based on the result that if a positive integer p is a divisor of two positive integers a and b, then it is also a divisor of their difference $c = |a-b|$. Here is a rather inefficient way of coding the algorithm in *TrueBasic*™.

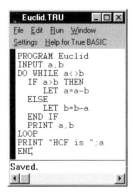

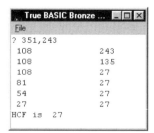

 Can you adapt the program to produce the least common multiple?

Note: Both of these algorithms are implemented within the software of the TI-83. They are found as 'lcm(' and 'gcd(' in the MATH NUM menu.

We conclude this section on factors with an idea for an extended task, or coursework project, on prime factorization. The starting point is to find numbers with exactly, say, four divisors, such as 15 which has the four divisors: {1,3,5,15}, or 343 which has the four divisors: {1,7,49,343}.

✎ *Can you find the smallest integer with exactly 4 divisors?*

✎ *Can you make up a table of the smallest number with exactly n divisors for, e.g. n = 1,2,3,4,5,6... ?*

✎ *Can you devise a way of finding the smallest number with any given number of divisors?*

✎ *Would you advise using ICT tools to help pose the problem, to help with the data-gathering, to check results, to communicate results . . .? If so, which tools would you think are most appropriate?*

Mental methods

By their very nature we might not expect to use ICT tools in this context! However they can be very useful aids to the teacher in finding resources, preparing materials, planning and record-keeping, etc. Mental methods can also be used alongside ICT, e.g. to estimate, round, check, etc. Here we take a simple example of the use of the internet. In almost any area of knowledge you can find one or more websites which give a good set of links to other sites. This is a cross between an index and having access to someone else's phone and address book! So we start with a visit to the Oundle school mathematics site created by Douglas Butler at:

`http://www.argonet.co.uk/oundlesch/mlink.html`

From there we find the page about Maths Resources and pick up the link to the MathsVR – Mathematics Virtual Resources Room (Hampshire) created by Karim Derrick at:

`http://www.mathsvr.demon.co.uk`

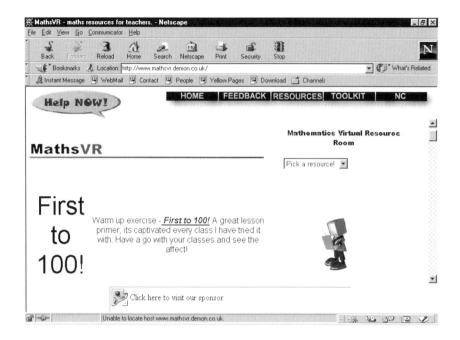

Clicking on the link to *First to 100!* you can now download the *Word*™ document giving the brief lesson plan for this activity, reproduced below.

The 'webmaster', and author, also invites you to contribute ideas and resources to the site. Why don't you visit the site and take up the challenge? Responses to:

```
Karim.Derrick@mathsvr.demon.co.uk
```

Algebra

Now we turn to some ideas to do with sequences of numbers and their relationships with functions, and, later, with graphs.

Again we can take an excerpt from the English national curriculum as a starting point:

Sequences, functions and graphs

6.   Pupils should be taught to:

Sequences

a)   generate common integer sequences (including sequences of odd or even integers, squared integers, powers of 2, powers of 10, triangular numbers); generate terms of a sequence using term-to-term and position-to-term definitions of the sequence; use linear expressions to describe the nth term of an arithmetic sequence, justifying its form by reference to the activity or context from which it was generated

Lesson Planner

Topic: Number (mental skills)   Date: 24/11/00 *Lesson: First to 100* (Warm up exercise)

Curriculum area: Number   Year Group: All years

Learning Objective: Practices basic addition but involves a quite complex game strategy .

Resources: A prize to serve as an incentive

This is a five-minute exercise and works best at the start and/or end of a lesson. It is a two-player game and can involve either the whole class or you and a volunteer. We think that it works best with just the teacher and a challenger, the aim being to beat the teacher (and win a prize!); with even the brightest class, this will still take a while.

The basics
The aim is to be the first player to get to 100. Players take it in turn to choose a whole number between 1 and 10. A cumulative score total is recorded on the white board/screen etc. The first player to score 100 wins.

Example
Player 1 chooses 10 making the cumulative score 10.
Player 2 chooses 10 making the cumulative score 20.
Player 1 then chooses 9 making a cumulative score of 29 . . . and so on.

Optimum Strategy
The first player to score 89 is effectively the winner because whatever happens that player will win (if I choose 1, you choose 10 etc). For the same reason the first player to score 78 will be the first player to score 89 . . . and 67 scored guarantees 78 etc. Keep backtracking and you can guarantee a win if you go first. Since most players will take a while to cotton on to this strategy, it need only be applied later on in the game, thus extending the suspense!

Sequences

Suppose we have a sequence such as 5, 8, 11, 14, 17 …

It is a common task to try to continue the pattern, and maybe to predict the tenth term etc. As a first step it might be helpful to visualize the pattern in terms of pins in the number line. So it should be easy to adapt our *Logo* number lines for this task.

 See if you can work out what to alter – or otherwise load the NumLine100 file.

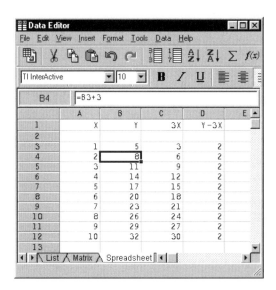

Clearly this is a sequence going up by adding 3 each time. So in a graphic calculator or spreadsheet we could enter the data and the 'term-to-term' rule. Here is an approach using the spreadsheet tool of *TI Interactive!* Cell A3 holds 1, and A4 the formula: =A3+1, which is copied down the A column. Cell B3 holds 5, and B4 the formula: =B3+2, which is copied down the B column. C3 holds: =3*A3, and D3 holds: =B3-C3. The labels in the first row are entered by hand.

So we can see that Y-3X = 2, in each case. So we can solve to give Y = 3X+2 as the 'position-term' rule. You could enter the formula '=3*A3+2' into E3 and copy down to confirm the identity between the two rules.

On the TI-83 there is a Sequence mode. Use 'MODE' and select 'Seq'. When you press 'Y=' you get a rather unusual form of editor. You have three sequences available, called *u*, *v* and *w*. The *n*th term of the *u* sequence is denoted by $u(n)$ so the rule which says that it is three more than the previous term becomes: $u(n) = u(n-1)+3$, which you enter into the editor. Note that *u* is '2nd' '7' and *n* is 'X,T,θ,*n*'. We also need to specify the starting value as 5.

In order to see the numeric output as a table we first use '2nd' 'WINDOW' for 'TBLSET' to setup the starting value and step for the sequence. Then press '2nd' 'GRAPH' for 'TABLE'.

When a student has a suggestion for an equivalent function in terms of *n* alone to try, it is a simple matter to put the potentially equivalent expression into the *v* sequence and to re-compute the table.

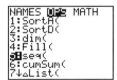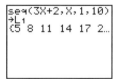

So now there is plenty of scope for a 'guess my rule' kind of tasksheet. Students can then work at producing their own suggestions for 'position–term' definitions, and check their conjectures using ICT, such as a spreadsheet or graphing calculator. We show a couple of variants on this idea, still with the TI-83.

In the '2nd' 'STAT' menu are a number of operations on lists. Choose '5:Seq('. We will enter our rule as:

Seq(3X+2,X,1,10)→L1

So you can see the list on the screen, or by using 'STAT' 'Edit'. Item 7 on the LIST OPS menu is a useful one. We can use it to make list L2, say, hold the differences of the numbers in list L1.

L1	L2	L3	2
5		------	
8			
11			
14			
17			
20			
23			
L2(1)=			

L1	▉L2	◆ L3	2
5	3	------	
8	3		
11	3		
14	3		
17	3		
20	3		
23	3		
L2 ="ΔList(L1)"			

If we change the MODE back to FUNC then we can use Y= to enter the function
Y1=3X+2 and view its table.

Plot1 Plot2 Plot3
\Y1◼3X+2◼
\Y2=
\Y3=
\Y4=
\Y5=
\Y6=
\Y7=

X	Y1	
0	2	
1	5	
2	8	
3	11	
4	14	
5	17	
6	20	
Y1◼3X+2		

Through exercises such as this we can use ICT to make a firm relationship between
the *symbolic* representation as a function (or, informally, as an 'equation') and its
numeric representation as a table or list of its values.

Once this is established we also have the tools at hand to make the links with a
third, *graphical*, representation. We already have the function in Y1, so just choose
a suitable WINDOW and press GRAPH. You can use TRACE to read off data from
the cursor position on the graph. Finally, from MODE, you opt to have the screen
split between a graph and a table with 'G↔T'.

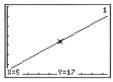
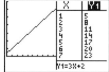

The final screen shows all three representations on the same screen.

Note that:

- We have to be careful about values for Xmin and Xmax to make sure (Xmax-
  Xmin) is a round multiple of the number of pixels across the screen, otherwise
  when you use TRACE the X values show an unhelpful number of decimals!
- We really ought to be careful about distinguishing between the discrete data
  from which we started, where the function $u(n)$ was only defined on the natural
  numbers, and the continuous function Y1(X) defined for all real X.
- Unless the WINDOW is chosen to match the aspect ratio of the display screen
  then the gradient of our linear function cannot be interpreted geometrically. For
  example Y=X will not be at 45° to the *x*-axis.
- The low resolution of the calculator's display screen gives rise to a rather
  stepladder graph in the last screen shot. Any graph shown on a computer
  display, or on paper, is only an approximation to our ideal mental image of the
  graph – after all the line drawing the graph should have no thickness!

Linear functions and their graphs

We now show the similar approach taken in *TI Interactive!* The fourth icon in the toolbar allows us to define a function and compute its table.

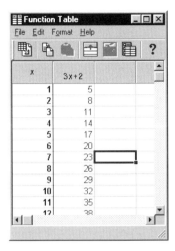

The fifth icon takes us into the List Editor. Clicking in 'formula' space under the title 'L1' of the first column opens the dialog box for information about L1, and we define it using exactly the same syntax as that for the TI-83.

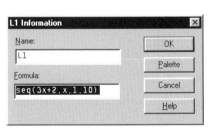

When you have entered the formula for L1, you can click on the function part of the L2 column to enter L2 as the differences of L1. From the L2 Information dialog select Palette, which opens up the Symbol Palette. Select the top-left icon which gives the Command Catalog. If you move the cursor down in the command list you will find the list operation 'deltaList(', with help about the syntax of the command i.e. that it just takes a single list as its argument. So enter 'deltaList(L1)' as the definition for L2.

The final version of the Data Editor screen is shown below. Notice that you can drag the gridlines to make more or less space for the entries in each list.

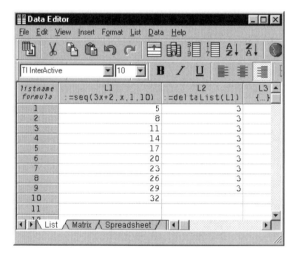

When you close the Data Editor the lists are pasted into your current document. Now select the third icon, the Grapher tool. Use the Functions editor to input your function: y1(x)–3x+2.

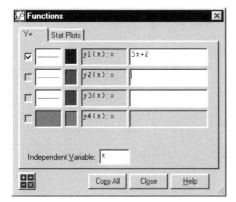

When the graph has been drawn you can edit the values used for the ends of the axes. Using the Grapher's Format button you also change the step sizes on each axis. Then you can use the Trace button to read off values from the curve. You can change, for example, the Trace Step in the Trace Value dialog box.

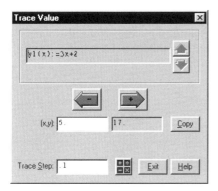

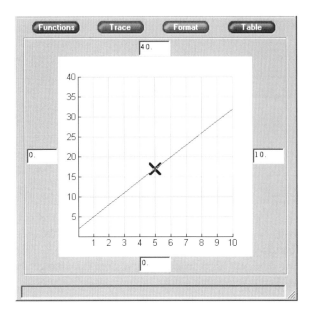

Finally when you close the Grapher window you can arrange your document so that it shows all three representations of the function Y=3X+2 i.e.

- Symbolic
- Numeric
- Graphic.

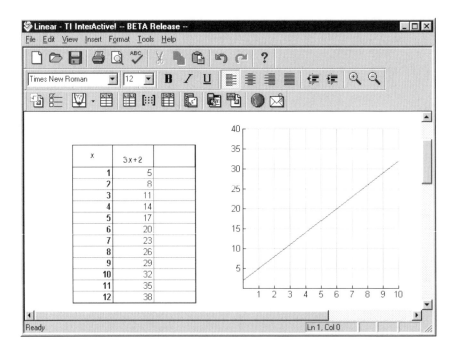

Similar output can be arranged in a spreadsheet such as *Excel*. Once the formulae have been evaluated in columns A and B, you can highlight the block of numbers to be graphed as (x,y) co-ordinates. The trick is to select Scattergram for the graph type, and then choose the format which joins the data points with line segments. You can then edit the title, axes, labels, etc. until you have a representation with which you are happy.

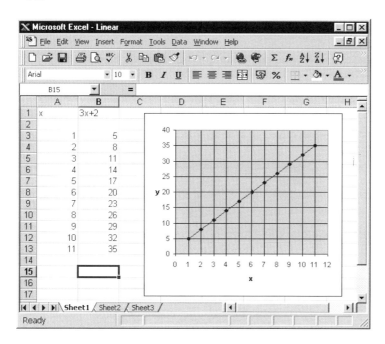

One major problem with using ICT tools with pupils to investigate sequences, functions, tables, graphs, etc. is that they can explore many cases very easily, without keeping any records of what they have been doing, what they have discovered, what problems they have encountered, etc. So another useful application of ICT could be for a teacher to produce a pro-forma on which students can record what they have been doing.

My Equations Name: Class: Date:

My sketch

Y1 =

Y2 =

Y3 =

My table

X	Y1	Y2	Y3

In summary we have reviewed some of the ways you can reinforce the links between different representations of linear functions:

- as a table of numbers with constant first differences

- as a straight line graph with constant gradient

- as an algebraic expression of the form $mx + c$.

In the case of linear sequences, which are discrete sets of numbers, they can be defined by

- a term-to-term rule such as $u_{n+1} = a.u_n + b$ and

- a position-to-term rule such as $u_n = p.n + q$

✎ *Investigate the cumulative sums of linear sequences, e.g. if $u = \{1, 3, 5, 7, 9,...\}$ then its sums are $S = \{1, 4, 9, 16, 25, ...\}$ – what sort of function generates this sequence?*

✎ *Investigate the differences of quadratic, cubic and other polynomial sequences.*

✎ *We leave it to you as an exercise first to develop some ICT approaches to the conventional interpretation of the m and c in y = mx + c, and then, using numeric and graphic representations, for the solution of linear simultaneous equations.*

Simultaneous linear equations

A different approach to simultaneous linear equations is afforded by the symbolic manipulation functions of CAS such as *Derive* and *TI Interactive!*

The following screen shows a step-by-step approach to the algorithm for solution by elimination and back-substitution. Step 9 involved substituting the value 1 for x and expanding. Can you adapt the approach to one where the equations are first reduced to the form $y = f(x)$ and $y = g(x)$?

```
┌─────────────────────────────────────────────┐
│ ▤ DERIVE for Windows - [Algebra C:\MY DOCUM...  ▢□▣ │
│ ▤  File  Edit  Author  Simplify  Solve  Calculus  Declare │
│ Options  Window  Help                    _▣✕ │
├─────────────────────────────────────────────┤
│  ▢ ☞ ▤ ▤ | #n #n #½ | ✐ b→a ▒▒ | = ≈ ⊕ ⁵ᵁᴮ │
├─────────────────────────────────────────────┤
│ #1:   2·x − y = −1                        ▲ │
│ #2:   x + 2·y = 7                           │
│ #3:   2·(2·x − y = −1)                      │
│ #4:   4·x − 2·y = −2                        │
│ #5:   (x + 2·y = 7) + (4·x − 2·y = −2)      │
│ #6:   5·x = 5                               │
│        1                                    │
│ #7:   ───·(5·x = 5)                         │
│        5                                    │
│ #8:   x = 1                                 │
│ #9:   2 − y = −1                            │
│ #10:  (2 − y = −1) − 2                      │
│ #11:  −y = −3                               │
│ #12:  − 1·(−y = −3)                         │
│ #13:  ▓y = 3▓                             ▼ │
├─────────────────────────────────────────────┤
│ Expd(#12)              ⊙     0.0s          │
└─────────────────────────────────────────────┘
```

Quadratic functions

Now we look at an approach to move from linear functions into quadratic functions.

The basic idea is to have a pair of simple linear functions defined in a graph plotter or graphic calculator as, say, $Y1(x)$ and $Y2(x)$ with their graphs drawn in a suitable window. The investigation is one on the 'arithmetic of lines'. For example can you predict the shape of the graph of the function $Y3(x) = Y1(x) + Y2(x)$? If it is a linear function, how are its gradient and y-intercept related to those of Y1 and Y2?

The surprise should come when we change to: $Y3(x) = Y1(x) * Y2(x)$!

We illustrate this with the TI-83, but again you can use other ICT tools similarly by now (we hope).

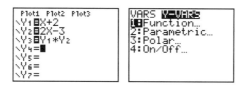

In order to enter the variables Y1 and Y2 you need to use the VARS menu and select Y-VARS and Function, then you can select, e.g. Y1 to paste into the equation for Y3.

Again you will need a judicious choice of WINDOW, depending on how important you judge maintaining the aspect ratio to be. By tracing you should be able to relate the zeros of Y3 to those of Y1 and Y2, and the sign of Y3 to the signs of Y1 and Y2.

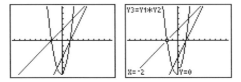

You can also change the screen representation. By moving the cursor over the '=' sign in Y1 and pressing 'ENTER' you can stop the graph of Y1 being displayed, and similarly for Y2. By moving to the left-hand edge of the screen on the Y3 line, and continually pressing 'ENTER' you can cycle through a range of possible graph types for Y3. We have chosen a dotted one. Now you could try to write an expanded version of Y3 as a quadratic function without brackets (or parentheses). If you can't distinguish whether the graphs are equivalent or note you might have to adjust the WINDOW.

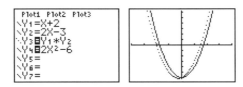

So in this example we are close, but not close enough!

Here we have an example of using ICT effectively to reverse a conventional teaching order. Instead of splitting a quadratic function into linear factors we have used a converse approach of arriving at a quadratic function by the product of two linear functions. Of course it is true that all products of linears are quadratic. Is the converse true? How would you demonstrate it? Of course we could extend the product of lines to produce cubics!

Transformations of functions

Another approach to quadratics is via the transformation of functions and graphs, which is usually only attempted with more able students in the 11–16 age range. Yet with ICT tools this becomes accessible to a wider range of students.

Suppose we start with the function $Y1(X) = X^2$. Then we can easily investigate transformations such as $Y2(X) = Y1(X) + 2$, or $Y3(X) = Y1(X+2)$.

 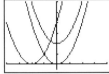

You can use TRACE to sort out which graph is which.

Of course Y1 can be any function, so the same technique can be used for older students, say, to explore the transformations of graphs of trigonometric functions, where terminology such as amplitude, phase shift, frequency etc. take on both graphical and symbolic meanings.

If we build up the general quadratic in terms of transformations then we arrive at the expression: $y(x) = a + b(x + c)^2$ as a much informative representation than the conventional: $ax^2 + bx + c$.

A popular activity to do with guessing functions, and their transforms, is to have a set of screen shots taken from the graphing calculator's screen and re-scaled so that they are the physical size of the calculator's display. These images can then be printed, and then photocopied onto overhead transparencies. These can be cut up with scissors and used for a 'match my graph' game. We provide here a set of 16 such images that you are welcome to use, but you may prefer to make up your own set.

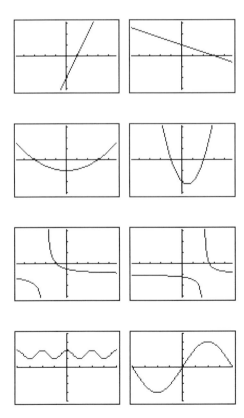

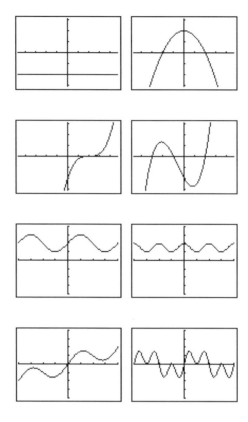

Note: we must stress that in this section we are being guided by the way that algebraic content is usually described in formal syllabuses and curricula. We have not chosen to give practical examples and contexts from which, say, linear, quadratic, polynomial, trigonometric or inverse functions might be derived. Instead we introduce these in Section c of this chapter, which is about statistics and modelling. Of course the handshake example in Chapter 1 could serve as a context for quadratics – can you find others?

Differences

We conclude this exploration on functions with a nice way of looking at the differences of linear, quadratic and other polynomial functions. Here we have chosen a spreadsheet, using *Excel* as our example. Here the three values in the F column correspond to the coefficients in the conventional representation of the quadratic polynomial as $y = ax^2 + bx + c$. A set of consecutive integers are generated in the A column. The formula for the quadratic is entered in cell B4 in terms of cell A4 using either the absolute references, such as $F$1, or the facility in *Excel* to define names for cells – which produces something more like conventional algebraic notation. This is copied down the B column. In column C we find the differences of the values in column B, and similarly column D has the differences from column C. Now we can enter different values for *a,b,* and/or *c* in cells F1:F3. We should find that D always has a constant value.

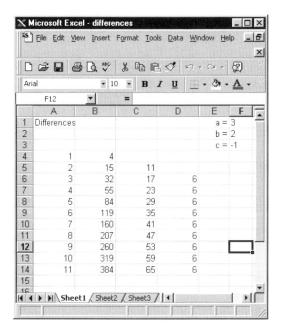

✎ *Can this be zero? How is it related to the value of* a, b *or* c*?*

✎ *Investigate changing the step-size* d *of the* x*-values in the A column, e.g. for 1, 3, 5, 7 . . . or for 1, 1.5, 2, 2.5, . . .*

✎ *Can you make a general rule for quadratics?*

✎ *Can you extend the idea to cubics? To higher order polynomials?*

Iteration and convergence

There is a very nice activity to be found in the NCET *IT Maths Pack* about iteration and convergence. This is described on pages 8 and 9 of the booklet: *Secondary Mathematics with a Graphic Calculator*.

In words and symbols the process is:

1.	choose two numbers A and B (with B ↑ 1)
2.	think of a number X
3.	add A to X to get Y
4.	divide the result by B to get Z
5.	If Z is different from X, replace X by Z and go back to step 3.
6.	Otherwise write down Z as the result.

We could investigate this using a spreadsheet, or *TI Interactive!* or a graphing calculator such as the TI-83. We can convert rules 3 and 4 into the single rule: (Ans+A)/B .

The following screen shows the start of a sequence which after a number of repeated presses of the 'ENTER' key produces 2 as the output.

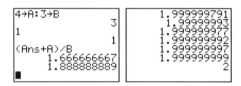

 Can you write programs in Logo, Basic *or the TI-83 to implement the algorithm?*

Results can be entered in a table:

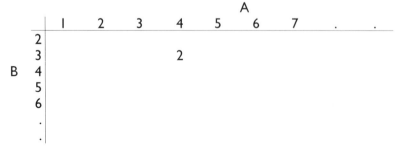

With A=1 and B=8 we get a result like 0.1428571429 so we also have an investigation which can lead into patterns in recurring decimals.

Of course this problem can be solved analytically by seeing if we can find a value X such that (X+A)/B = X which we could illustrate graphically for any given values of A and B as the intersection of two straight lines. Solving algebraically we have X = A/(B-1) , so we can see why the restriction that B ≠ 1 was needed. Graphically we see that we would then have a pair of parallel lines, with no intersection.

Do now have a good look through your own Number and Algebra schemes of work for classes which you teach and see where these, and other ICT approaches could be integrated.

In the bridge between the last chapter and this one you have seen an example of an approach to finding the maximum of a function using graphic calculators.

 Can you think of other ways of approaching this if, say, your only available tool was a spreadsheet, or TI Interactive! ?

We conclude this section on number and algebra with an unusual application of dynamic geometry software. Here we will use *Cabri* to try to find the isosceles triangle of side 5 with the greatest area. This is the problem described in Section 3 of the TTA's book on *ICT Needs Identification in Secondary Mathematics*, and also one of the case studies on their CD-ROM.

Algebraic modelling with dynamic geometry

First we construct a segment, labelled *VW* to represent a section of a straight wall.

Then another segment *FG* to represent the length of a fence. We measure the length of *FG*, and drag *G*, say, until it is as near 5 cm as we can get. In algebraic terms this length is a *parameter* for the problem. We can now construct the midpoint *M* of *VW*, and the perpendicular bisector of *VW*. Using the Compass tool from the Construction menu we can describe a circle centre *M* whose radius is the segment *FG*. We must drag *V* and *W* sufficiently far apart for the circle to intersect the segment *VW* in *B* and *C*. It also intersects the perpendicular bisector in *A*. Now we have made the perpendicular bisector and the circle appear in dotted format. The top vertex of the triangle can slide on the perpendicular bisector, but cannot leave the circle. So we construct the segment *MA* and choose a point *P* on it as the vertex. In algebraic language, *MA* is the *domain* of the *independent variable P*. Now we use the Compass tool again to draw a circle centre *P* with *FG* as radius. It intersects *VW* in points *Q* and *R*. Now we use the Triangle tool to define the triangle *PQR*. This has been filled with colour, and its area has been measured. We now draw the segment *MP* and measure its length i.e. the height of the triangle. As *P* slides on *MA* the height and area both change. So we can fairly easily find the geometric configuration which maximizes the area (i.e. when angle *QPR* is a right angle) and we could illustrate this by reflecting the triangle in *VW* as mirror line to get a rhombus *PQP'R*.

We can also construct the graph of area against height geometrically! First we Show Axes, and drag the origin *O* to a suitable position. Then we can drag one or both

Unit Points on the axes to choose suitable scales to fit the screen. From the Construction menu choose Measurement Transfer and point first at the height measurement, and then the *x*-axis to define point *X*. Repeat with the area measurement and the *y*-axis to define point *Y*. Now we just have to turn these two points into point *Z*. You could do this by drawing perpendiculars to each axis through *X* and *Y* and finding their intersection *Z*. Another approach is to define the vectors *OX* and *OY* and then construct their Vector Sum *OZ* starting from *O*. So now *Z* is a variable point *dependent* on *P*. As you drag *P* so the point *Z* describes a curve. If you construct the Locus of *Z* with *P* then you get the desired *graph* of the area as a function of the height. So here is a way of constructing graphs of functions without using the conventional symbolism of algebra. Given the Calculator tool in the Measurement menu, we can actually compute out all sorts of functions based on variable measurements. So we now have another analytical tool in the armoury. The power of this representation is that as soon as the parameter *FG* is altered, by sliding either of the points *F* or *G*, the whole locus deforms dynamically.

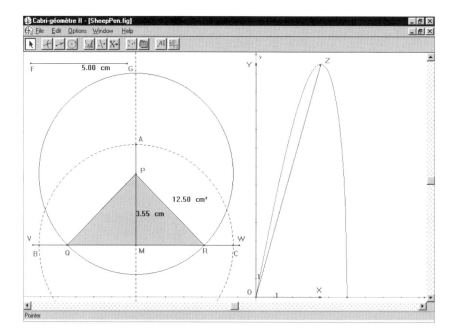

ICT and the teaching of algebra

The availability of ICT tools can clearly impact both on the way algebra is taught, and on the way it is applied. The UK's Royal Society asked the Joint Mathematical Council of the United Kingdom (JMC) to carry out a review of the teaching of Algebra. The report of a working group chaired by Prof. Rosamund Sutherland, *Teaching and Learning Algebra pre-19*, was published by the Royal Society in 1995. Section 1.5 contains the following quotation:

> The growth of IT has made it possible for students to manipulate many different types of external representations on the screen, involving

symbolic, graphical and tabular forms. It is now possible to manipulate graphical representations in ways which were not possible on paper. Harnessing this new power within mathematics and school mathematics is the challenge for the 21st century.

A subcommittee of the Mathematical Association studied aspects of the use of Computer Algebra Systems and reported in 1996 in the book *Symbolic Manipulation by Computers and Calculators* edited by Adrian Oldknow and Jean Flower. There are now graphic calculators (such as the TI-89) which have functions for symbolic manipulation, similar to *Derive*. So it is becoming a real issue for examination boards to be able to specify just what sorts of ICT tools may be permitted in examinations. Conclusions from that report are:

> One thing is clear, the effectiveness of technology in supporting students' learning and understanding depends almost entirely on how it is used. An often repeated cliché perhaps, a self-evident 'axiom', but one which is forgotten all too easily when we focus on the technology itself.

> Teachers and lecturers need planned support to help them gain the necessary expertise to explore the full potential of using such IT tools. They will need to involve students in the use of new technological devices in a variety of mathematical situations. Students should be encouraged to evaluate critically the use of technology and make informed judgements in their use.

> Examiners will need to develop an awareness of the facilities offered by such machines. Current syllabuses and assessment methods will need to be reviewed.

2b   GEOMETRY AND TRIGONOMETRY

In the English National Curriculum the very word 'geometry' is hard to find! The area of the curriculum, known as Ma3, is headed 'Shape, Space and Measures' – but it does contain some familiar geometric content, such as applications of Pythagoras' theorem, circle properties, transformations, co-ordinates, construction, locus etc. However, following its revision in 1999, there are now specific references to the use of ICT by students. For example, in Key Stage 3 (age 11–14) we find:

Using and applying shape, space and measures

1.   *Pupils should be taught to:*

Problem solving

a)   *select problem-solving strategies and resources, including ICT, to use in geometrical work, and monitor their effectiveness*

and

Measures and construction

4.   *Pupils should be taught to:*

   .....

   ### Loci

   j)   *find loci, both by reasoning and by using ICT to produce shapes and paths*

We have already seen that one of the case studies on the TTA Needs Identification CD-ROM for secondary mathematics is based on a lesson where 11-year-old students use dynamic geometry software to explore angles in parallel lines, leading to the angle sum of the triangle. Obviously *Cabri* will be our major ICT tool in this section, but we shall use *Logo* for angle, and TI-83, *TI Interactive!*, spreadsheets and *True Basic* for work on co-ordinates, trigonometry etc.

   As with the last section we shall begin by taking an extract from the English National Curriculum and seeing how ICT might be used to support its teaching and learning.

Geometrical reasoning

2. *Pupils should be taught to:*

   .....

   ### Properties of triangles and other rectilinear shapes

   e) *use their knowledge of rectangles, parallelograms and triangles to deduce formulae for the area of a parallelogram, and a triangle, from the formula for the area of a rectangle*

   f) *recall the essential properties of special types of quadrilateral, including square, rectangle, parallelogram, trapezium and rhombus; classify quadrilaterals by their geometric properties*

   g   *calculate and use the sums of the interior and exterior angles of quadrilaterals, pentagons and hexagons; calculate and use the angles of regular polygons*

   h) *understand, recall and use Pythagoras' theorem*

Calculating area

One great advantage of the measurement tools within dynamic geometry software is that we now have the means of measuring areas of closed shapes such as rectangles, triangles, polygons and circles. So our first example is just a sort of *Cabri* test-bed for carrying out investigations into areas for (e) above. It could be used by a teacher as an 'electronic blackboard' or you could develop some tasks for students to tackle using some parts of the basic idea.

First we use Numerical Edit to enter the dimensions of a base rectangle: here we use 8 by 5. We construct a long line AX across the screen and also define the vector AX. Then we can transfer the eight measurement to AX to define B. Similarly we construct a perpendicular to AX through A and a point Y on it. Define the vector AY and transfer the five measurement to it to define D. Perpendiculars through B and D meet at C. We can define the polygon (rectangle) $ABCD$ and measure its area to check it agrees with the known formula of: area = base x height. Now define any point D' on the line CD. Construct the segment AD' and a parallel line to it through B. This meets the line DC in C'. So we can construct the polygon (parallelogram) $ABC'D'$ and measure its area. We can also construct a diagonal BD', and then define the triangle ABD' and measure its area. We can also drop perpendiculars to define the segments PC' and QD'. Hence we can define the (congruent) triangles $AD'D$ and BPC', and measure their area. Now, as D' slides on DC, we can see which areas change, which do not, and which are equal. Then we can start to use visual imagery to find explanations for these phenomena.

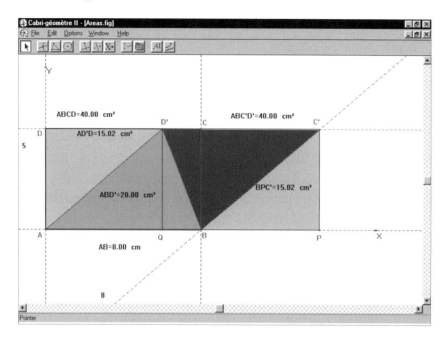

In the above diagram we have used a judicious mixture of line styles (thick, thin and dotted) and colours to try and bring out the features for attention. Of course our static picture is just a snapshot of what is now a dynamic image dependent on the position of D'. If you change either of the defining numbers (5 or 8) then the picture should change size without losing any of its essential properties.

Properties of shapes

A quite different use of *Cabri* is by students themselves, starting with blank 'paper', to create the standard shapes in (f) in such a way that they are robust, i.e. you can't move any of the defining points or edges in such a way that the figure loses its essential shape. As an example the diagram below shows a construction for a rhombus of side 6 based on some of the known properties of a rhombus. Of course the way in which we construct such a figure gives us insight into its properties, and *vice versa*!

 Can you work out how the figure was constructed? Can you think of alternative ways to construct it using different properties? How about other common shapes?

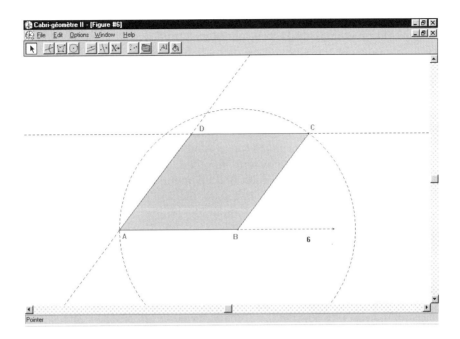

Below is another *Cabri* test-bed. Here six random points A,B,C,D,E,F have been joined using Rays (half-lines). Points A',B',C',D',E',F' have been constructed on these rays so that external angles like $A'BC$ can be marked and measured. Using the Calculator tool in the Measurement menu you can find the sum of the six external angles. Now you deform the position of any of the defining points to see that although some of the angles change, the sum remains an *invariant*. Of course such software cannot prove results like this are always true. (Is it true if the hexagon is concave? Just what do we mean by a hexagon? Can it cross over itself?)

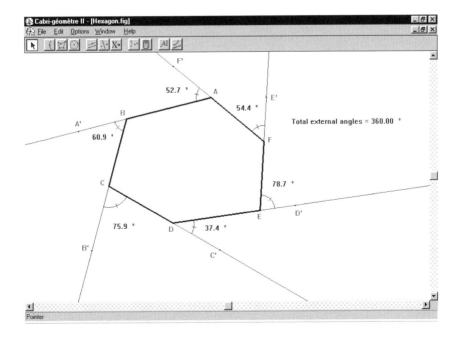

Now we consider how *Logo* handles polygons. First, can we draw a general hexagon? The procedure called Hex below shows a 'hit and hope' approach. It would have been a matter of pure chance if the sixth side had actually been exactly the right length and at exactly the right angle to close the polygon. *Logo* provides a very useful command called TOWARDS which returns the angle at which we need to head to be in the direction of a given point. So first we have to store the co-ordinates of the initial point, using POS to find them. The modified procedure, Modhex, uses this idea to close, but overshoot, the polygon. We have adjusted the angle, but not the length, of the final side. In our final version, Modmodhex, we use the DISTANCE function to calculate how far we need to move with the final side to return to the original position. If, though, we want to finish pointing in the same direction as we started then we can use the known fact about the sum of the external angles to calculate the last amount of turn.

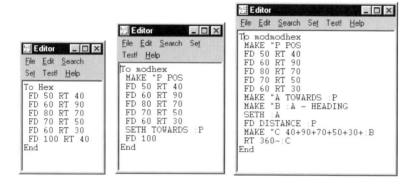

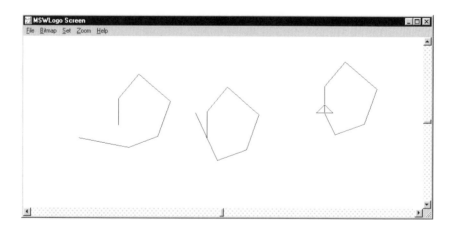

A general form of *Logo* procedure for a regular polygon is given below, and this uses the content of section (g) of Geometrical Reasoning in the National Curriculum for England.

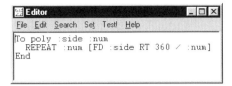

Pythagoras

And so to Pythagoras! Below is one example of another dynamic test-bed. We started by constructing the hypotenuse *BC*.

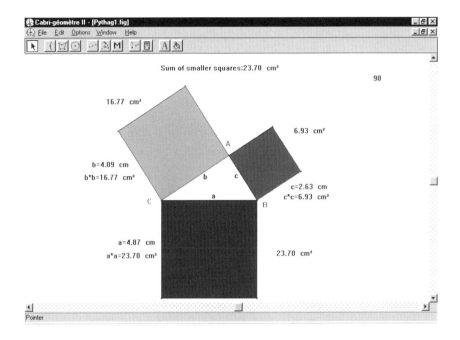

✎ *Can you think how* A *was constructed so that triangle* ABC *is always right-angled at* A*? In order to simplify the drawing of squares on the sides we used a powerful device, called a Macro. This is just like a little program or procedure to do something new using instructions already defined. This makes the software* **extensible***. We will run over how to get a red square drawn on side* AB, *and then how to turn it into a macro to use to get a green square on* CA *and a purple square on side* BC.

First we use Numerical Edit to enter 90 as the angle for rotation. Select the Rotate tool from the Transformation menu and click in turn on point *B*, point *A* and the number 90. This rotates *B* anti-clockwise around *A* through 90° to *P*. Then repeat the process to rotate *A* around *P* to *Q*. Select the Polygon tool and click in turn on *A,B,Q,P,A*. Now we have constructed the square on side *AB*.

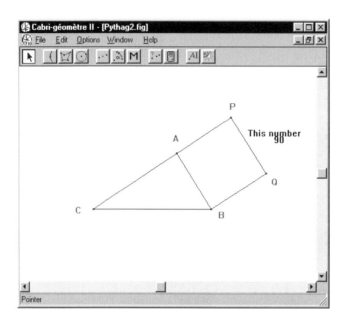

To turn this into a macro select the Macro tool (the seventh icon, shown as X→) and select Initial Objects. We need just three things to define the macro: so click in turn on points *A* and *B* and then the number 90. Use the Macro tool again and select Final Objects (the icon changes to →Y). Just click on the polygon *ABQP* as the output. Finally use the Macro tool and select Define Macro (the icon changes to X→Y).

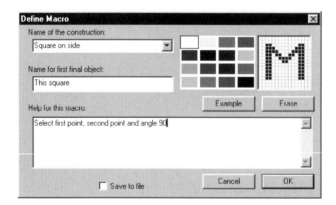

You need to give a name for the new macro, such as 'Square on side' and the message which *Cabri* will show when you point to the object created by the macro, e.g. 'This square'. You can also add some helpful comments in case you forget what the macro was supposed to do! It's a good idea also to tick the little 'Save to file' box, so that you keep your macros saved on your disk. Now when you use the Macro tool you will see 'Square on side' at the bottom of the list. Select this, and point in turn to *C, A* and 90. With luck you will now get the required square. What do you think would happen if you selected *A, C* and 90 instead? Then you can use the macro again with *B, C* and 90.

How many different proofs of Pythagoras' theorem can you find? Can you construct *Cabri* figures to illustrate them? You will find some interesting information in David Wells' *Penguin Book of Curious and Interesting Geometry*. For example there is a very nice one attributed to Leonardo da Vinci. Another copy of triangle *ABC* is added to the bottom of the figure at *XWV* (how could you do this?). Segments *CV, UXY* and *TZ* are added to the figure. The quadrilateral *BXVC* is shown filled. Can you see three other identical ones in the figure? If you rotate it through 90° about *B* can you prove it will fit exactly over *BAUY*? How does this help you prove Pythagoras' theorem?

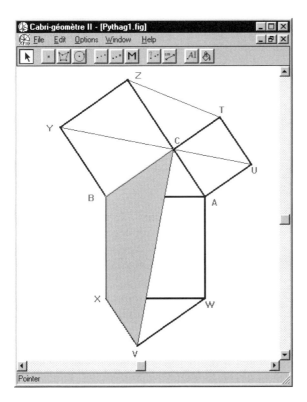

Further ideas

A nice activity is to take a design with a certain amount of symmetry and to try to construct it in *Cabri*. Flags and logos are nice starting points.

*Can you construct the European Union flag: 12 yellow
pentagrams evenly spaced round a circle within a blue rectangle?*

As an example here is a *Cabri* version of the NatWest bank logo.

 Can you work out how to construct it?

Ideas such as these are regularly to be found in *SYMmetry plus*, the Mathematical
Association's magazine for young mathematicians.

An interesting investigation is concerned with Golden ratio, equiangular spirals
and constructions for the pentagon. Robert Dixon's *Mathographics*, Basil Blackwell,
1987, is another excellent source of geometric ideas such as these.

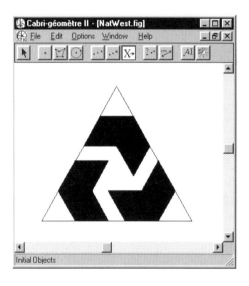

Before we leave this kind of geometry we first mention some unusual theorems to
explore (and explain?) and a nice activity. Wells quotes the following theorems due
to Aubel, Napoleon and Thébault.

 See if you can construct Cabri *test-beds for them.*

Aubel's Theorem: Draw any quadrilateral. On each side construct a square
facing outwards. Join the neighbouring centres of these squares to form a
quadrilateral, and show that its diagonals are always equal in length and are
perpendicular.

Napoleon's Theorem: Draw any triangle. On each side construct an equilateral triangle facing outwards. Join their centres to form a triangle, and show that it is always equilateral. (Note: this construction can also be used to find Fermat's point – can you find out what it is and why it is interesting?)

Thébault's Theorem: Draw any parallelogram. On each side construct a square facing outwards. Join the neighbouring centres of these squares to form a quadrilateral, and show that it is always a square.

Circles and other loci

Now we will take a look at some ideas to do with circles. Here is a conventional diagram, shown in many textbooks, to establish the relationship between the angles subtended by a chord *AB* of a circle at its centre *O* and at a point *C* on the major arc *AB*. We can mark and measure appropriate angles and explore what happens as *C* is dragged round the circle.

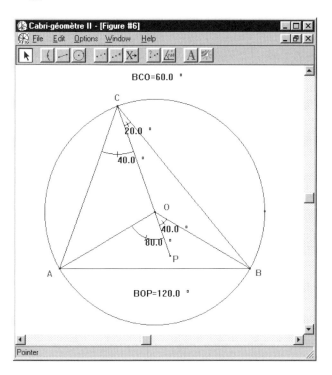

Of course we can use this to suggest the usual 'proof' that angle *BOP* is twice angle *BCO*. But what happens as *C* moves towards *B*, and *P* no longer lies inside triangle *AOB*? Can you adapt the proof to cope with this kind of case?

Can you extend the ideas to showing why angles in the same segment are equal, why the angle in a semicircle is a right-angle, and why opposite angles in a cyclic quadrilateral add up to 180°?

As an alternative to reproducing dynamic versions of static diagrams, we can approach problems from unconventional directions. Suppose you are adrift in a small sailing boat with only a compass as an aid. You see two landmarks on the shore, maybe a church spire and a power station chimney. You take the bearings of each, and work out that they are 60° apart. If you use your mobile phone to tell the coastguard, what can they deduce about your position?

In balder terms we seek the locus of a point *P* which subtends a given angle from two fixed points *A* and *B*. We will try to talk through a general strategy for tackling such problems with dynamic geometry software such as *Cabri*.

First we construct the points *A* and *B* and use Numerical Edit to write the required angle, e.g. 60°. The technique is to define a circle centre *A* and a point *D* on it – we have used an arbitrary point *C* on *AB* as a radius point for the circle. The line *AD* is then like a bi-directional radar beam which we can use to scan over the plane. Our next problem is to be able to draw a line through *B* which makes the given angle with *AD*. This is easy. We just rotate *D* with centre *A* and angle 60° to give *E*. Now we draw the segment *AE*, and a line parallel to it through *B*. This intersects *AD* in *P*. So as we 'crank' the handle *D* round the 'wheel' centre *A* we see the point *P* describe a path. But what is it? One way is to choose the Trace On/Off option and make *P* leave a trail as it moves. Another alternative is to use the Locus option in the Construction tool menu. Just choose the locus of *P* with *D* (on its domain, the circle centre *A* through *C*). Once again we have only really partially solved the problem. The internal angle *APB* is 60° when *P* is on the major arc *AB*, but flips to the external angle for the minor arc.

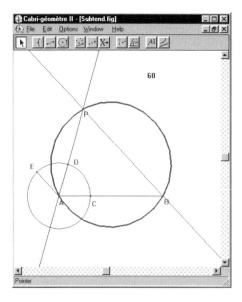

Congruence and similarity

A standard piece of 'traditional' geometry, now resurrected in the new English national curriculum is to '*understand and use SSS, SAS, ASA and RHS conditions to prove the congruence of triangles using formal arguments..*'. Another way into this is to prepare a task-sheet for use together with dynamic geometry to see whether individual, or groups of, students can produce different shaped triangles given any three of the six lengths and angles of a triangle. In this way it should be possible to see why ASA also includes SAA (because of the angle sum of a triangle) and why RHS is rather different from ASS.

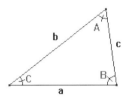

Construct a triangle from the following data, if possible. Measure and record the missing data. Make a sketch in your exercise book. If you think there are other triangles with different shapes using the same data then sketch them too.

a cm.	b cm.	c cm.	A°	B°	C°
3	6	5			
4	5				70
		4	60	50	
5	6		40		
3	4				90
		4	70		
			60	80	40

Another aspect is 'establish the validity of standard ruler and compass constructions'. Obviously the key concept is that a circle is the locus of points in the plane equidistant from a given point. Another is that locus of points equidistant from two given points is their perpendicular bisector. Can you devise activities to establish and/or apply these ideas?

So now suppose we consider the standard ruler-and-compass construction for an angle bisector. A very powerful image here is the rhombus together with the properties of its diagonals, i.e. that they are perpendicular and bisect each other. So if we have an angle *ABC* defined by the half-lines *BA* and *BC* we just need to find a way of 'fitting a rhombus into the corner *ABC*'. So if you define a point *D* on *BA*, say, then you can construct a circle centre *B* through *D* to meet *BC* in *E*. So triangle *DBE* is isosceles. To complete a rhombus we need to construct another, congruent, isosceles triangle *DFE* on *DE* as base, so draw the circles centre *D* through *B* and centre *E* through *B* to meet in a second point of intersection at *F*. Then *DBEF* is a suitable rhombus and hence its diagonal *BF* bisects the angle *DBE = ABC*. As you drag *D* on *BA* only the size of the rhombus alters, not the direction of its diagonals.

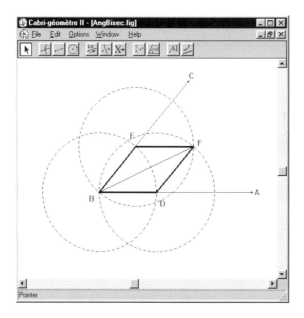

A good investigation for more able students is to use these constructions on the sides and angles of a triangle. For example suppose the angle bisectors of angles *A* and *B* of a triangle meet in a point *P* – what can we say about *P*? Is it obvious that the angle bisector of *C* must pass through *P*? Is *P* the same distance away from corners (vertices) of the triangle? Is it the same distance away from the sides? How could you construct a circle to touch each of the sides? How is its radius related to the area and perimeter of the triangle? Repeat a similar exercise for the perpendicular bisectors of the sides. How about the medians of a triangle (e.g. the segment from vertex *A* to the mid-point *D* of the opposite side *BC*, etc.)? How about the altitudes of a triangle (e.g. the perpendiculars from the vertices to the opposite sides)? Can you construct a circle which passes through the mid-points *D,E,F* of the sides? Where is its centre? What happens to these various 'centres' as the triangle *ABC* is deformed? Are any lines concurrent, or any points collinear?

Transformation geometry

We turn from traditional geometry to studying geometric transformations. In chapter 1 we chose a simple transformation geometry program as an example of small software. Most of the current dynamic geometry software packages, including *Cabri*, provide tools for transformations. For example we can show axes, and display a grid. On this we can define a polygon, such as a 'flag-pole'. Using Numeric Edit you can enter an angle to define a rotation. Using the Rotation tool from the Transformation menu you can rotate your polygon through the given angle around a given centre. In the following figure we have taken an object polygon and shown three successive rotations around the origin through the given angle, currently 30°. As you edit this angle you can see the images deform dynamically.

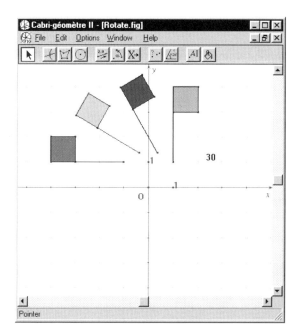

Of course this same test-bed can be used by teacher or student to illustrate or explore properties of various transformations. In fact the new version of the English national curriculum draws specific attention to the ICT opportunities offered by the use of software to explore transformation geometry. For example, we can easily investigate the product of reflections in parallel and non-parallel lines.

In the next figure two mirror lines and an object polygon have been defined. The object (coloured blue) is reflected in the first mirror (coloured red) to give the first image. This is then reflected in the second mirror (coloured magenta) to give the final image. What single transformation could map the blue object to the magenta image? If it was a rotation then corresponding points, like E and E'' would be the same distance away from the centre P. Hence EE' would be a chord of a circle centre P, and hence their perpendicular bisector passes through P. The same argument applies for each pair of corresponding points such as AA'' etc. Hence the perpendicular bisectors of AA'' etc. should all pass through P. Do they? If so, where is P? Does this *prove* that there is a rotation centre X which takes the object to the second image? If X is the centre, how can you find the angle of rotation?

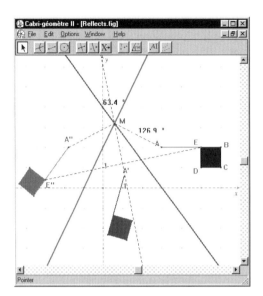

Another aspect to explore about combinations of transformations is whether or not the order matters (i.e. are they commutative?). For example the following screen shows two different ways to reflect in lines *m* and *n*. Under what circumstances will the images marked *Rnm* and *Rmn* be identical? Will this stay true for whatever position the object *R* is placed?

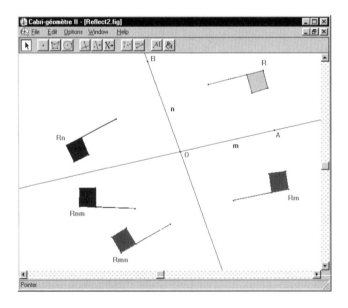

Interactive white-boards

If the school has access to interactive white-board technology, then dynamic geometry is probably the area in mathematics which best exploits its potential. If not then a reasonable simulation can be made by projecting the computer's output onto an ordinary classroom white board on which you can also write with, e.g. non-permanent dry colour markers. Then, for example, students can draw freehand suggestions which can be confirmed (or negated) by displaying computer generated results. As an example we could explore lines of symmetry of standard geometric objects, such as a parallelogram. Suppose we have the parallelogram *ABCD* projected together with the mid-points of its sides *P,Q,R,S*. A student might very well propose that, e.g. *PR* or *AC* is a line of symmetry and superimpose it on the projected image. The class can see whether they agree or not. If required then you can use *Cabri's* Reflect tool in the suggested mirror line to test the hypothesis. An even cheaper solution would to be use the dynamic geometry application in, e.g. a TI-92 graphing calculator together with an OHP display pad.

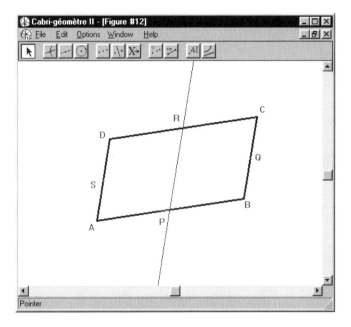

Co-ordinates and vectors

Naturally, similar approaches can be used with co-ordinates. For example we can easily illustrate how to calculate the distance between two points whose co-ordinates we know. Here *A* and *B* are attached to grid-points, but they could just be floating points. Lines through *A* parallel to the *x*-axis and *B* parallel to the *y*-axis are constructed to meet in *C* (what happens if *AB* is parallel to the *y*-axis, or the *x*-axis?)

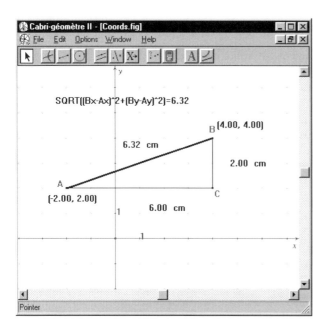

Similarly, higher level students may use the same software to explore vectors. For example we can look at various vector properties of the regular polygon. Here $AB = \mathbf{a}$ is shown in red and $AF = \mathbf{b}$ is shown in green. Can you define each of the other vectors in terms of $\mathbf{a}$ and $\mathbf{b}$?

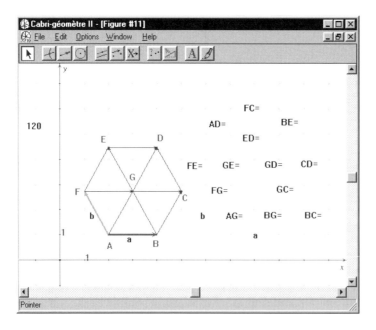

Further ideas: transformations, co-ordinates and Pythagoras

Many of the transformation, co-ordinate and vector ideas can also be explored using, say, *TrueBasic*, but most are more easily explored with graphic calculators such as the TI-83 and versatile graph plotting software, such as that contained in *TI Interactive!* For example we shall use the lists of the TI-83 to hold the co-ordinates of an object shape which we plot using a joined-up scattergram (called an *xy*-line). The idea is to use STAT PLOT to draw the object shape whose *x*-coordinates are held in list L1 and *y*-co-ordinates in list L2. The problem is to work out what combinations of L1 and L2 should go in list L3 and L4 if they are to hold the (*x*,*y*) co-ordinates of the image shape under different transformations, such as a reflection in the *y*-axis. You will need to define a second STAT PLOT to display the image.

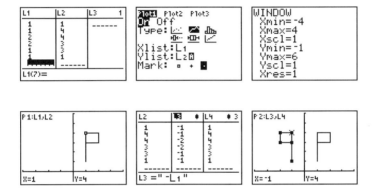

A different approach is to create a program to draw a shape using the Line(x1,y1,x2,y2) command. For example the four-line program 'PYTHAG' draws a right-angled triangle. You will need to choose a suitable WINDOW and FORMAT for the screen and make sure that any function and statistics plotting is disabled. The problem is to extend the program to create the 'Pythagoras diagram' as shown.

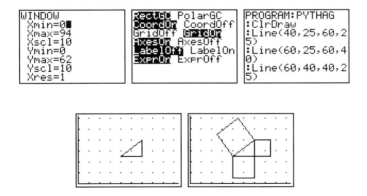

There are many variations on this theme, such as creating letters of the alphabet, symmetric shapes, etc. which are of popular appeal to students.

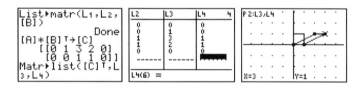

Although neither shears, nor the use of matrices, appears in the latest English national curriculum in mathematics for students aged 11–16, they are still in other nations' curricula. In any case the post-school literature in many subjects, such as physics, geography, statistics, etc. makes use of matrix notation and students can be very disadvantaged if they have not encountered it at school. The NCET task-sheet refers to some small-software from the *Smile* project, called *Matrices*. The activity can be undertaken using other ICT tools, such as the graph-plotting software *Omnigraph™*, or with spread-sheets or graphing calculators. It can also be carried out using dynamic geometry software. We just include a few screens to illustrate the idea and leave you to work out the fine detail. The first group of screens are taken using the lists and matrices of a TI-83 and Stat Plots for the object and image using first L1, L2 and then L3, L4.

A similar approach can be taken in most spreadsheets. However we have to make the rules of matrix multiplication explicit when entering the formulae (not strictly true, as some sheets do provide matrix multiplication as a function). We need to make use of the ideas of absolute reference to cells again. To produce the graph you need to start with a scattergram of columns C and D, and then insert the additional data for a second 'series' from columns E and F. It can take a bit of practice to get control over the layout of the axes, and you will need to drag the corners and sides of the chart window until the unit square appears square!

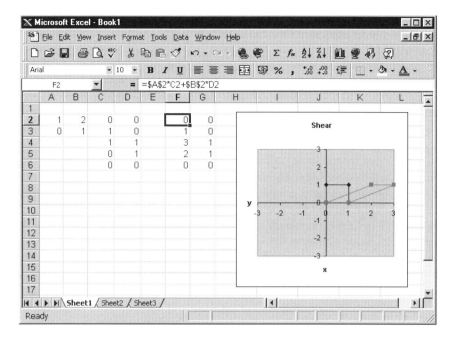

In *Cabri* we use a similar idea, using Numeric Edit to enter the four values of the matrix. Then you can define your object, and measure its co-ordinates. Using the calculator you can 'teach' *Cabri* the rules of matrix multiplication to obtain the co-ordinates of the sheared image. Transferring these values to the axes you can draw the image. Of course now you can measure areas.

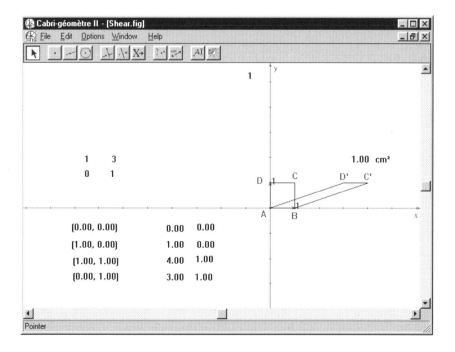

There are also plenty of applications for geometry in realistic situations and some of these will be included in sections 2c on modelling and 2e on links with other subjects. We conclude the part of this section on geometry by taking a look at some of the activities in the book *Geometry with Computers*, and accompanying Activity Sheets, included in the NCET *The IT Maths Pack*. The book refers to some software which is available from BECTa and other sources, but many of the ideas can be explored within *Cabri* and *MSW Logo*.

Further ideas: Locus

Chasing games is an activity based on what are technically called 'curves of pursuit'. In *MSW Logo* we can have several turtles all performing on the same screen. Just use SETTURTLE followed by a number to give instructions to this turtle alone. So we will have turtle #0 to represent Jean who chases Jayne leaving a red trail. Turtle #1 represents Jayne who moves along some path leaving a blue trail. We define just four procedures for this *Logo* microworld. SETUP moves Jayne and Jean to their starting position. CHASE has two arguments. The first is the number of steps to take in the chase, and the second is the length of a step.

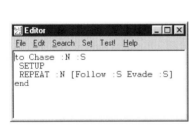

CHASE uses two procedures. FOLLOW makes Jayne turn towards Jean and move forward a distance S. EVADE makes Jean travel a distance S along some path.

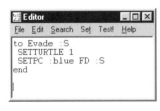

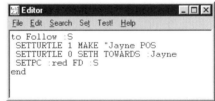

The command CHASE 50 5 results in the following output.

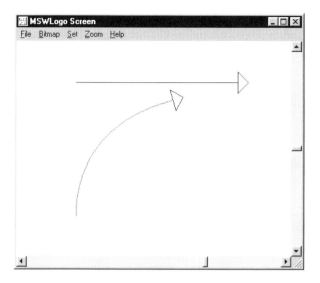

Equal areas: Take points *X* and *Y* on two different lines through *Z*. Choose any point *P* and construct the triangles *PXZ* and *PYZ*. Measure their areas. Drag *P* until they are roughly equal. Can you predict the set of points *P* for which the areas are exactly equal? Can you explain why?

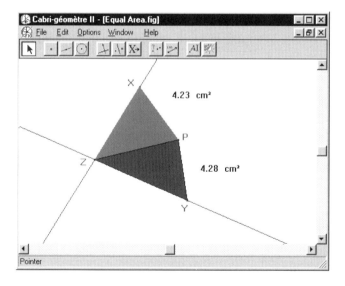

Imagine a clock: This consists of some activities to do with imagining loci and then confirming or amending your ideas when you use software to produce them. There is a piece of small software called *Arms* which was developed by members of the Association of Teachers of Mathematics and is contained in the NCET *Locus* software pack. However, the activity is equally one which can be carried out using the facilities of dynamic geometry such as *Cabri*. The essential idea is to have two circles of radii *r* and *r'*, say. Each has a radius vector (the '*arm of a clock*') which starts from bearings B and B', say. One radius vector rotates at a constant rate in a clockwise direction. The other rotates at a multiple m of this rate (possibly a negative multiple). The ends of the radii are joined by an 'elastic' segment PP'. The activity is to predict the locus of its mid-point M.

The task-sheet suggests you start with OB at 12 o'clock (or at a bearing of 000°), $O'B'$ at 6 o'clock (180°) and take $m = 1$. Then try changing $O'B'$ to 3 o'clock (090°). Now try changing both initial bearings to 000° but change m to 2.

We will run through a way to set up the test-bed for this activity and leave you to perform the 'thought experiments' and confirmation with the software. Start by constructing the line XX' and points O,O' on it. Construct vectors OX and OX'. Use Numerical Edit to enter values, such as 3 and 3 for the radii of the circles, and add Comments as required. Use Measurement Transfer to create points R, R' on OX and OX'. Construct the circles centre O through R, and centre O' through R'. Construct perpendiculars to XX' through O and O' to meet the circles in N and N'. Hide the lines XX', ON, ON' and vectors OX, OX'. Now use Numerical Edit to enter initial values of the bearings of B from N and B' from N', and annotate as required. Use the Calculator to multiply each bearing by -1 and call the results *rot1* and *rot2*. Rotate N about O by *rot1* to get B, and N' about O' by *rot2* to get B'.

Construct vectors OB and $O'B'$. Use Numerical Edit to enter a value for the multiplier m and the angle θ to turn OB through. Use the calculator to multiply θ by -1 to get *rot3*, and by $-m$ to get *rot4*. Rotate B about O by *rot3* to get P, and B' about O' by *rot4* to get P'. Construct vectors OP and $O'P'$, and make them thick. Construct the segment PP' and its midpoint M. Select Trace On/Off and select M. Finally select Animation, and select the turn angle θ, dragging out a rather short 'spring'. When you release this you should see the 'arms' OB and $O'B'$ rotating reasonably slowly on their 'clock faces', and the locus of M being traced out as a thick red line. Just click on the mouse button to stop the animation. To clear a locus just select Hide/Show and then click on the pointer icon. Now you can double click on any of the numerical parameters to set another problem. Reset θ to 0, and use Animate again.

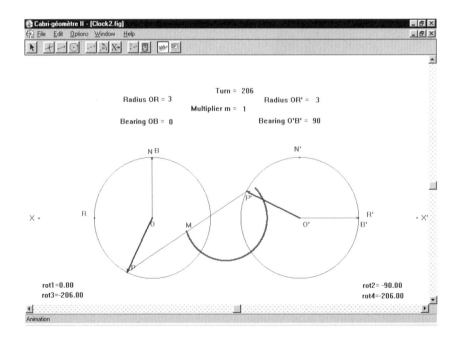

The tethered goat: A goat is tied to the corner of a shed measuring 4m by 3m. The
rope tethering the goat is 5m long. What is the shape of the grass that the goat can
reach? What would happen if the goat was tethered to a different part of the shed.

Of course this is something which you can investigate with a variety of practical
apparatus, starting with a pencil and ruler, before moving to ICT. It is a nice problem,
though, for testing your problem-solving strategies, e.g. using *Cabri*.

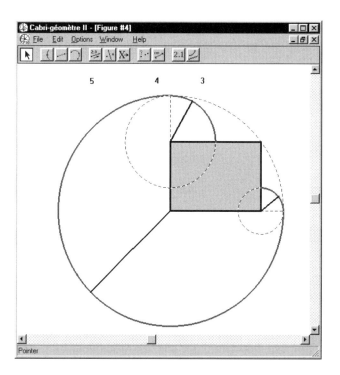

Circles: This activity is described in an article by Greg Morris, which first appeared
in the NCET *Locus Pack*. This describes some 'thought experiments' to do with
touching circles. Again there are a variety of practical ways to investigate this sort of
problem without using ICT. The article describes the use of some small software
dedicated to this problem. However with *Cabri* we can again make a useful test-bed.
Points *O* and *R* define the 'blue' circle. *Q* is any point. *P* is a point on the blue circle.

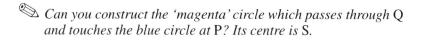 *Can you construct the 'magenta' circle which passes through* Q
and touches the blue circle at P*? Its centre is* S.

What is the locus of S *as* P *is dragged round the blue circle?*

How does the locus change as Q *moves inside or outside the blue
circle?*

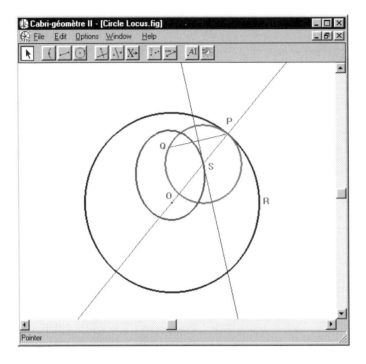

Trigonometry

Starting with right-angled triangles a useful tool is a 'dynamic set square'. Here we have a little *Cabri* test-bed with just two major variables. The point *P* can be moved on arc *QR* to define the angle ∠*A*, and the point *A* can slide horizontally in and out towards *C* to define the base *AC*. The sides of the triangle *ABC* can be measured, and their ratios calculated. Dragging the point *A* keeps the angles constant, so we have similar triangles *ABC* and *OPS*. We can see that ratios are invariants (and that *ABC* is an enlargement of *OPS*). Dragging the point *P* keeps the base constant, and changes the vertical and hypotenuse of the triangle, and hence the ratios.

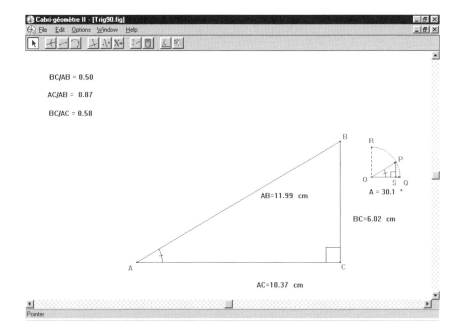

The ratios could be copied down and tabulated against ∠*A* in a spreadsheet or graphing calculator. Needless to say *Cabri* has a Tabulate tool in the Measurement menu to make this easier.

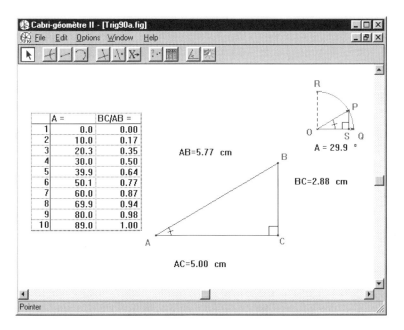

Once the table has been constructed it can be 'cut and pasted' to another application such as the *Excel* spreadsheet.

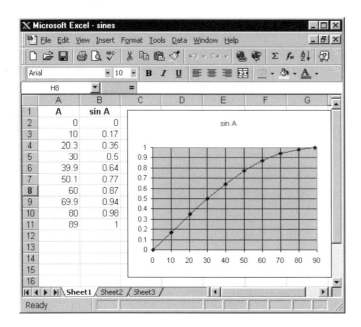

A similar idea can be used to illustrate the trigonometric functions for any angle. Here we start by showing axes and dragging the origin O to a suitable position. Now our x-co-ordinates will be angles in degrees, so we need to reduce the x-co-ordinate's unit length by dragging its unit point towards O. However the y-co-ordinates will be in the interval $[-1,1]$ so we need to increase the y-co-ordinate's unit length by dragging its unit point away from O. With Numerical Edit we can transfer the measurement -1 to the y-axis and hence create a 'unit' circle (in the y-sense!). We can create the point of intersection E of the circle with the x-axis. Using Numerical Edit we can now enter a rotation angle, such as 397. Then we can rotate E about O by this angle to get P, and construct the triangle OPQ. For the sine function we just need to measure the y-co-ordinate of P. (We measured P's co-ordinates and then used the Calculator tool to extract just its y-co-ordinate.) Now we transfer this measurement to y-axis to obtain point Y and the rotation angle to the x-axis to obtain point X. Using perpendiculars we can construct the graph point S. Now mark S as Trace On, edit the rotation angle to -100, say, and then Animate this number. As the 'rotor' P sweeps round the circle, so the point S traces out the graph of the sine function.

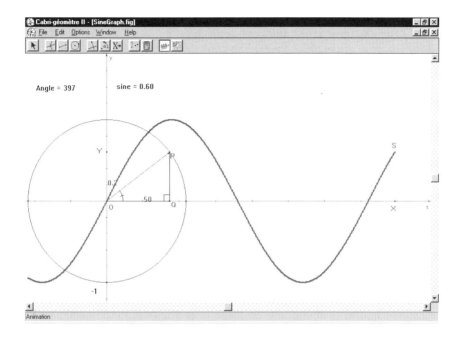

You will need to be just a bit more cunning to get the correct measurements for the cosine function! Within the English higher level curriculum 14–16-year-old students are expected to meet the sine and cosine rules, and also know that area of a triangle is ½ *ab* sin *C* . The following *Cabri* screen suggests one possible useful visual aid for investigating both the cosine rule (as Pythagoras with an error term) and the area.

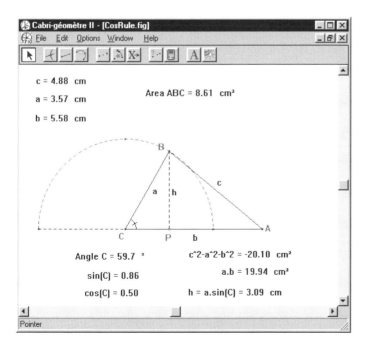

A nice application of trigonometric functions is in exploring parametric and polar curves. For example, using the parametric plotting mode of the TI-83 or *TI Interactive!*, you can explore graphs of the form $x = \cos^p(t)$, $y = \sin^q(t)$ for various values of p and q.

2c STATISTICS AND MODELLING

Handling data

The attainment target Ma4 of the newly revised English national curriculum in mathematics at ages 11–16 (Key Stages 3 and 4) is called *Handling Data*. As with the word 'geometry' in Ma3, the word 'statistics' appears very infrequently, and 'modelling' not at all! The NCET *IT Maths Pack* contains a book entitled *Mathematics in Context*, subtitled *IT in Mathematics across the Curriculum*. An article entitled *Why Data Handling?* describes the **PCIA** data handling cycle, introduced by Alan Graham in *Investigating Statistics*, Hodder & Stoughton, 1990. That cycle forms the basis of the approach taken in the national curriculum.

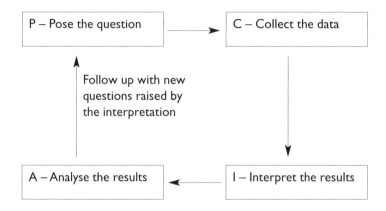

PCIA data handling cycle

In the terminology of the national curriculum this becomes:

- Specifying the problem and planning.
- Collecting data.
- Processing and representing data.
- Interpreting and discussing results.

There is considerable scope for the use of ICT tools within the aspects C, A and I:

C as sources of data and ICT tools for storing and retrieving data;
A to compute statistics from data and to display data graphically;
I to communicate results.

Note: the efficient and rapid exploration that ICT affords can often encourage pupils to pose further questions for themselves, and so impacts on aspect P as well.

To start this section we will take a close look at how far the facilities in just one ICT tool, *TI Interactive!*, can support work in data handling and statistics. We will start with a data source which was included on a disk within the NCET *IT Maths Pack*. This contains versions of a file called *Cities*, which is described in the article *City Life* in the *Mathematics in Context* book from that pack. This data file contains ten data sets from 50 of the world's largest cities, and was published by the Population Crisis Committee in 1990. (See the Appendix for details.)

The article suggests providing opportunities for students to formulate their own questions in both whole-class and small group discussion and gives as examples:

> 'I wonder which city has the highest murder rate.'
> 'Which is the noisiest city..'
> '... and the most congested?'
> 'Why don't you put in order all the data on murders and we'll do the data on noise?'
> 'Yes, then someone else can do traffic flow.'

Obviously we need to care with this, and any other secondary sources of data, whether stored electronically or not. There may be errors, either in the way the data were collected or in the way the data were entered. The data may have been approximated, incomplete, too far out of date to be useful, etc.

Before you can pose and explore your own questions you need to know something about the data that are available to you. The data file is organized as a table with 51 rows and 12 columns. The first row contains the headings for the columns, which are known as the 'Field names'. They are as follows:

Field name	
CITY	Name of city
COUNTRY	Name of country
POPULATION	Population of city
MURDERS	Number of murders per year per 100,000 people
FOODCOSTS	Average % of income spent on food
LIVINGSPACE	Average number of people per room
WATER/ELEC	% of homes with water and electricity
TELEPHONES	Number of telephones per 100 people
SECSCHOOL	% of children (age 14–17) in secondary schools
INFDEATH	Infant deaths (age 0–1) per 1000 live births
NOISE	Level of background noise (1–10) (low-high)
TRAFFICFLOW	Average miles per hour in rush hour

Unfortunately this is not a fully interactive book! So we will make some decisions about the questions we are going to use to illustrate an ICT-assisted data handling approach. Of course you are quite at liberty to choose a completely different set of questions.

One question we often ask secondary school students, if we want to collect a quick data set, is: 'How many telephones (mobile and conventional) do you have at home'. Clearly this number has escalated enormously in many countries over the past five years or so. So this data file gives us some data about the spread of telephones ten years or so ago. Our first problem then is to get a feel for just what that eighth column of data, headed TELEPHONES, actually tells us. We will start by opening the *Cities* file in the *TI Interactive!* spreadsheet. (We will abbreviate *TI Interactive!* to TII from now on.) Here you can see a small extract of the file, and you can scroll across and down to see more of it. We will do the data analysis and display in TII's List Editor. You can also do the same kind of things using the TI-83's STAT Editor. So our first task will be to highlight the data in column H ready to copy and paste it from the spreadsheet into column L1 of the List Editor.

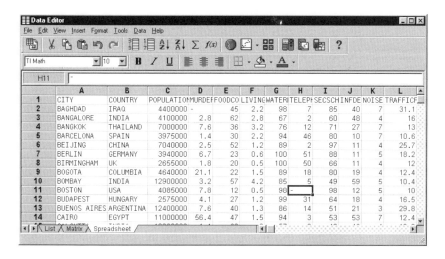

The first problem is that two of the entries on column H are undefined (Boston and Tehran), and marked with a dash, which is not a 'numeric character'. So we will get a syntax error when pasting the data into L1. Just remove the dashes and leave these two cells, H11 and H49, empty. Now when you paste the cells H2:H51 the two empty cells will be ignored. So now our data set has 48, not 50 entries.

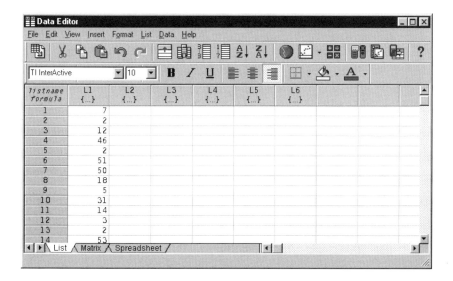

Next we can copy L1 into L2 and sort it. Just click in the Formula field under the listname L1 and enter the formula for L2 in terms of L1.

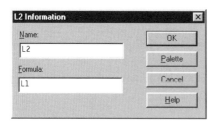

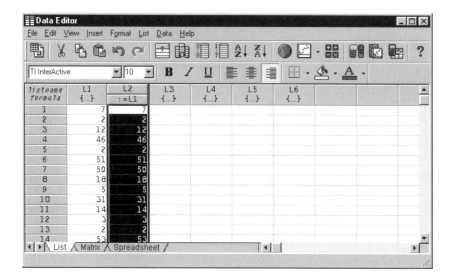

Now with L2 already highlighted just click on the icon with a blue A above a red Z and a downward arrow. This will sort L2 into ascending order.

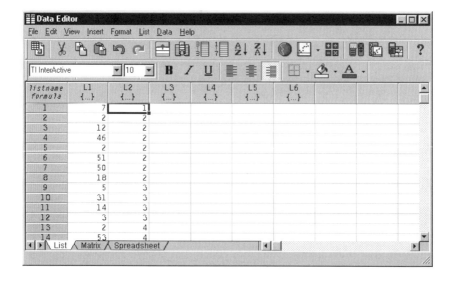

Here we see that the minimum value is 1 phone per 100 people (corresponding to which city?). Of course we might have had some cities where the data recorded were 0 phones per 100 people – would that have meant that there were no phones at all in the city?

Now there are a whole lot of list operations which produce statistics from a given list. In the first cell of L3 we typed 'mean(L1)' and in the second cell 'median(L1)'.

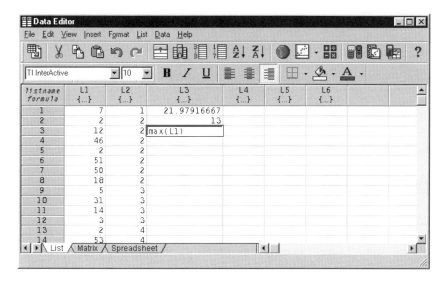

Using this technique we find that:

$$
\begin{aligned}
\min(L1) &= 1 \\
\max(L1) &= 75 \\
\mathrm{mean}(L1) &= 21.98 \\
\mathrm{median}(L1) &= 13 \\
\mathrm{stdDev}(L1) &= 20.66 \\
\mathrm{variance}(L1) &= 426.96 \\
\dim(L1) &= 48
\end{aligned}
$$

The icon third from the right opens the Statistics Regression Calculation window. From Regression Setup you can select the Calculation Type as One-Variable Statistics, and enter L1 for the X List.

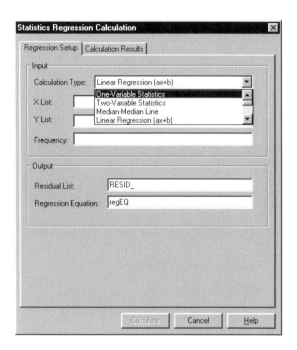

When you click on the Calculate button the display changes to Calculation Results. Here you now get a very full set of statistics for our data set. These include the sum of the elements, and the sum of their squares, the population and sample standard deviations, and the quartiles.

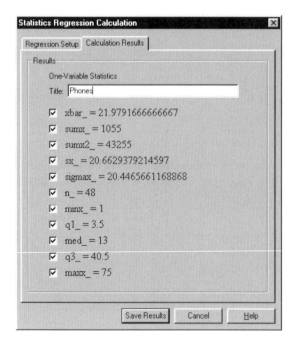

As we all know, a picture is worth a thousand words, so we next look at some ways of displaying this data. The first is the histogram. So just click on the Graph icon, which shows a scattergram. Change the Stat Plot Style to Histogram and enter L1 for Xlist.

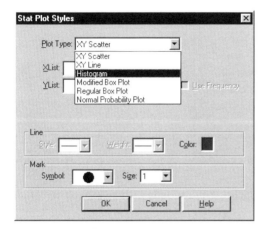

You can edit the Line and Fill details, but the most important thing is to choose the Class Edge and Class Width values appropriately. If we want the number of phones to be sorted into the 'bins' $0 \le x < 10$, $10 \le x < 20$ etc., we then want the Edge to be at zero, and the width to be 10.

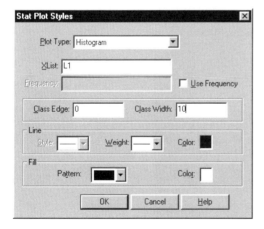

Of course we are going to need to adjust the limits on the axes to get a sensible graph.

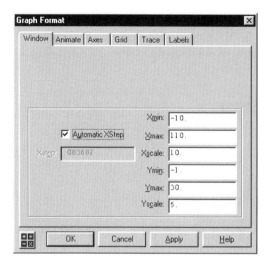

This should produce a suitable histogram. You can read off values with the Trace button.

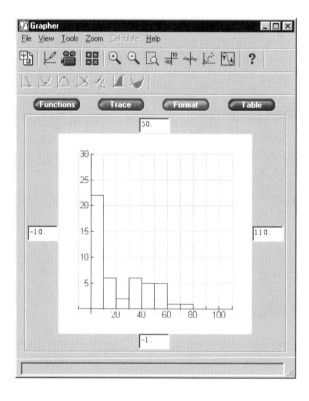

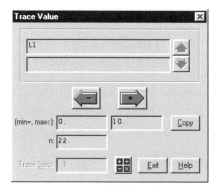

This confirms that the modal class is the half-open interval [0,10) – or, for discrete data 0–9, with a count of 22 (out of 48). Of course both the shape of the histogram, and the value of the mode, change if you re-plot with different Class Edges or Class Widths. Another useful representation is the Box Plot (or box-and-whisker diagram). We can superimpose one over the histogram.

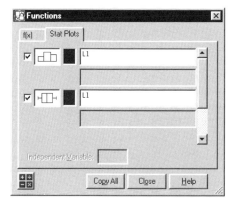

Tracing this you can read off the min, max, median and quartiles, as shown on the following page.

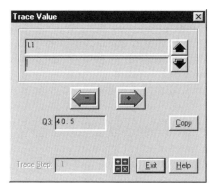

Hence you can also calculate the range as max − min = 75 - 1 = 74, and also the inter-quartile range as Q3 - Q1 = 40.5 - 3.5 = 37. So now you have seen most of the tools of trade for working with a single data set. There is another display type called 'Modified Box Plot' which you might explore. This is very similar to a 'Regular Box Plot' except where there are values called 'outliers' which might unduly distort the data. An example often quoted is the salary data for a small company, where the Managing Director or Chief Executive might earn in the order of ten times the average salary. In this example there are no such outliers.

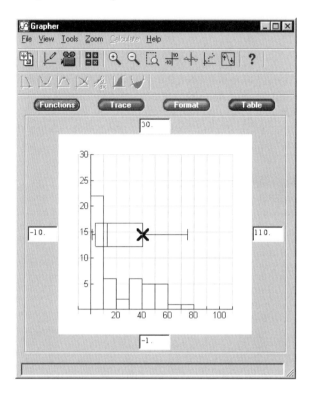

The box plot is particularly useful for comparing data about the same aspect taken from different groups. For example we can split our list of data on telephones from 48 cities between three new lists corresponding to Europe, the Americas and the Rest of the World. The respective box-plots can be superimposed on the same axes. Only the scale on the horizontal axis is important. Can you guess which box plot corresponds to which international grouping? Do you think a similar result would hold true if data were collected now?

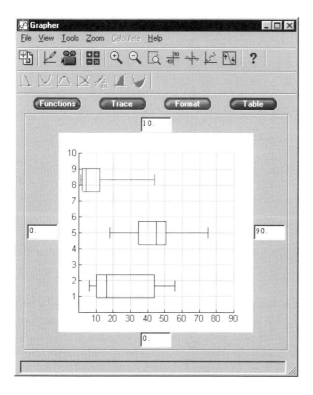

Another important aspect of data handling is in looking for associations between data. For example the data on telephones might be regarded as associated with the relative wealth of the people in the cities included in the data set. But there is no data directly giving comparisons on, e.g. income per capita. So we could choose another set of data which we also think might be related to wealth, such as LIVINGSPACE, i.e. the average number of people per room. Whereas the number of phones might be expected to increase with wealth, the number of people per room might be expected to decrease. So we might make the hypothesis that there is an inverse association between TELEPHONES and LIVINGSPACE, i.e. that the more phones there are per 100 people, the less people there are per room, on average.

So we will now look first at producing a scattergram, and then at fitting some models, both 'by eye', and using the TII's built-in regression models.

Before we rush into copying and pasting the LIVINGSPACE data into the List editor we must not forget Boston and Tehran! Remember that we did not have any TELEPHONE data for these two cities, so they must be struck off our list of comparisons. Just remove the data from cells F11 and F49 so these are empty. Then you can copy and paste the F column data into list L3, and copy and sort it in list L4. So before we go onto the next stage can you find the values of the min, max, mean and median for the LIVINGSPACE data from our remaining 48 cities?

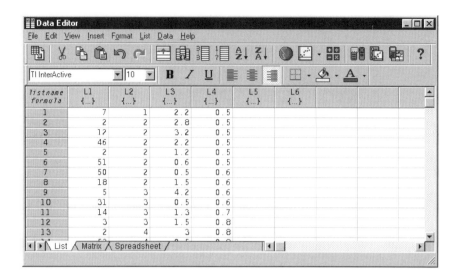

The key features of the current Data Editor are that once lists L2 and L4 have been sorted independently they have lost all association between them. We have to use the unsorted data in lists L1 and L3 since they each refer to the same city. Select the Graph icon and make a scatterplot of the co-ordinate data pairs (L1(n),L3(n)) for n = 1, 2,. . ., 48.

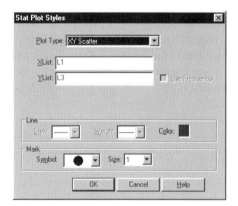

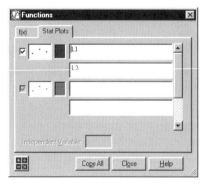

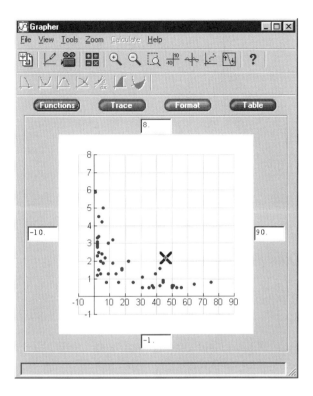

You can use Trace to step through the points of the scatterplot. Here Madrid is being shown as (46,2.2).

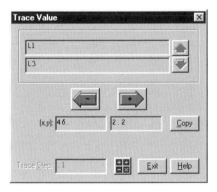

The data do seem to show an inverse relationship, though not necessarily a linear one! Click on the Function button, and the f(x) tab of the Functions window. Now you can enter any function you like, and its graph will be superimposed on the scatterplot. Here we try a linear function with a negative gradient.

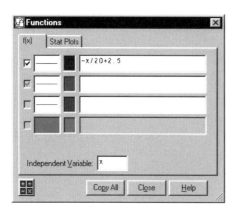

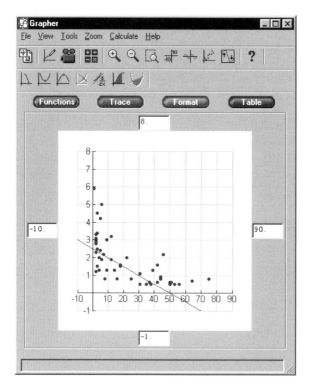

If you think that an inverse function, such as $y = k/x$, would be a better fit, then you can compute values of xy by forming list L5 as the product L1*L3 of the lists L1 and L3. Then you can compute the mean of L5 to give a value for k of about 23. So we can also plot the graph of the function $23/x$ for comparison.

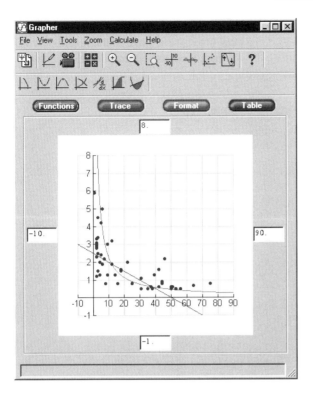

Now you can get TII to compute regression models for you. First a linear one, and then a power law of the form $y = ax^b$.

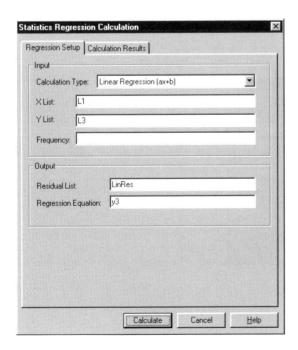

So, from the Statistics Regression Calculation window you just select Linear Regression using lists L1 and L3. You can also give a name to the resulting list of residuals which will automatically be computed and stored, and also to the function which will store the computed regression model.

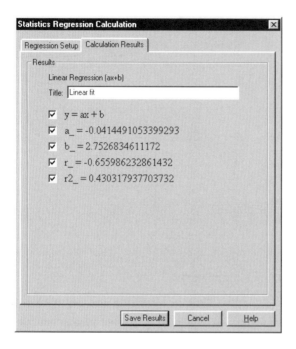

So the 'line of best fit' is roughly $y = -0.04x + 2.75$, with a correlation coefficient of about -0.66 . This is a bit less steep and intercepts the y-axis a little higher up than our 'by eye' fit. So now we can graph the function stored in $y3(x)$.

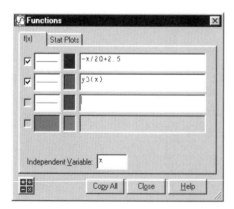

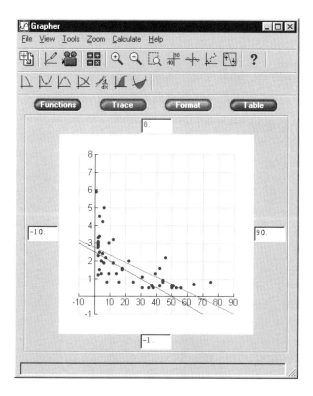

We can also try fitting a power regression model.

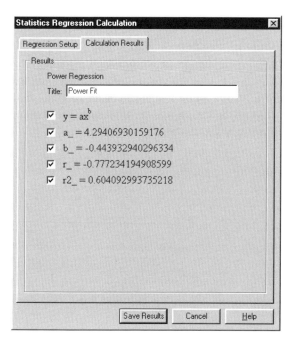

Here we see that this model is roughly $y = 4.3\,x^{-0.44}$ with a correlation coefficient of -0.78 .

You can plot this over the scatterplot – and change the line style of the 'by eye' fit to give a broken line.

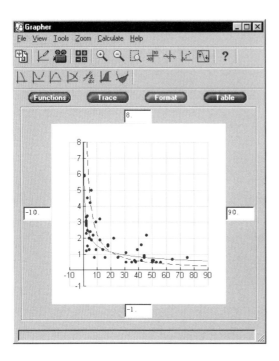

In the Data Editor you can view the list of residuals, shown here as list L5, and compute their squares, as in L6. You can use the stored regression equation, $y4(x)$, to compute a list of predicted y-values in L7. Also you could plot a scattergram of L3 against a transformed version of L1 to see if a linear fit would be appropriate. Here L8 holds L1 raised to the power -0.44, so the line $y = 4.3x$ should be an approximation to the line of best fit on the scattergram of L3 against L8

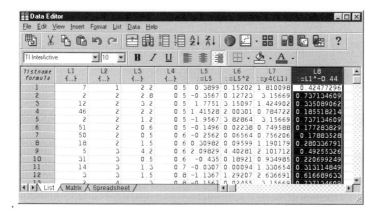

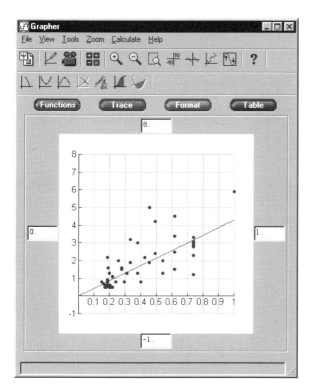

The really amazing thing is that pretty well all that we have just done in TII can also be carried out in a graphing calculator such as a TI-83. We will just show a few screens corresponding to the last stages of this analysis. Of course the TI-83 can exchange data with TII. You can save the TII lists on disk in TI-83 format and use TI Graphlink to transfer the data. You can also export the data directly to a TI-83 from the TII's Data Editor File menu.

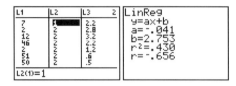

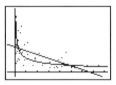

Armed with both TII and a set of TI-83s you have enormous flexibility in how to plan for work in data handling. Enhanced with data-loggers such as the Texas Instruments' CBR and CBL you also have the means of capturing real-data first hand. In the next section on modelling there are some other suggestions for ways of data-capture, such as taking readings from photographs.

The TI-73 calculator will also draw pie-charts and pictograms. It might be useful to have a PIECHART program for the TI-83. This program takes the data from list L1 and draws a pie-chart clockwise starting from 12 o'clock.

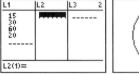

Note: the flash-Rom technology of modern GCs such as the TI-83+ means that new applications software may well be developed to extend the built-in range of functions.

Simulation with random numbers

We conclude the statistics part of this section with an illustration of the use of TII to simulate the rolls of dice using random numbers for which we used a graphing calculator in Chapter 1. In the List Editor you can define L1 to hold randInt(1,6,100) – i.e. 100 simulated rolls of a dice (integers from 1 to 6 inclusive).

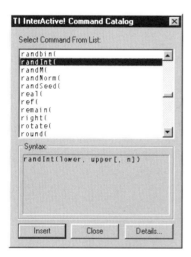

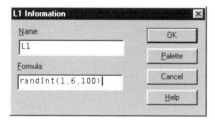

Repeat this for list L2, and then make L3 the sum L1+L2 of L1 and L2.

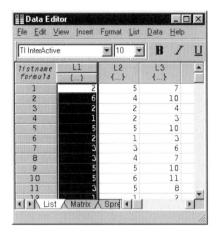

✎ *Can you now produce box plots for each list?*

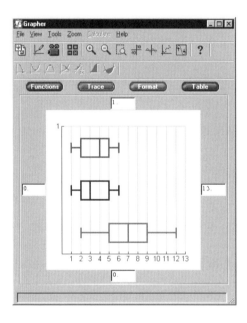

Modelling using captured images

One good source of data for modelling can come from pictures, posters, photographs, etc. For example all or part of an image from a photographic print can be scanned in to a computer, such as the one of Sydney harbour bridge below.

With the image saved in a conventional JPEG or TIFF format you can open it in an image editor, such as *MS Paint*™, and read off co-ordinates measured in pixels from the top right-hand corner of the screen.

We have sampled the data for the 32 points where the vertical struts meet the lower front curved girder, which looks fairly like a parabola. Entering these into TII we can perform a quadratic regression. Here x-data like 869 are stored in L1 and y-data like 244 in L2. However, the origin for the picture data is at the top left-hand corner of the picture, which is 721 pixels deep. Hence we form L3 as 721−L2 to invert y-co-ordinates to be taken from the bottom of the screen. L4 is found from L1/100 and

L5 from L3/100. Fitting a quadratic regression model we get the approximate relationship:

$$y = -0.059x^2 + 0.834x + 1.962$$

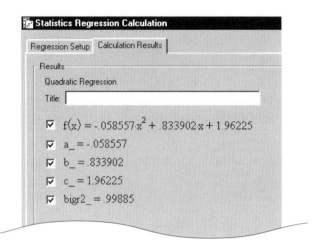

with a correlation coefficient given by $\sqrt{0.9988} \approx 0.9994$ – pretty remarkable!

The resulting quadratic function can be superimposed over the scattergram of L5 against L4. Here it is geometrically important to choose scales for the axes so that units are the same length on both *x*- and *y*-axes.

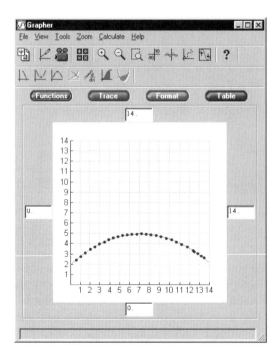

If you have any of the following:

- a digital camera;
- a conventional camera and a computer with a scanner;
- a conventional video camera and a computer with a video card accepting video input;
- a digital cam-corder.

you too can be in the image capture business! Another good example for a parabola should be an image taken of water coming out of a hosepipe or drinking water fountain.

With a video camera (and with some still digital cameras) you can take a succession of images of a moving body at a known number of frames per second (usually 25). For example instead of (or as well as) using a motion detector to collect sensed data from a swinging pendulum you could also capture images and digitize its position at known time intervals. Below are eight successive frames from such a video clip.

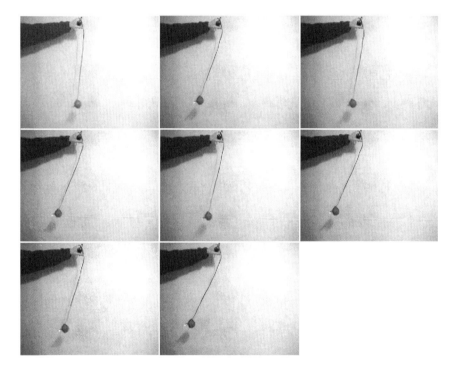

Data can be measured and extracted from these using an image editor. This can be scaled to give actual measurements if the size of any part of the image is known, e.g. the diameter of the ball, or the length of the string.

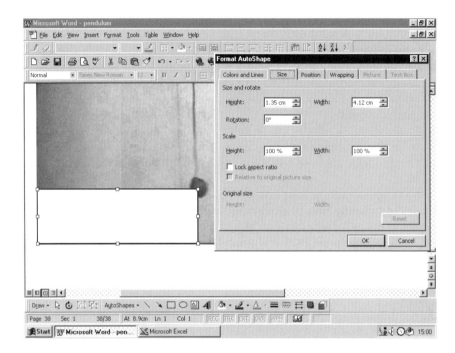

Here is the resulting image from the data entered into a *MSExcel™* spreadsheet.

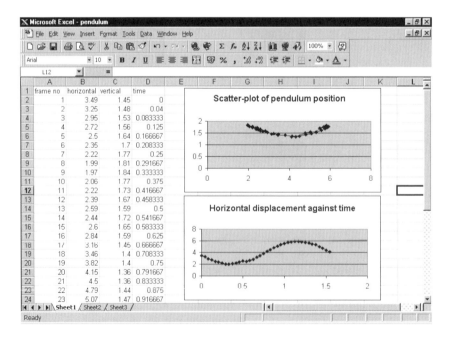

For ease of modelling we can export the data to the lists of TII, with horizontal measurements in L1, vertical measurements in L2, and time in L3, say. As usual we can show the scattergram of L1 against L3 and try to fit a function 'by eye' – in this case a transform of the sine function of the form $y = a + b \sin(c(x + d))$ where we need to match the period, amplitude and phase shift.

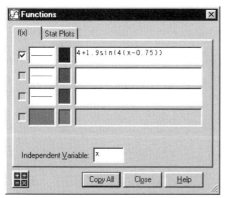

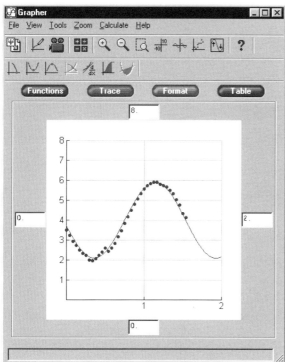

So it looks as if we have a pretty good fit! But we can also use the TII's Sinusoid Regression model. This gives an approximate fit by the function:

$$y = 3.95 + 1.93 \sin(3.88x - 2.94).$$

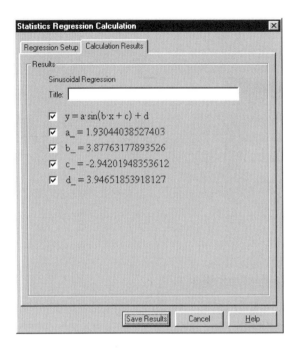

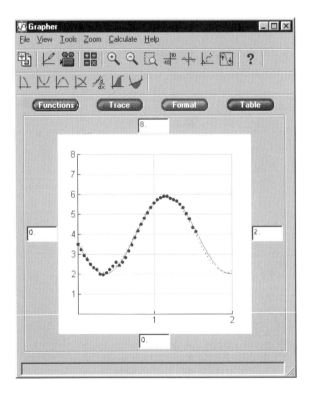

Modelling using practical activities and other contexts

Another good way of gathering data practically is by flexing a long plastic ruler over a large sheet of squared paper. You should be able to get a good approximation to a quadratic curve by just pulling the ends a short way towards each other. You can also make a cubic curve, with a point of inflection by pushing the ends in opposite and parallel directions. Just hold these shapes over the paper and run a felt-tip pen along them. Then you can read off co-ordinates afterwards from the squared paper.

Another practical approach is to use a piece of hardboard, some chain and a couple of cup-hooks. Screw the hooks into the board a metre or so apart and use them to suspend a chain some 20 per cent longer than the gap. Again you can read off co-ordinates from the chain. It is made easier if squared paper is placed on the hardboard beforehand. A similar result can be obtained by suspending a length of thick rope between two points. The theoretical model is actually a curve called a 'catenary', but you should find that it is well approximated by a quadratic.

Bouncing and swinging

A good source of quadratic models comes from sensing motion. Anything falling under gravity, ignoring friction, etc., should have constant acceleration, and hence its velocity should be given by a linear function, and its displacement by a quadratic one. The CBR motion detector includes a program called *Ranger*. One of the applications offered within the program is called Ball Bounce. In the next chapter we give a case study about the use of this application. Using Ball Bounce you can hold the CBR above the point of release of a ball and, with a little practice, capture data from successive rebounds. The software then uses the greatest distance value captured as its estimate of the distance to the ground, and subtracts all the distance data from it. Hence the images show heights of bounce against time.

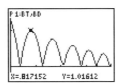

Another feature of the software's Plot Tools is the facility to extract a subset of the data. So you can select data from just one bounce in order to try to fit a quadratic model.

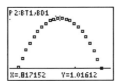

When you leave the program, the data are stored in lists L1 (time), L2 (displacement), L3 (velocity) and L4 (acceleration). So now you can analyse and display them just as you like. The first thing to note is that we have discrete data collected from a continuous process. The program originally sampled around 100 readings at regular intervals within a 4-second span. We have extracted around 20 readings within about a 1-second span. Using the Stat Plot you can display the data as a scattergram, and then do some 'by eye' fitting of quadratic functions. Of course it helps to use Trace to find an approximation to the maximum point for the graph.

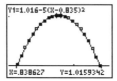

Remember that the quadratic function only models the vertical displacement y of the ball for positive values of y! Remember, too, that the graph does not show the path of the ball. It is not a trajectory in space.

Of course you can also use the built-in regression models to fit a quadratic function to the data. Also you could transfer the data to a computer and use TII for the analysis.

The correlation coefficient (0.999987) is so close to 1 to suggest that we might have 'cooked' the data, but honestly we have not. This is just a very robust experiment. From the theory we know that the acceleration is given by $-g$, assuming no air-resistance, etc. Hence the velocity is given by a linear function $-gt + b$, and displacement by a quadratic function $-1/2gt^2 + bt + c$. So we have also found an approximate value for g as $2(-4.934) = -9.868$ ms^{-2}.

It is also interesting to study the maximum heights of the bounces and the times at which they occur. Now this time we really do have discrete data, so we must approach curve fitting with care. What sort of function would you expect to model this data?

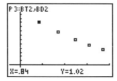

Here is a table of the extracted data for you to use for your own analysis.

N	x (s)	y (m)
0	0.00	1.30
1	0.84	1.02
2	1.68	0.78
3	2.45	0.60
4	3.10	0.46
5	3.69	0.37

While carrying out some work like this, some students had begun to get the impression that every curve might be a quadratic! So they tried fitting a quadratic function to this data. Would you expect it to be a good fit?

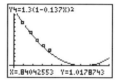

Once again the correlation coefficient is phenomenally close to 1! The corresponding second-degree equation is :

$$y \approx 0.028x^2 - 0.356x + 1.300 \approx 1.300\,(1 - 0.137x)^2 .$$

Clearly we have to be cautious about not using such a function to interpolate between data points, nor to extrapolate beyond $t \approx 1/0.137 \approx 7.3$ seconds. If you have met the 'coefficient of restitution' you might like to use the data to estimate its value, and also to see if you can confirm theoretically that the quadratic model for maximum height against time is not such a surprise.

One group of students decided to see if they could simulate a quadratic displacement curve by walking towards, and then away from, a CBR. Their results became a little confused when they got very close to the CBR, but they generated a reasonable data set on which the class arrived at a 'by eye' fit using transformations of x^2.

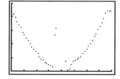
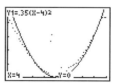

The CBR can also be set up to log data from a variety of dynamics experiments, such as with spring–mass systems and pendulums. These oscillations make a good way of introducing the trigonometric functions outside the range $0°$ to $90°$.

Now we look at some examples of modelling and problem solving which have formed the basis of successful pieces of coursework by 15- and 16-year-old students. In each case we will illustrate the activity by using a different ICT tool, but you might like to think how you could approach the task using a different ICT tool.

Swimming and running

A girl is swimming off a beach which has a straight shoreline. When she is at point G, 100m from the nearest point N on the shore, she is stung by a jellyfish. She wants to get back to shore and pick up her towel as quickly as possible. Her towel is on the shore at a point T, 200m from N. The fastest she can swim is 2 m/s and the fastest she can run is 5 m/s. What is the best route for her to follow from G to T, and how long will it take her?

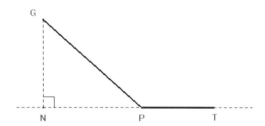

Using Pythagoras you can calculate the time taken to swim directly from G to T. Even though this is a shorter route, it takes longer than swimming directly from G to N, and then running to T – a total of 90 seconds. Can you find some point P between N and T for which the journey $GP + PT$ takes the shortest possible time?

Clearly you will need to make one of the lengths, say NP, as the independent variable x, say, and find the other distances and times as functions of x. One way to approach this is by using the spreadsheet facility of TII. The screenshot shows one possible layout. Can you suggest what formulae are used for, e.g. cells A3, B2, C2, D2, E2 and F2? With this layout you can easily 'zoom' in on the table by changing the initial value A2 and the step length G2. You can easily set up a different problem by varying either the swimming speed or the running speed. You could also turn the other constants, GN and NT into parameters.

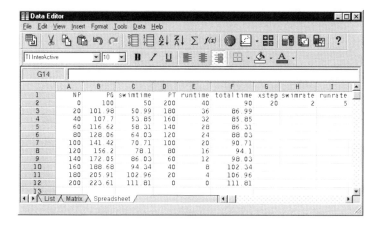

To graph the data you will need to use the cells A2:A12 as the *x*-list and F2:F12 as the *y*-list for a scattergram. You could also write down the symbolic expression for the values in the F column in terms of the variable *x* (= *NP*) and superimpose the graph of this function.

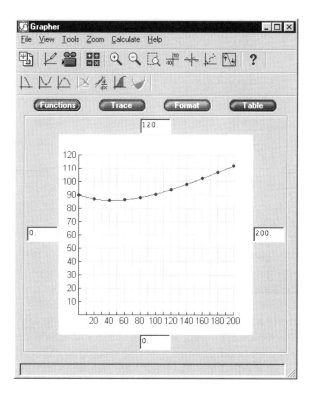

The 'missing' region

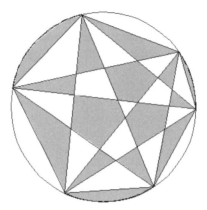

The diagram shows six points arranged irregularly around a circle, and chords are drawn to join every pair of points. We know that there are $^6C_2 = 15$ such lines. But how many regions do they divide the circle into? By counting it appears the answer is 31. Can you build up a table of the number of points against the number of regions and suggest what sort of function might model this (discrete!) data? Can you find a good fit (a perfect one?). Can you explain geometrically why it takes the form it does?

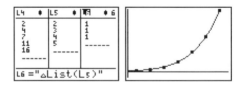

Here we have put the data into the lists of the TI-83 and formed their differences.

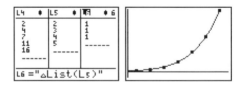

The pattern in list L2 appeared to be doubling, until the 'missing region' disrupted things at $n = 6$. If the pattern in list L6 continued, what sort of function would you expect in L2? To relate any results to the geometry we can record the changing numbers of geometric objects. Can you find, and prove, formulae for both the number of Lines and Crossings, and hence derive the formula for the number of Regions?

Points	Lines	Crossings	Regions
2	1	0	2
3	3	0	4
4	6	1	8
5	10	5	16
6	15	15	31
7	21	35	57
8	28	70	99

The old max-box

There are a whole variety of modelling problems based upon maximizing one measurement of an object subject to constraints on other ones. A simple example is to find the rectangle of greatest area contained in a rope of length 4m. This gives another quadratic model. Working in 3D with volumes of boxes yields cubic models. These ideas can easily be extended to volumes of cylinders and cones. Here we take a very well-known example of the largest open tray which can be cut from a sheet of card. This time we will make use of the dynamic properties of *Cabri Géomètre*. You will have to construct your own version to make it behave dynamically!

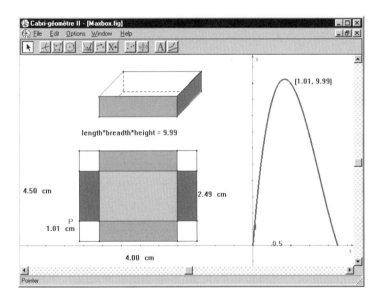

Measures

We conclude this section with a couple of ideas to do with 'Measures'. Using the lists of the TI-83 or TII it is very easy indeed to change between units. For example, suppose list L1 has a series of temperatures recorded in degrees Fahrenheit and you want list L2 to hold the corresponding conversion into degrees Celsius.

✎ *At what temperature are the Fahrenheit and Celsius readings
   identical?*

You might like to construct yourself a dynamic temperature converter using *Cabri*.
Can you work out how this was constructed?

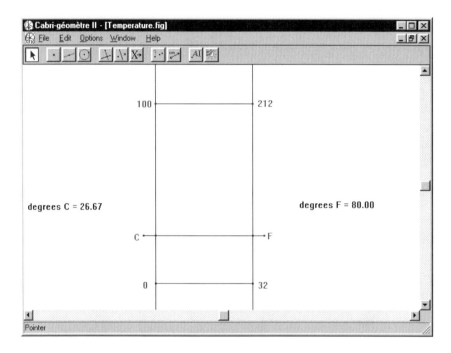

2d   MORE ADVANCED MATHEMATICS

In the UK, the Nuffield Foundation supported the development of a set of text books called *Nuffield Advanced Mathematics*, published by Longmans in 1994. Along with project groups such as SMP (the School Mathematics Project) and MEI (Mathematics in Education and Industry) this course aimed to integrate the use of ICT tools in the teaching and learning process. Unfortunately these books are, at the time of writing, out of print. They contain a number of useful activities which can be carried out using a variety of mathematical ICT tools and we include a few examples here. The first is some numerical approaches to the derivative of a function.

Differentiation and integration

The first idea is that of an Approximate Gradient Function (AGF). This uses the idea that the gradient of a function f(x) can be approximated by (f(x + h) - f(x))/h for small, finite, h. We will explore the idea with a TI-83 graphing calculator, but you can follow the same path using any suitable graph-plotting software, including TII. We will find approximations to the gradient of $Y1(x) = x^3 - 4x^2 + 3$ at the point where $x = 0.5$. With the function entered in the Y= editor as Y1, you can conveniently enter a value for *h* in Y2. The definition of the AGF in Y3 uses the values of Y1 and Y2 already defined. (These are recalled using the Vars, Y-Vars, Function menus.) The line style of Y3 has been selected as dotted. (Move the cursor over the symbol to the left of Y3 and repeatedly press ENTER to cycle through the list of possible line styles.) The graph of Y2 will not be displayed since the '=' sign has had its highlight removed.

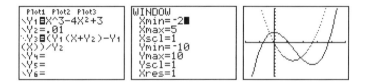

Now you can trace over the graph of Y1 describing its gradient as you go, and comparing it with the *y*-co-ordinates from the Y3 graph. The TI-83 has a CALC menu from which you can compute the numerical derivative of a graph at a given *x* value. Just select 6:dy/dx and enter 0.5 for the *x* value. Here the TI-83's numerical algorithm gives -3.249999 as its approximation. Selecting Trace and moving to the graph of Y3 you can enter 0.5 for the *x* value and read off -3.2749 as the AGF value with *h* = 0.01. Try a smaller value in Y2.

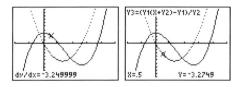

Another approach to the derivative for a smooth function is the idea of 'local straightness'. First trace Y1 and select 0.5, then use Zoom In, accepting the suggested co-ordinates for the centre of enlargement. Then use Zsquare to make sure that the units on both axes are the same length. This will help to ensure that a line of gradient 1 does make a 45° angle with the *x*-axis. Now repeatedly Trace to $x = 0.5$ and Zoom In until the curve looks like a straight line. Using Trace you can explore co-ordinates of neighbouring points to $x = 0.5$. For example we see that the 'curve' passes through (0.5,2.125) and (0.51,2.092251) from which we can find another numerical approximation of -3.2749 to the gradient at 0.5.

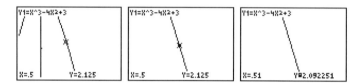

The TI-83 has a built-in function called 'nDeriv' which is in the MATH MATH menu. So 'nDeriv(Y1,X,0.5)' will return the value of the numerical derivative of Y1 with X at X = 0.5. Similarly: 'Y4 = nDeriv(Y1,X,X)' will compute values of the numerical derivative at each of the values of X used for plotting a graph.

The Nuffield approach to integration is to start with the solution of differential equations as anti-derivatives. Later this is seen to be equivalent (the fundamental theorem of calculus) to finding areas under graphs. In this example the area under the function $Y1(x) = 1 + x^2$ is approximated by rectangles. Here we can use the function-plotting and statistics (histogram) plotting of TII (or the TI-83) to illustrate the idea.

✎ *Try using different step lengths, different ranges and/or different functions.*

In the following image the list L3 is the sum of L2, and L4 is given by L3 $\times$ 0.1 i.e. the area.

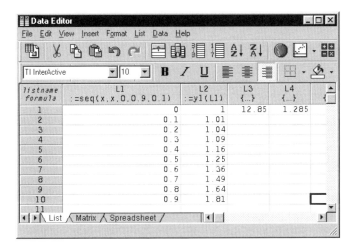

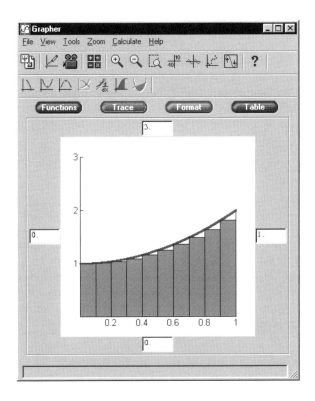

Just as there was a built-in function for numeric differentiation, so the TI-83 has one for numeric integration.

Again we do not know the exact algorithm used by the TI-83, but we can easily write a little program to accumulate and plot the approximate area function for the function stored in Y1, using the values of Xmin and Xmax set in the WINDOW. (These are found in the VARS, Window menu.)

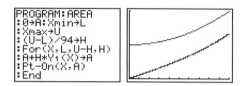

You could compare the output from the program with the graph generated by fnInt to check the closeness of the fit. Can you adapt the program to compute numerical approximations to definite integrals using, e.g. trapezium, midpoint and/or Simpson's rules?

Iterative processes

Fixed-point iteration is a common topic on many post-16 syllabuses. Here the use of a 'cobweb' or 'staircase' diagram provides a graphic illustration of whether or not the process converges. Using the 'Seq' mode on the TI-83 you can set up an iteration in the Y= editor and a suitable WINDOW.

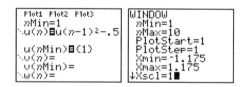

Use '2nd' and 'WINDOW' to select 'FORMAT' and set the display to 'Web'. When you graph the function you now get both the graph of $y = x^2 - 0.5$ and that of $y = x$. Their points of intersection are the fixed points of the iteration. Use 'TRACE' and each time you move the cursor right you will open up another line of the cobweb.

Here we see that the intersection near -0.366 seems to be an attractor for the iteration, while that near 1.366 seems to be a repellor.

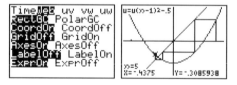

A similar, but more dynamic tool, can be created in *Cabri*. A macro has been defined to draw successive pairs of line segments from the curve to the line and back to the curve. Now you can just slide point *P* to change the initial value for the iteration.

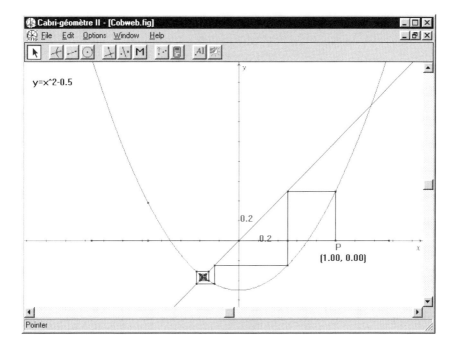

Complex variables

Just to show off, we can also use the TI-83 to explore functions of a complex variable! One of the Nuffield books 'Complex Numbers and Numerical Methods' has an investigation into the mapping of shapes such as a cardioid under a complex function such e^{x+iy}.

First use MODE to select parametric plotting, angles measured in radians, graphs plotted simultaneously and complex numbers enabled in the form $a + bi$. The parametric equation for a small cardioid is entered in the Y= editor. The formula for its transform uses the Complex functions real and imag from the MATH menu. The line style is dotted.

With a suitable WINDOW you can see both the object and its image.

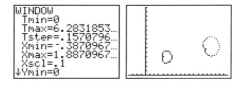

Of course now the calculator can be used for complex arithmetic as well!

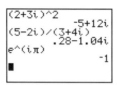

Naturally the graphic output looks better on the higher resolution colour TII display.

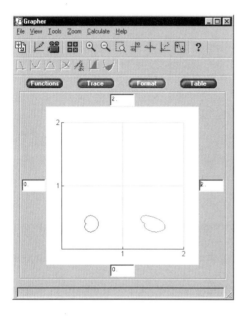

Co-ordinate geometry, conics and parametric equations

A good starting point for work in co-ordinate geometry leading to conic sections and to parametric equations is afforded by the locus of a falling ladder (see the picture below). *FT* is a 2m ladder whose foot *F* can slide in contact with a slippery floor *OE*, and whose top *T* can slide in contact with a slippery wall *ON*. The starting point is a 'thought experiment'. Concentrate on the midpoint *M* of *ON*.

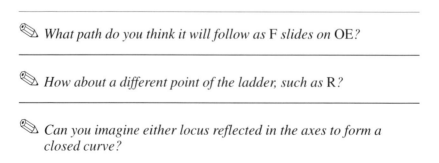

What path do you think it will follow as F slides on OE?

How about a different point of the ladder, such as R?

Can you imagine either locus reflected in the axes to form a closed curve?

✎ *Can you imagine how the locus generated by* R *will deform as* R *slides on* FT*?*

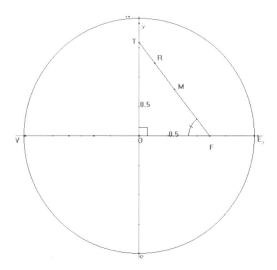

You know that *FM* = *MT* = 1. If *P* is the point on the floor directly below *M*, what can you say about the lengths *OP* and *PF*? Can you find the length *OM*? Another useful image is to imagine a point *Q* such *OTQF* is a rectangle, and to consider its diagonal *OQ*.

If the co-ordinates of *M* are (*x*,*y*) can you find the equation of the locus of *M*? If the angle *OFT* is given by the parameter *t*, can you find *x* and *y* as functions of *t* ? Try checking this out using the parametric plotting mode of a graphic calculator, like the TI-83, or graphing software like TII.

✎ *What does the locus look like if* t *can take all values between 0°
and 360°?*

✎ *Could you make a* Cabri *construction which models this?*

✎ *Could you use angle* FTO *instead?*

✎ *Suppose the distance* FR *is given by another parameter* p, *can
you find both the Cartesian and parametric equations of the
locus of* R*?*

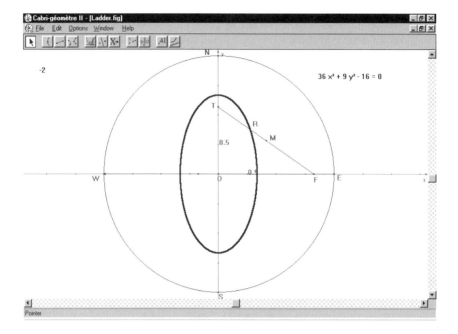

In addition to circles and arcs, *Cabri* has the ability to construct conics. This tool is based upon a construction by Blaise Pascal, and needs five points to define the conic. Reflecting *R* in the axes provides four of them and just choosing any other point of locus does the trick. Using the Equation and Coordinates tools from the measurement menu you can now check out the Cartesian equation of the locus of *R* and see how it varies as you slide *R* on *FT*.

The curve that many people see in their 'mind's eye' when trying the thought experiment is not the locus of *M*, but the curve which has *FT* as its tangent. If you reflect *FT* in the axes and construct the four loci of these segments with *F* you will not actually see a curve, but your eye will detect a smooth edge hinted out at by the boundary of this bunch of segments. To show this curve you need to work with lines, rather than segments. In the Preferences window from the Option menu you can select whether the locus of lines will be shown as the Envelope, or not. So the next image shows the curve enveloped by the bundle of tangent lines like *FT*. This curve is called an 'astroid' and its parametric equations are:

$x = 2 \cos^3 t$

$y = 2 \sin^3 t.$

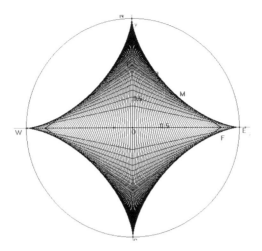

'*Astroid*' *curve*

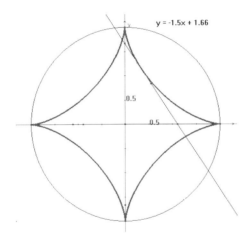

'*Astroid*' *curve*

An excellent source of ideas for constructions and curves is E. H. Lockwood's *A Book of Curves*, CUP 1967. The other 'classic' is *Mathematical Models*, H. M. Cundy & A. P. Rollett, Tarquin 1987.

We conclude this section on co-ordinate geometry with another example of the power of *Cabri*, this time to illustrate the focus–directrix definition of the conics. We have used Numerical Edit to enter values for the parameters a and e (the eccentricity). Using the Calculator tool we have computed the co-ordinates of the focus F $(ae,0)$ and the point D on the directrix $(-a/e,0)$. A segment XX' has been constructed along the x-axis as the domain for the independent variable P. Distance PD has been measured and we now seek if there are points Q such that $FQ = e.PD$, i.e. such that e is the ratio between the distances from Q to the focus and from Q to the directrix. Using the calculator we can compute $e.PD$ and transfer this measurement to a vector from F. The circle through that last point is the locus of all points distance $e.PD$

from F. If this intersects the perpendicular to the x-axis through P at points Q and Q' then these points belong to the locus.

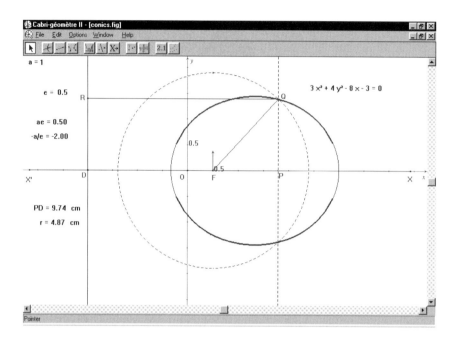

Using Q, Q' and three other points on the locus we can define a five-point conic and read off its equation. Now, if you double-click on the value for e you can increase and decrease this to see what happens as e first reaches 1 and then gets bigger.

Trigonometric functions and relationships

The next example is from trigonometry, and has a sting in its tail! The idea is to use a graphical approach to 'discovering' trigonometric identities, such as $\sin 2x = 2\sin x \cos x$.

On the TI-83 we have plotted the graphs of $\sin x$ and $\cos x$ in degrees in [-360,360] and superimposed the graph of their product. Clearly the zeros of this function are the unions of the zeros of both sine and cosine, and so it looks like a sine wave but with twice the frequency. However its amplitude is smaller than those of either sine or cosine. One of its maxima is at $x = 45°$, so the amplitude is $\sin 45° \cos 45° = (1/\sqrt{2}).(1/\sqrt{2}) = 1/2$. This suggests the identity: $\sin x \cos x = 1/2 \sin 2x$, which you can check by graphing 'both sides of the equation' to see if they appear identical.

The following is a true story! Kate, a newly qualified teacher, had used this approach with a class of 16/17 year olds and was very pleased with the results. But there had been an absentee. When this girl, Sam, returned, the teacher explained the task and left Sam to get on by herself. After a short while Sam showed Kate her results. She had discovered that sin 45x has the same zeros as sin x cos x, double the amplitude, and with the sign changed. So Sam's 'identity' was: sin 45x = -2 sin x cos x. How would you have coped with this situation? Fortunately Kate was sure of her mathematical ground, even if she could not figure out what the calculator had done 'wrong'. So she changed the WINDOW to [-90,90] and was able to show that sin 45x was really very wiggly indeed!

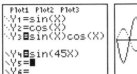 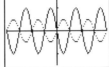 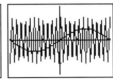

The calculator's 'mistake' is easy to explain. It uses the same sort of algorithm as we used for a *TrueBasic* graph-plotting program in Chapter 1. It evaluates the function at each of the 94 or so pixels across the screen. Provided this is not too far away from the last point it joins them with a 'blobby' line segment. For certain values of k in sin kx, this will be exactly 'in sync' with -sin 2x at the points where x is an integral multiple of 720/94. (720 is Xmax-Xmin and 94 is the number of pixels.) So whatever the screen resolution there will always be some function which has this property. In fact you may know how to expand sin 45x + sin 2x as 2 sin 47/2 x cos 43/2 x .

 Can you calculate the value of k *if, say, there were 100 pixels across the screen?*

Another useful example in trigonometry concerns motivating the use of radians. If you use nDeriv to explore the derivative of the sine function when x is measured in degrees in [-360,360] the result is very unexciting! Tracing the nDeriv function reveals that it is virtually indistinguishable from the x-axis, with a maximum value of only 0.01745329 . Of course this is not particularly surprising since the line joining (0,0) to the first maximum (90,1) has a gradient of 1/90, so the gradient of sin x at x = 0 is not going to be much larger. In fact the reciprocal of 0.01745329 is 57.29579, so the slope is about 1 in 60. We can easily change the unit from degrees, say, to right-angles. This just means we divide the Window's Xmin and Xmax by 90 to get the interval [-4,4] and graph the function given by y = sin 90 x. Here we see that the graph of nDeriv now looks like a cosine function, but with an amplitude greater than 1. (Actually 1.5707957.)

```
Plot1 Plot2 Plot3     WINDOW
\Y1◘sin(90X)          Xmin=-4
\Y2◘nDeriv(Y1,X,      Xmax=4
X)                    Xscl=1
\Y3=                  Ymin=-2
\Y4=                  Ymax=2
\Y5=                  Yscl=1
\Y6=                  Xres=1
```

✎ *Try re-graphing in multiples of 60°.*

✎ *What is the significance of 57.2979?*

✎ *What familiar number appears if you double 1.570957?*

A historical problem

We conclude this section on ICT use to explore more advanced mathematics with an interesting historical problem. As you know, Isaac Newton (1642–1727) and Gottfried Leibniz (1646–1716) are both credited with the invention of differential and integral calculus independently at about the same time. On the continent of Europe it was the Swiss brothers Jean (1667–1748) and Jacques (1654–1705) Bernoulli who did most to publicize Leibniz's work. Jean was engaged as tutor by the Marquis Guillaume François Antoine l'Hôpital (1661–1708) in Paris in 1692. In return for a regular salary, Jean agreed to keep l'Hôpital informed of his mathematical discoveries and to let him do as he liked with them. L'Hôpital published the first textbook on differential calculus *Analyse des Infiniements Petits*, published in 1696. This includes what we now call 'l'Hôpital's rule', which had actually been discovered by Jean Bernoulli! As one of his examples to illustrate the power of differential calculus l'Hôpital solved the following problem in mechanics.

Here a rope of length a is attached at A, and its free end C carries a small pulley. Another rope of length b is attached at B, on the same level as A and 1m away. This rope passes over the pulley at C and carries a mass at its free end D. L'Hôpital used differential calculus to determine the minimum value of the y-co-ordinate of D, i.e. the point of equilibrium of the system. Can you do this? (Maybe the symbolic manipulation of *Derive* or TII would help?) L'Hôpital used values of $a = 0.4$m and $b = 1$m. You could use the angle $BAC - t$ as parameter to find the parametric equation of the locus of D. Actually we are seeing an arc of a closed curve. If b is greater than $1 + a$ then the locus is the whole curve, but the part above the horizontal axis only makes sense if AC is a stiff rod, rather than a piece of rope. Do you think this curve is an ellipse?

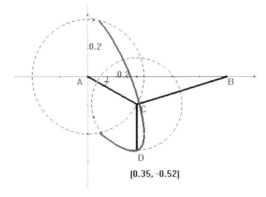

(0.35, -0.52)

We would be very surprised if Newton was impressed by this analytic technique. He would have known that the tensions in the parts of the rope *CB* and *CD* would have to be equal, and that, in equilibrium, their components along the tangent to the circle at A would have to be equal. Hence *AC* produced must be the angle bisector of ∠*DCB*. So that gives a means of constructing the solution geometrically.

 Can you construct the solution geometrically?

2e   CROSS-CURRICULAR WORK

The most obvious scope for co-operation between other subjects and mathematics is in the choice of data sets to use for data handling work, e.g. in Ma5 of the English national curriculum in mathematics. The example of the cities data we used in section 2c of this chapter could typify cross-curricular linking mathematics and geography.

As well as sharing secondary data sources, there is also plenty of scope for collaborating in capturing experimental data. For example some 15-year-old students in one school are working on a project involving bouncing balls and the CBR. Their project reports will be entered as assessable coursework both for science and for mathematics in the General Certificate of Secondary Education (GCSE) examinations at the end of Year 11. We give more details about this kind of work in Case Study 3 in the next Chapter.

Using the CBL there is a wide variety of experiments which can help prompt study of important mathematical functions as models. For example, using a pressure sensor together with plastic veterinary syringe you can record volumes in cm³ in L1 and pressure in atmospheres in L2. As usual you can produce a scatterplot and try a 'by eye' fit. Here it looks as if a model such as xy = constant might be appropriate. L3 is defined as the product L1*L2 and we can see that its values are fairly close to each other. The plotted graph is of the function Y1= mean(L3)/X .

 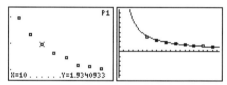

So we have a mathematical model as an inverse relationship, which the scientists can help explain theoretically from physical principles.

A very important kind of model is that of exponential growth or decay. Here are similar looking results obtained from a CBL. The first uses a temperature probe to record a hot object cooling in air; the second uses a voltage probe to record the discharge of a capacitor through a resistor.

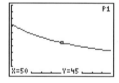 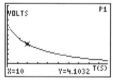

In one school all the pupils in Year 10 took part in a Health and Fitness programme as part of an area of the curriculum known as Personal, Social and Health Education (PSHE). Within this they all used a CBL and a simple probe attached to the ear lobe to record their heart rates before and after exercise. This large data set was analysed as part of the mathematics data handling work by all the students involved.

A group of schools in Hampshire have been working on a project to integrate handheld technology within their schools' ICT strategy concentrating on subjects such as mathematics, science, geography and D&T. Some of the teachers' findings from this project are to be published on the TTA website:

`www.teach-tta.gov.uk/research/grant/index.htm`

The project built upon work already published by NCET is now to be found at:

`www.vtc.ngfl.gov.uk/resource/cits/maths/support.html`

There is plenty of scope for work linking geometry and Design and Technology. Brian Bolt's *Mathematics meets Technology*, Cambridge, 1992 is an excellent source of ideas. Mechanisms, such as pistons, cranks, etc. are a rich field for exploring, e.g. with the help of dynamic geometry software. As an example the diagram below was produced in *Cabri* to model the steering geometry of a car.

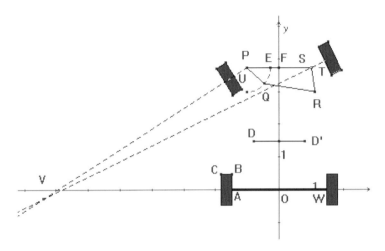

Ackerman steering

The system, known as Ackermann steering, is based on a trapezium. When the front wheels are pointing straight ahead, the quadrilateral *PQRS* forms a trapezium. For a given wheelbase *AW* and length between axles *OF*, the shape of the trapezium is defined by the two parameters $p = PE$, the length of the track rod ends, and $q = DD'$, the length of the tie bar. As *Q* slides on the arc through *E*, the 'stub axles' *PU* and *ST* turn through different angles. This is because the four circles to which the tyres are tangents should all have the same centre, otherwise the front tyres will soon lose their tread. The design problem is to choose *p* and *q* so that the point *V* of intersection of the stub axles produced lies as close to the line *AW* as possible for all positions of *Q*. Of course there also physical constraints on the maximum sizes of *p* and *q*.

The diagram above suggests making a dynamic model, e.g. in *Cabri*. You could also make an analytic model using the angle $QPS = \theta$ as independent variable, and splitting the quadrilateral *PQRS* into two triangles. Using the sine and cosine rules you can find the angle $QRS = \phi$ as a function of θ (perhaps in a spreadsheet?), and compare it with the desired value ϕ' found when *V* is on *AW*.

BRIDGE TWO

As a bridge into the next chapter we examine more deeply some of the issues raised about ICT use in the TTA case studies. We will include much of the detail from just one of the four studies, including the lesson plan, and refer to the key aspects identified within the others. If possible, you should refer to the original TTA CD-ROM for the full details. We will work in reverse order this time!

Case study 4: Algebra at Y10 using graphing calculators

> Lesson Plan
> Subject: Mathematics
> Age group: 14 to 15 years
> Topic: Algebra

Background information
The class is a top examination set of higher attaining pupils. This lesson marks the transition from work on the area of polygons to work on quadratic functions. In the previous lesson, the class had tackled the problem of making an enclosure of maximum area using a 10 m rope, a post and a long straight wall. Pupils have used graphical calculators previously to study linear functions, a variety of forms of distance–time graphs and for data handling applications, e.g. drawing scattergrams and associated lines of best fit.

Teaching/learning objectives
Pupils should:
• be able to compute accurate tables and graphs based on manipulating an algebraic expression for a given area;
• know how to find a numeric solution to the problem;
• be able to validate and interpret numerical results using scale diagrams;
• be able to offer a proof of why a particular shape will enclose a maximum area;
• be able to communicate clearly and concisely what they have done.

Methodology and organization
   1. A résumé with the whole class on the methods used in the previous lesson to solve the triangle problem using the OHP graphic calculator.
   2. Introduction to the task: to find the largest rectangular area that can be enclosed by a 10m rope, two posts and a long, straight wall.
   3. Pupils work in pairs to find a solution to the rectangle task. They:
      (a) devise a system to record their investigation methodically;
      (b) review their work and locate steps which may have generated errors;
      (c) improve the strategies that they used to solve the problem;
      (d) produce a display to communicate their solutions and methodology to others.
   4. Monitor progress and question or challenge where needed.

5. Selected pupils present their solution to the rest of the class.

Differentiation
The class has some high attaining pupils who will make good progress. An extension activity is provided which requires them to apply what they have learned in the triangle and rectangle investigations to a trapezium.

Assessment opportunities/criteria
Questioning pupils orally during summary of previous work.
Observing and questioning pupils while carrying out group work.
Checking through final work handed in for presentation.
Pupils:

- are able to derive correct and precise algebraic formulations using conventional symbols and syntax;
- are able to produce and interpret tables and/or graphs to help them find an accurate numeric solution to the problem;
- are able to draw and use scale diagrams to validate and interpret the numerical results;
- explain how they proved that their solution was correct;
- explain the methodology and outcome of their investigation.

Resources
Work sheets and blank A4 paper.

A half-class set of 16 graphic calculators.

The teacher's graphic calculator linked to an overhead projection panel, OHP and display screen.

Rulers, pencils, compasses etc.

Training needs
The TTA identify the following as possible aspects you may identify as training needs:

- using hand-held ICT such as graphical calculators to teach aspects of mathematics;

- using ICT to present information, give instructions and explain ideas to a whole class;

- using ICT to help assess pupils' progress and to build a record of attainment.

The main issues identified about the use of ICT in this case study are (a) the effective use of time and (b) ensuring that learning is not masked.

Effective use of time

In his analysis, the teacher describes how using graphical calculators helps him to make more effective use of the time available for mathematics teaching.

The pupils are already competent and accurate with the mathematical processes needed to generate tables of values from formulae, and are skilled at drawing graphs. The calculator performs these data processing tasks automatically. For example, once pupils have entered a function in algebraic notation and specified sets of values, the graphical calculator automatically generates a table of values and plots the graph. The automated search facility speeds up their search for maximum values. Pupils are, therefore, able to spend more time on the mathematical objectives for the lesson, which require them to formulate functions correctly and to interpret, validate and explain their results.

By changing the values entered, the teacher and pupils are able to produce many different examples quickly and easily. The teacher uses this to demonstrate particular teaching points, to explore with pupils their suggestions about the values to be used, and to help pupils having difficulty by matching his examples to their understanding. Pupils are able to ask 'what if . . .?' questions, experiment with different values and get rapid results to aid their learning.

The teacher uses the graphical calculators to illustrate the relationship between numerical, algebraic and graphical representations. The 'split screen' facility helps pupils see and understand the relationship between the graph, its function and how it had been created from the table of values.

The graphical calculators are used alongside pencil, paper and other mathematical equipment in the teacher's mathematics classroom. He has enough calculators for pupils to work in pairs. This enables all pupils to practise what they have been taught and to continue to hypothesize and to explore the mathematical relationships between number, algebra and graphs in the context of the problems given.

The teacher uses an overhead projector pad or tablet so that the whole class can see the display from one graphical calculator. This helps him to explain particular points and encourages discussions between pupils and with the teacher. He projects the image onto his whiteboard so that he can annotate the images. The teacher involves pupils in the whole class teaching, by inviting them to demonstrate using the graphical calculator and large screen during the lesson, and to present and explain their results to the class.

Ensuring that learning is not masked

In his analysis, the teacher describes how activities using ICT need to be carefully planned to ensure that the intended mathematical learning is achieved.

By automating some processes, he enabled pupils to focus on higher level mathematical thinking and the identified objectives. The important decisions in mathematics are not carried out automatically by the graphical calculator. For example, in order to produce tables and graphs using ICT, pupils have to derive correct and precise algebraic formulations using conventional symbols and syntax, and in order to make sense of the results generated pupils need to validate their solutions.

He keeps track of pupils' progress towards his teaching objectives by structuring the activity so that it is essential for them to record their work. This enables them to go back, review their work and locate steps that may have generated errors. As a consequence, the pupils improve the strategies they use to solve problems. The record of their work provides the teacher with evidence for assessment and feedback, and enables the pupils to communicate their solutions and methodology to the rest of the class.

The teacher intervenes to question pupils while they are working in order to assess their progress and understanding, to identify any misconceptions and to undertake focused mathematics teaching. Sometimes he stops the group work and uses the large screen to explain particular points.

Case study 3: Number at Y9 using small software

Teaching objectives
Pupils should:

- be able to demonstrate instant recall and mental agility in number;
- achieve a deeper understanding of the number system, place value and metric measurements;
- be able to think strategically about this problem.

Lesson activities
The teacher begins the lesson by recapping previous work on place value and multiplying and dividing by 10, 100 and 1000. She uses numbers greater and less than one as the basis for questions to assess the pupils' current level of understanding. She quickly describes how to operate the mathematics software program. Pupils work in pairs competing against each other or the computer. The teacher uses the plenary session to consolidate their learning and apply it to calculating conversions in the metric system.

The main issues identified about the use of ICT in this case study are (a) selecting and using ICT, and (b) extending ability with number.

Training needs
The TTA identify the following as possible aspects you may identify as training needs:

- using the internet to access sources of information and software to support mathematics teaching;

- using a portable computer and OHP, or other ICT resources, for whole class teaching;

- using small mathematics software programs to teach aspects of number;

- using programs that set up competitive situations to improve pupils' mental arithmetic.

Selecting and using ICT

In her commentary, the teacher describes how she selects ICT to help her to meet her teaching objectives in mathematics.

She uses the internet as a source of information and mathematics software that she can evaluate against her objectives and use as appropriate.

The teacher demonstrates the software to the whole class to make sure they understand the mathematics behind the program before they divide into pairs to use it. She uses a portable computer with a detachable screen that can act as a projection tablet on the overhead projector. This enables her to project the image from the desktop computer onto a large screen that all the class can see clearly. While demonstrating the mathematics involved, all pupils can benefit from the questions she asks and the answers given by individual pupils. The whole class can benefit from her interaction through questions and answers.

The teacher decides to book and use an equipped IT room in the school so that pupils can work together in pairs on the computers.

Extending ability with number

The teacher intervenes while pupils are working to check that they can explain the mathematics behind their answers, to address mistakes and misconceptions and to re-teach any mathematics as necessary. In her analysis, she describes how ICT helps to extend pupils' knowledge, understanding and ability to apply number.

The mathematics software program provides a stimulating context for pupils to practise operations with decimals and to consolidate their understanding. The teacher considers that the practice examples available on worksheets and in textbooks are rather unimaginative and repetitive. Pupils find playing an interactive game against the computer stimulating. They want to win the game and therefore try hard to get the mathematics correct.

The text book practice examples only ask pupils to carry out particular operations. When using the computer program, pupils have to decide for themselves which operation is appropriate and then carry it out correctly using mental methods. The program also develops pupils' strategic thinking since they need to win certain places on the grid and block their opponent in order to win the game.

Case Study 2: Data handling at Y9 with a spreadsheet

Teaching objectives
Pupils should:

- collect and record data accurately;
- find, from a set of data, the range, mean and median;
- select an appropriate graphical form to represent the data;
- find a relationship between two data sets using the line of best fit;
- generalize the investigation and decide whether the relationship is valid across a wider population.

Training needs
The TTA identify the following as possible aspects you may identify as training needs:

- using a spreadsheet to teach about possible relationships between two data sets;

- using a spreadsheet to very rapidly produce graphical representation of the relationship between two data sets, to scale and re-scale the graphs and to explore lines of best fit;

- matching pupils' IT capability to the knowledge, skills and understanding they will require to use ICT for mathematical purposes;

- selecting and using ICT for whole class teaching.

Lesson activities

The teacher introduces the pupils to the task and clarifies the objectives. The pupils are to explore the relationship between wrist and neck circumference. They measure each other and then enter their data into a spreadsheet. Analysis of the two data sets using a scattergram leads to discussion about how they might explore whether the findings are valid more generally and how the data might then be employed.

The main issue identified about the use of ICT in this case study is the effective use of time.

Effective use of time

In her analysis the teacher describes how it is important that the pupils are already familiar with the ICT so that they can focus on the mathematics. She does not have to teach them how to use a spreadsheet or to select, sort or graph data. The computer network enables the teacher to prepare appropriate files for the pupils to use so that they can gain quick and easy access to them.

The teacher also explains that the pupils already have a good mathematical understanding of a scattergraph which enables them to make informed decisions about how to use it to aid their analysis and interpretation of data.

The teacher emphasizes that the ICT allows the pupils to work quickly in recording, analysing and presenting the two data sets in graphical form. This enables them to spend more time discussing the possible relationships between the two data sets, hypothesizing and testing their hypotheses rather than drawing and redrawing graphs by hand. The teacher is able to use the time gained to extend the pupils' mathematical understanding.

Whilst the teacher is aware that ICT does not help pupils to be able to draw accurate scattergraphs, she points out that the accuracy of the graphs avoids the possibility of pupils being misled in their interpretation. They are also able to employ ICT to scale and re-scale their graphs quickly and accurately and try a variety of lines of best fit without recalculating or redrawing. The teacher puts the pupils into pairs to consider their data.

The teacher describes how using the large display monitor allows her to make specific teaching points and discuss the pupils' conclusions with the whole class as part of the plenary session.

Case Study 1: Geometry at Y7 with dynamic geometry software

Teaching objectives
Pupils should:

- develop a strong visual imagery to support the concept of 'parallelism';
- be able to derive the angle properties of intersecting and parallel lines;
- be able to use dynamic geometry software to demonstrate that the angles of a triangle sum to those of a straight line.

Lesson activities
The teacher begins by involving the whole class in a short task based on a Z-shape drawn on the whiteboard. On a large screen, she then displays images produced from the dynamic geometry software. She questions pupils to focus their thinking and assess their initial understanding. Pupils are given a brief description of how to use the software. They work in pairs on the tasks which relate to properties of intersecting and parallel lines. The worksheets contain different levels of guidance. The lesson ends with a plenary session where pupils share their findings and the teacher reinforces key points. Pupils are set homework to produce an argument for why the angles in a triangle always add up to the same figure.

Training needs
The TTA identify the following as possible aspects you may identify as training needs:

- selecting subject-specific software to meet particular teaching objectives in mathematics;

- using dynamic geometry software to teach mathematics;

- deciding how and when to combine the use of ICT with conventional teaching of geometry;

- using ICT to present information, give instructions and explain ideas to a whole class;

- using ICT to prepare differentiated materials to guide pupils' learning.

The main issues identified about the use of ICT in this case study are (a) advantages and disadvantages of using ICT and (b) maintaining the focus on mathematics.

Advantages and disadvantages of using ICT

In her analysis, the teacher considers the advantages and disadvantages of using dynamic geometry software to help her meet her teaching objectives.

She decides to use dynamic geometry software because it provides a number of advantages over working with geometric figures on paper.

The software allows the teacher and pupils to deform shapes dynamically and observe which of their properties change and which stay the same. The teacher considers that the vivid and dynamic images produced help pupils to form mental images on which to base their understanding of concepts, such as parallelism.

By changing variables, the teacher is able to demonstrate a wide range of examples without having to draw them physically. Pupils are able to explore many more cases in a shorter time, giving them greater opportunity to consider general rules and test and reformulate hypotheses.

The software requires pupils to construct figures accurately. Visual feedback enables them to recognize quickly when they have made a mistake and they are able to undo and correct it easily. The pupils can concentrate more on mathematical relationships rather than on the mechanics of construction, enabling her to intervene more productively and have higher expectations of pupils' progress.

The teacher wishes to make use of features that would not be possible using conventional means. For example, zooming in on different levels of detail, and automatic measurement of angles or areas of figures.

The teacher takes into account the disadvantages of using the ICT, including problems caused by the quality and accuracy of the screen display. Dynamic geometry software simulates reality. The images produced on the screen are sometimes inaccurate, e.g. proportions are sometimes wrong, so it is difficult to accurately measure lines and angles directly off the screen. Similarly, because of the resolution and curvature of the screen, lines are not always straight. The teacher is aware of the difficulties and misconceptions that this might cause and addresses them in her introduction and as pupils work in pairs. She teaches pupils to question and check the accuracy of the computer generated images in the same way that they check their own constructions on paper.

Maintaining the focus on mathematics

In her analysis, the teacher describes how she ensures that the focus remains on the objectives in mathematics.

She projects the computer screen image onto a large screen so that all the class can see clearly. This enables her to ask focused questions, involve pupils in discussions, and explain key points while everyone in the class is looking at the same images.

She involves pupils actively in whole class mathematics teaching, both by inviting them to demonstrate using the software and large screen during the lesson, and to present and explain and justify their conclusions to the class.

She uses the program to provide pupils with a wide range of examples and to help give immediate feedback on their work. This maintains the mathematical focus of the lesson and allows the teacher to increase the pace of the lesson by moving quickly from specific examples to generalizations.

The teacher is aware that pupils could very easily run through a large number of different images without keeping a record of what they did and what they understood. So that she can keep track of pupils' progress the teacher structures the activity so that it is essential for pupils to record their work. The printed worksheets instruct pupils to make a record that helps them to go back and review their work, locate steps which may have generated errors, provide evidence of their processes and solutions for the teacher to assess, and communicate their findings and proofs to each other and their teacher.

Although the program has many helpful features, the teacher intervenes while pupils are working to question them about their understanding. This enables her to quickly identify misconceptions and to undertake focused mathematics teaching. This intervention, and asking pupils to explain to the rest of the class, enables them to clarify their thinking and challenge each other's hypotheses and proofs. Sometimes she stops the group work and uses the large screen to bring the discovery of one pair of pupils to the notice of the whole class or to address a common misconception.

Expected outcomes for training in the use of information and communications technology in secondary mathematics

A.   Effective teaching and assessment methods

1.   **Teachers should know when the use of ICT is beneficial to achieve teaching objectives in secondary mathematics, and when the use of ICT would be less effective or inappropriate. In making these decisions, they should know how to take account of the functions of ICT and the ways that these can be used by teachers in achieving mathematics teaching and learning objectives. This includes:**
   (a) how the speed and automatic functions of ICT can enable teachers to demonstrate, explore or explain aspects of mathematics to make pupils' learning more effective;
   (b) how the capacity and range of ICT can enable teachers and pupils to gain access to historical, recent or immediate information;
   (c) how the provisional nature of information stored, processed and presented using ICT allows work to be changed easily;
   (d) how the interactive way in which information is stored, processed and presented can enable teachers and pupils to explore models, communicate effectively with others and present and represent information effectively for different audiences.

2.   **Teachers should know how to use ICT effectively to achieve mathematics teaching objectives, including:**
   (a) using ICT because it is the most effective way to achieve teaching and learning objectives, not simply for motivation, reward or sanction;
   (b) avoiding the use of ICT for simple or routine tasks which would be better accomplished by other means;

(c) where ICT is to be used, what appropriate preparation of equipment, content and methodology is required;

(d) avoiding giving the impression that the quality of presentation is of overriding importance and supersedes the importance of content;

(e) structuring pupils' work to focus on relevant aspects and to maximize use of time and resource;

(f) having high expectations of the outcomes of pupils' work with ICT, including:

- expecting pupils to use ICT to answer valid questions appropriate to the subject matter being taught;
- when appropriate, requiring pupils to save work, and evaluate and improve it;

(g) making explicit the links between the ICT application and the subject matter it is being used to teach as well as the impact of ICT on everyday applications.

3. **For those aspects of lessons where ICT is to be used, teachers should be able to identify in their planning:**

(a) the way(s) in which ICT will be used to meet teaching and learning objectives in mathematics;

(b) key questions to ask and opportunities for teacher intervention in order to stimulate and direct pupils' learning;

(c) the way(s) in which pupils' progress will be assessed and recorded;

(d) criteria to ensure that judgements about pupils' attainment and progress in mathematics are not masked because ICT has been used;

(e) any impact of the use of ICT on the organization and conduct of the mathematics lesson and how this is to be managed;

(f) how the ICT used is appropriate to the particular mathematical objectives in hand and to pupils' capabilities, taking account of the fact that some pupils may already be very competent, and some may need additional support.

4. **Teachers should know how to organize classroom ICT resources effectively to meet learning objectives in mathematics, including how to:**

(a) use ICT with the whole class or a group for introducing or reviewing a topic and ensuring that all pupils cover the key conceptual features of the topic;

(b) organize individuals, pairs or groups of children working with ICT to ensure that each participant is engaged, that collaborative effort is balanced, and that teacher intervention and reporting back by pupils takes place where appropriate;

(c) make ICT resources available to pupils for research or other purposes which may arise either spontaneously during lessons or as part of planned activity, ensuring that the resource is used profitably to achieve mathematics-related objectives;

(d) position resources for ease of use, to minimize distraction, and with due regard to health and safety;

(e) ensure that work done using ICT is linked to work away from the screen, allowing ICT to support teaching rather than dominate activities.

5.   **Teachers should be able to recognize the specific contribution that ICT can make to teaching pupils with special educational needs in mainstream classrooms based upon the need to provide access to the curriculum in a manner appropriate to pupils' needs, and to identify where ICT can provide mathematics-specific support.**

6.   **Teachers should be able to choose and use the most suitable ICT to meet teaching objectives, by reviewing a range of generic and mathematics-specific software critically.**

7.   **Teachers should know how to contribute to the development and consolidation of pupils' ICT capability within the context of mathematics through:**
   (a) explicit discussion and, where necessary, teaching of the ICT skills and applications which are used in mathematics;
   (b) using terminology accurately and appropriately, and explaining to pupils any terminology which arises from the application of ICT to mathematics;
   (c) using ICT in ways which provide models of good practice for pupils, and ensuring that pupils employ correct procedures when using applications.

8.   **Teachers should understand how to monitor and assess pupils' learning in mathematics when ICT is being used, and how to evaluate the contribution that ICT has made to the teaching of mathematics. They should be able to:**
   (a) monitor pupils' progress by:
      i. being clear about teaching objectives and the use of ICT in achieving them;
      ii. observing and intervening in pupils' ICT-based activities to monitor and support their progression towards the identified objectives;
      iii. asking key questions which require pupils to reflect on the appropriateness of their use of ICT.
   (b) recognize standards of attainment in the mathematics when ICT resources are used, including:
      i. recognizing how access to computer functions might change teacher expectation of pupil achievements;
      ii. identifying criteria by which pupils can show what they have learnt as a result of using ICT-based resources from the Internet or CD-ROM, and insisting that pupils acknowledge the reference sources used in their work;
      iii. how to determine the achievement of individuals when the 'product' is the result of a collaborative effort, for example through observation, record keeping, teacher intervention and pupil–teacher dialogue;

iv. how to ensure that assessment of ICT-based work reflects pupils' learning and the quality of their work within mathematics rather than just the quality of presentation or the complexity of the technology used;

(c) use formative, diagnostic and summative methods of assessing pupils' progress in mathematics where ICT has been used, including how to set up ICT activities with targeted objectives for assessment and make provision in those activities for all pupils to demonstrate achievement, conceptual understanding and learning through the use of ICT.

9. **This section of the Expected Outcomes has been omitted since it refers only to pupils aged 3-8 and 3-11.**

B. **Teachers' knowledge and understanding of, and competence with, information and communications technology**

10. **In relation to the ICT content set out in paragraphs 11 to 18, teachers should be able to:**
   (a) evaluate a range of information and communication technologies, and the content associated with them, justifying the selection and use of ICT in relation to aspects of their planning, teaching, assessment and class management, including for personal professional use;
   (b) understand and use correctly the specialist terms associated with the ICT used in the mathematics which are necessary to enable them to be precise in their explanations to pupils, to discuss ICT in relation to mathematics at a professional level, and to read inspection and classroom-focused research evidence with understanding.

11. **Teachers should be competent in those areas of ICT which support pedagogy in every subject, including that they:**
   (a) can employ common ICT tools for their own and pupils' benefit and can use a range of ICT resources, at the level of general users (rather than as network or system managers), including:
      i. the common user interfaces, using menus, selecting and swapping between applications, cutting, pasting and copying files, and cutting copying and pasting data within and between applications;
      ii. successfully connecting and setting up ICT equipment, including input and output devices;
      iii. loading and running software;
      iv. file management;
      v. seeking and using operating information, including from on-line help facilities and user guides;
      vi. coping with everyday problems and undertaking simple, routine maintenance, with due consideration to health and safety;
      vii. understanding the importance of passwords and the general security of equipment and access to it.
   (b) know and understand the characteristics of information, including:

    i. that information must be evaluated in terms of its accuracy, validity, reliability, plausibility, bias;

    ii. that information has to be stored somewhere, it takes up memory (storage space) and that there are implications when saving and compressing files;

    iii. that ICT systems can present static information or changing information;

    iv. that information can be directly and dynamically linked between applications;

    v. that applications and information can be shared with other people at remote locations.

12.   Teachers should, in relation to secondary mathematics and ages of pupils:

  (a) know how to use ICT to find things out, including

    i. identifying sources of information and discriminating between them;

    ii. planning and putting together a search strategy, including framing useful questions, widening and narrowing down searches;

    iii. how to search for information, including using key words and strings and logical operators such as AND, OR and NOT, indexes and directories;

    iv. collecting and structuring data and storing it for later retrieval, interpretation and correction;

    v. interpreting what is retrieved;

    vi. considering validity, reliability and reasonableness of outcomes;

  (b) know how to use ICT to try things out, make things happen and understand how they happen including:

    i. exploring alternatives;

    ii. modelling relationships;

    iii. considering cause and effect;

    iv. predicting patterns and rules recognizing patterns, and hypothesizing;

    v. knowing how to give instructions;

    vi. sequencing actions;

    vii. defining conditions, e.g. '*if this happens, do that..*';

    viii. understanding how feedback works and the difference between things that do and do not rely on feedback;

  (c) know how to use ICT to communicate and exchange ideas:

    i. presenting ideas, including: identification of audience and purpose; deciding the best means with which to communicate;

    ii. exchanging ideas, including identifying the most appropriate medium, and information.

13.   Teachers should know those features of ICT which can be used, separately or together, to support teaching and learning in mathematics, including:

  (a) speed and automatic functions – the function of ICT which enables routine tasks to be completed and repeated quickly, allowing the user to concentrate on thinking and on tasks such as analysing and looking for patterns within data, asking questions and looking for answers, and explaining and presenting results, as appropriate to secondary mathematics, including how ICT can be used to:

    i. measure events at long or short time intervals in order to compress or expand events which would normally take very short or long periods of time, and illustrate them to pupils at speeds appropriate to their pace of learning;

    ii. measure and record events which might otherwise be impossible to gather within a classroom environment;

    iii. explore sequences of actions and link the sensing of events with the control of actions

(b) capacity and range – the function of ICT, as appropriate to secondary mathematics, to access and to handle large amounts of information; change timescales, or remove barriers of distance; give teachers and pupils access to and control over situations which would normally be outside their everyday experience, including:

    i. the range of forms in which ICT can present information;

    ii. the range of possible appropriate ICT sources, including local sources such as CD-ROM, and remote databases such as the Internet and the National Grid for Learning;

    iii. how to judge the accuracy of the information and the credibility of its source;

    iv. how ICT can be used to gain access to expertise outside the classroom, the school and the local community through communications with experts;

(c) provisionality – the function of ICT which allows changes to be made easily and enables alternatives to be explored readily, and as appropriate to secondary mathematics:

    i. how to make best use of the ability to make rapid changes, including how to create text, designs and models which may be explored and improved in the light of evaluation;

    ii. how to judge when and when not to encourage exploration and change using ICT;

    iii. how saving work at different stages enables a record to be kept of the development of ideas;

(d) interactivity – the function of ICT which enables rapid and dynamic feedback and response, as appropriate to secondary mathematics, including how to determine the most appropriate media to use.

14. **Teachers should understand the potential of ICT to make the preparation and presentation of their teaching more effective, taking account of:**

  (a) the intended audience, including matching and adapting work to subject matter and objectives, pupils' prior attainment, reading ability or special educational needs; recognizing the efficiency with which such adaptations can be made using ICT;

  (b) the most appropriate forms of presentation to meet teaching objectives;

15. Teachers should:

(a) in relation to secondary mathematics, understand the ICT requirements of the statutory curriculum for pupils and the application of ICT as a key skill;

(b) be familiar with the expectations of pupils' ICT capability, relevant to secondary mathematics, and know the level of ICT capability they should expect of pupils when applying ICT in mathematics.

16.   Teachers should know how each of the following is relevant to secondary mathematics:

(a) generic procedures and tools, including:
  i. understanding the key features and functions used within mathematics;
  ii. using ICT to prepare material for pupil use;

(b) reference resources, including:
  i. how to search reference resources;
  ii. how to incorporate the use of reference resources into teaching;

(c) the ICT specific to mathematics;

(d) the contribution made by ICT to the professional, commercial and industrial applications of their subject;

(e) the major teaching programs or 'courseware' to ensure that material is matched to the pupils' capabilities:
  i. where content and activities are presented in sequence to teach specific topics;
  ii. where teaching activities are combined with assessment tasks and tests.

17.   Teachers should be aware of:

(a) the current health and safety legislation relating to the use of computers, and be able to identify potential hazards and minimize risks;

(b) legal considerations including those related to:
  i. keeping personal information on computers, as set out in the Data Protection Act;
  ii. copyright legislation relating to text, images and sounds and that relating to copying software;
  iii. material which is illegal in this country;

(c) ethical issues including:
  i. access to illegal and/or unsuitable material through the internet;
  ii. acknowledging sources; confidentiality of personal data;
  iii. the ways in which users of information sources can be (and are) monitored;
  iv. material which may be socially or morally unacceptable.

18.   Teachers should know how to use ICT to improve their own professional efficiency and to reduce administrative and bureaucratic burdens, including:

(a) using ICT to aid administration, record-keeping, reporting and transfer of information;

(b) knowing about current classroom-focused research and inspection evidence about the application of ICT to teaching mathematics, and where it can be found;

(c) knowing how to use ICT to join in professional discussions and to locate and access teaching plans, material and other sources of help and support, including through the National Grid for Learning;

(d) knowing how ICT can support them in their continuing professional development.

Chapter 3

How to plan for effective ICT use

This chapter builds on the practical experience from Chapters 1 and 2 in developing a more analytical structure for the planning, implementation and evaluation of ICT use in teaching and learning. By the end of this chapter you should be in a strong position to know how to select and plan for its effective pedagogic use. We will also ask you to review your progress and to draw up an action plan for your future continued professional development (CPD) in the use of ICT in your teaching.

In this chapter we will consider a number of case studies and examples in which ICT has been used to enhance the teaching and learning of mathematics. We will analyse each example/case study to judge the extent to which they address the outcomes in parts A and B section 2, of the TTA document *Use of ICT in Secondary Mathematics (Identification of Training Needs)*. The level of detail of this analysis diminishes throughout the chapter as we hope that you will be getting more confident and expert in deciding professional issues for yourself.

We will keep in mind the three key aspects of ICT use outlined in chapter 1b:

- **Pedagogical**: can it be used to help teach content, to develop concepts, to increase knowledge, to improve understanding, to practise and reinforce skills . . .?
- **Mathematical**: can it be used to compute results, to produce tables, to draw graphs, to solve problems, to manipulate expressions, to compute statistics . . .?
- **Organizational**: can it help me more efficiently to produce materials, to keep records, to manage time, to communicate with others, to find resources . . .?

Another useful checklist is provided by the BECTa/NCET Pupil's Entitlement:

ICT: A pupils' entitlement

The NCET document: *Mathematics and IT – a Pupil's Entitlement* categorizes ICT tools by the nature of the mathematical activity involved. The six categories are:

Learning from feedback: The computer often provides fast and reliable feedback which is non-judgmental and impartial. This can encourage students to make their own conjectures and to test out and modify their ideas.

Observing patterns: The speed of computers and calculators enables students to produce many examples when exploring mathematical problems. This supports their observations of patterns and the making and justifying of generalizations.

Seeing connections: The computer enables formulae, tables of numbers and graphs to be linked readily. Changing one representation and seeing changes in the others helps students to understand the connections between them.

Working with dynamic images: Students can use computers to manipulate diagrams dynamically. This encourages them to visualize the geometry as they generate their own mental images.

Exploring data: Computers enable students to work with real data which can be represented in a variety of ways. This supports interpretation and analysis.

'Teaching' the computer: When students design an algorithm (a set of instructions) to make a computer achieve a particular result, they are compelled to express their commands unambiguously and in the correct order; they make their thinking explicit as they refine their ideas.

The following table summarizes this analysis. We have also included references within the body of the text of the case study where this is relevant, for example {**A1a**}

TTA Expected Outcomes

Case Study	A1	A2	A3	A4	A5	A6	A7	A8	B10	B11	B12	B13	B14	B15	B16	B17	B18
1. Not just building a Fence-Skeletowers	d	b	a,b,f					a			b						
2. Polygon Stars-T cup ride	c	f	c					b		a		d	a				
3. Distance match, Ball bounce, modelling	b	a,c,g	e		SEN					b		a		a			
4. Neck-wrists	a	e		c		b	a	c		b	a,b,c	b	b	a			
5. Garage door		d					b			a		c		b			

3a   NOT JUST BUILDING A FENCE

How many posts? How many rails?

Background

The following case study was written by a newly qualified teacher. This activity arose from the mathematics department's desire to develop pupils' reasoning and idea of proof/justification. Currently most pupils are able to organize data and tabulate it in ways that enable them to spot patterns and describe simple inductive rules and/or formulate simple generalizations. However, they would rarely give reasons on why their rule or formula worked. The department also wanted to increase their confidence in using algebra to model situations and their knowledge of algebraic conventions and techniques. The following is an account of the work done with a mixed ability set of Year 9 pupils to help them make progress in these aspects of the mathematics curriculum. The school is an inner-city all-girls comprehensive. However, it has been tried with both lower ability Year 7 and higher ability Year 8 pupils using slightly different starting points and extensions. Pupils had access to various grid papers, matchsticks and TI-80 graphic calculators (GC).

Lesson Plan

Teaching/learning objectives

Pupils should:

- be able to formulate linear rules based on geometric patterns;
- be able to explain why their rules work in terms of the way they see the patterns grow;
- collaborate with other pupils to pool and compare results;
- be able to present their findings clearly and concisely to a group/whole class.

Methodology and organization

1. Introduction to whole class using context of 'growing matchstick triangles' to establish pupils' understanding of number patterns and rules (use OHP). Ask for next pattern, ten triangles how many matches. Initially pupils to work in pairs explaining and justifying answers.

2. Tabulate results with whole class and ask for 'rule'. Demonstrate how this data can be entered and the 'rule' can be checked on the graphic calculator. {**A3a**}

3. Pupils to work in pairs on a range of problems (some similar so that different 'equivalent' forms can be compared) and combine to form a group of four to share findings and prepare poster/OHT for rest of class. They will have GCs to help them establish and/or check their rules. {**A4b**}

4. Check on progress and question or challenge pupils (such as looking for the inverse) have a range of different growth patterns of increasing difficulty including some leading to quadratic formulae. {**A3b**}

5. Overall time on topic 2/3 50-minute lessons including pupils' presentations and feedback.

Differentiation
Having a range of different growing patterns of increasing difficulty, including some involving quadratics, will ensure all pupils are appropriately challenged. Also, ask them to generate some of their own patterns.

Assessment opportunities/criteria
The initial interaction and discussion with pupils will help to establish pupils' knowledge understanding.

Observing and questioning individual pupils and groups while they are carrying out the work.

Listening to the presentations and looking at their work including the posters summarizing their findings

Pupils:

- are able to find and write down their generalizations in conventional algebraic form, some progressing to inverses and quadratic forms;
- carry out simple algebraic manipulations to check for equivalent expressions;
- can give reasons, explain and justify their rules in terms of the spatial patterns/arrangements.

Resources
Matchsticks, range of different grid papers such as square and isometric dotty paper
Variety of diagrams of growing patterns
16 graphic calculators, sufficient for 1 between two
Teacher's graphic calculator and view screen for whole class display on OHP.

The white board display will be useful for writing the pupils' rules as well as showing the graphic calculator display and will be helpful for linking the form and notation used by the GC compared to the pupils' own notation.

Other points

This is the first time most pupils have used the data handling/spreadsheet facilities of the graphic calculator. Pupils working in pairs should help alleviate the difficulties about 'which keys to press'.{A3f} The large poster of the GC indicating the menus 'under each key' will also act as a reminder. Also, the GCs can be easily used in the maths classroom so there is no need to book the computer suite.

At a later stage we can plot the table of results and look at the links between the graphs and their formulae.

The starting point – tricky triangles

Ten triangles, how many matches? Why?

The activity was introduced by looking at tricky triangles. The first few diagrams were formed on the OHP using matchsticks and pupils were asked to work out the number of matches for ten triangles. In the first instance they worked in pairs and were asked to explain and justify their answers. All could continue the pattern 'by adding two matches each time'. It was then decided that a rule was needed to speed up the process, and enable prediction of the number of matches for greater numbers of triangles. The pupils offered several different suggestions. In order to familiarize pupils with the TI-80 for use with further work and, to display the results for all to see, the data were entered into an OHP version of the graphic calculator.

L₁	L₂	**L₃**		L₁	L₂	L₃
1	3	------		1	3	3
2	5			2	5	5
3	7			3	7	7
4	9			4	9	9
5	11			5	11	11
10	21			10	21	21
L₃=L₁*2+1∎				L₃(1)=3		

The pupils were able to draw up the tables of results in lists L1 and L2 using the calculator STAT function. They then tried out their rules in L₃ and checked the results against those entered in L2. {A2d} This initially encouraged a trial and improvement method for getting the solution. It was interesting to note that in later presentations to the class, pupils used this phrase naturally when describing their work.

The calculator accepts the conventional algebraic hierarchy and will allow L1 × 3 + 1, 3L1+1 or even L1 3+1. This has the advantage that pupils are not forced to write their rules according to some 'textbook' convention and allows for development and discussion about acceptable forms. Pupils had little problem converting their own formula, which might have been written in terms of say a symbol t or n, into one using L1 etc. The main advantage of the calculator is the rapid feedback pupils receive. Lack of, or misuse of brackets, for example, is soon picked up.

Pupils were given a variety of different spatial sequences, ranging in difficulty, to work on. They quickly devised their own methods for finding rules. A number used the difference method and recognized that the number you add on to get the pattern must have some bearing on the formula. Others relied on the spatial arrangements and began grouping dots or lines to help find a rule. While some discontinued using the calculator to check results others, less confident, continued to use it for trial and improvement. Also, those concerned with presentation found it quicker to enter their results into the 'calculator tables' than to spend time drawing one in their books.

For some of the harder problems the pupils again returned to the calculator. They only used the technology when it was relevant and helpful rather than for the sake of it. **{A2b}{A4e}** The more able pupils were challenged to find the inverse rules or to move on to more difficult arrangements.

The same idea was used with three classes but with spatial arrangements and rules (linear, quadratic . . .) appropriate to the ability of the pupils. As a means of sharing their findings one class went on to produce posters. Another class (slightly lower ability) used the OHP to present their findings. This encouraged them to explain their thinking and justify their results. Pupils expressed their rules in several different ways; 2 x n was written as n x 2, 2n, or even n2 all of which were accepted by the calculator. Some pupils had discovered this for themselves and took great delight in explaining this to the rest of the class, especially when they were told that this also demonstrated the commutative law.

In her presentation one girl wrote her 'linear' rule as n^3. When asked whether this looked confusing pupils were quick to point out that this 'looks like n to the power 3, Miss, which means n x n x n, not n x 3'. This led to the class deciding that the shorthand form of n x 3 was best written 3n (the 'textbook' convention). Other points that came up in the various presentations were that one pupil had expressed their rule as 3a + a while the same sequence was expressed by another pupil as 4a – are these the same I asked? A rule was written 3n + 3 by one group and (n + 1) x 3 by another, are these the same? These presented further opportunities to return to the calculator to explore 'different' equivalent forms. Algebraic manipulation had been given ownership and the pupils were eager to find out if someone else's version of a rule really does work. Wanting to try out more algebra! – that really is a worthwhile outcome!

Review and evaluation – activity review

The following is an analysis**{A8a}** of the lesson(s) using the ACTIVITY REVIEW prompt. The purpose of this sheet is to provide some prompts to guide your analysis of the activity.

1. What did you expect to get from the task, i.e. purpose and learning intentions?

   These are defined in the Teaching/learning objectives in the lesson plan

2. What additional knowledge and skills did **you** need :

   about the technology

   Using the data handling facilities associated with the 'stat' key and the calculator's ability to manipulate 'lists'. For the follow up lesson, how to plot data and superimpose functions.

   about the mathematics

   Fairly confident with the mathematics, but talked to mentor about the expectations and level of challenge appropriate for this Year 9 group.

   about teaching strategies and approaches?

   How to engage all pupils in the whole class interaction, use of the growing design and matchsticks as an initial task accessible to all pupils. The use of more open-ended questioning at the start of the lesson to establish what pupils already know. Getting the pupils to discuss in pairs to ensure everyone is involved was a good idea. I like collaborative work and often use this approach in my lessons. Pupils learn so much when they have to explain their thinking to others. It also improves their listening skills.

3. What additional knowledge and skills did the **pupils** need:

   about the technology

   How to enter, edit and manipulate data in lists.

   about the mathematics

   An ability to analyse growing patterns and convert observations in words into conventional mathematical symbols

   about learning strategies and approaches?

   Be prepared to explore, {B12b} look for patterns and try things out, develop their use of visual imagery to explain their thinking. Work and co-operate with other pupils in their group. Explain and communicate ideas to other pupils in the class

4. Was the focus of your teaching on developing skills or understanding?

Both: I wanted pupils to develop pupils reasoning and communication skills through an accessible context. I also wanted to develop pupils understanding of equivalent algebraic expressions and introduce them to algebraic manipulation and give purpose for further work on this topic. Although I think it is much more important that pupils can use algebra to formulate/model situations.

5. Did the pupils focus on understanding or pressing buttons?

At the beginning of the first lesson some time was spent getting used to the data handling facilities on the GC. However, pupils were quick to come to terms with these and after an initial hiatus were able to use the GC with confidence to explore, check and validate their algebraic rules.

6. In what ways were your answers to questions 4 and 5 affected by the use of the technology for the topic?

The technology acted as an extra 'teacher'. Pupils were able to try out their ideas on the calculator and it provided them with instant feedback on the validity of their conjectures and formulae.

7. Would the use of the technology for this topic change the order in which concepts were taught?

Might try to introduce simple modelling and formal algebraic conventions earlier. Pupils coped well with the symbolism in the context of growing geometric patterns and had little difficulty using the GC.

8. What were the benefits/disadvantages of using the technology?

Benefits: see 5,6 and 7. Disadvantages: some initial problems getting to know the GC. I had considered using 'mouseplotter' and/or a spreadsheet in the school's computer room but chose the GC because of its easy use in the classroom and the similarity of the GC's notation with the standard algebraic convention.

9. What would you do differently next time?

As pupils become familiar with the GC I will get the pupils to plot the results and link the graphs to the rules such as the kind of rule that produces a straight line and the connection with the gradient and the intercept.

3 b   MODELLING SKELETON TOWERS

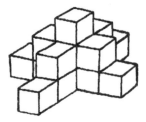

We have included here another example of a teacher using a practical context to help Year 10 pupils develop their algebraic modelling skills. As you read through the following account try to identify which of the 'Individual Training Needs' apply to this activity.

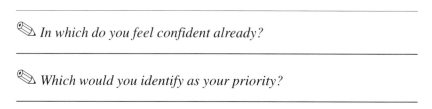

✎ In which do you feel confident already?

✎ Which would you identify as your priority?

You might like to use the Activity Review Sheet to help you with this process.

Background

Following the purchase of our TI-82 calculators, I was very keen to develop activities that related to Ma3 (Algebra) and in particular, modelling sequences.

I had in mind an activity that used the STAT Plot facility to scattergraph a sequence and then 'fit' this data to an equation using the function graphing facility.

I was aiming this activity at a set 1 Year 10 class.

If I was to develop this activity, I needed to accomplish two things:

- Spend some time investigating numbers generated from a series of linear, quadratic, cubic, quartic . . . functions and then investigate the differences. This was a prerequisite as I wanted pupils to discover that this could be a key to the type of function that they were dealing with.
- Generate the sequence that the pupils were going to fit from a practical situation as I wanted pupils to be able to prove their function both geometrically and algebraically.

The following Task Sheet summarizes the two activities:

Exploring Sequences using the TI-82

Make a growing pattern using multilink cubes.

Record the cumulative number of cubes needed for each layer.

Enter the layer number in List 1 and the cumulative number of cubes in List 2.

Select a suitable window and plot the data as a scattergraph.

Explore the differences in your sequence to try to determine the type of function that it could be;

i.e. linear, quadratic, cubic, quartic etc.

Try to determine the exact function by superimposing your guess using the Y = button.

Check for accuracy using zoom.

Once you have found your equation, can you 'prove' it geometrically by remaking your shape?

Why does your equation work

Activity 1

This was a mammoth task in itself, as I was asking pupils to investigate $y = mx + c$, $y = ax^2 + bx + c$ and $y = ax^3 + bx^2 + cx + d$ in about three fifty-minute lessons, so I used a teaching method that is very successful when you wish pupils to discover things through investigation in a short timescale. I delegated each table of 3–4 pupils a function to investigate and within the group each pupil would change one variable at a time. This also meant that I could differentiate, with more able pupils investigating the most challenging equation. Each pupil set up a master spreadsheet that allowed them to put in a sequence of numbers and watch the differences pan across. I gave the pupils two options for generating their sequence. Having chosen an equation, they took x values from 1 to 7 and either typed the equation into the spreadsheet to generate the sequence or used the TI-82s to define L2 as a function of L1.

Each group collated their results and presented their findings to the rest of the class. I then co-ordinated the whole class collection of results into a table for future reference.

Activity 2

The next part of the task was to generate a sequence from a practical activity and I decided that an extension of the 'growing patterns' work in Year 8 was in order. Pupils had previously investigated linear growing patterns, graphed their results and come up with some rules. We discussed these models and how we could 'put them together' to make something more interesting. We talked about counting the number of cubes cumulatively and looking for patterns. The pupils expected there to be a 'rule' for any pattern that was building up in an orderly way and I did not put restrictions on the type of pattern they chose. The group discussion seemed to throw out any dodgy models!

The class was already familiar with putting sequences into STAT memory and I then showed them how to do a STAT Plot, plotting the data as a scattergram. We discussed the idea of modelling the curve by choosing a function in the $Y =$ graphing mode and trying to make it go through the points. Very quickly it became obvious that there were an infinite number of equations to try, so pupils looked at the differences in their sequences to get some clues as to the type of function they were looking for. This is where the table of results in Activity 1 became invaluable.

Having found their function, pupils used the zoom function to check for accuracy. Some interesting points came out . . .

If each layer of the model was constructed from a linear growing pattern they were looking for a quadratic function. (These I called the skeleton models as they built up in two dimensions.) If each layer of their model was built up from a quadratic growing pattern (i.e. a space filling one) the function was a cubic one. This gave my most able pupils something to bite on as they were thinking how they could generate a quartic function. Other ideas that we discussed were:

- taking a step back to the original Year 8 growing pattern graphs and investigating the areas beneath the lines (or curves) and looking for connections;
- investigating the gradients of the modelled curves at different x-values;
- some of the pupils were looking for an equation for the sum of the square numbers so they were directed to 'A' level text for research.

The final part of the project was to prove the shape geometrically by rebuilding the model from the equation and there was immense satisfaction from the pupils if they were successful.

Extension

It would be an ideal opportunity to introduce some calculus. Initially, pupils would need to explore the linear function of their growing pattern by looking at each layer separately. They could explore the area under the line between zero and different values of x. These could be related back to the x-values of the linear function.

Evaluation

This is definitely an activity that is firmly on our Year 10 scheme of work. It enabled pupils to make great progress in their understanding of the nature of functions both graphically and algebraically. The multilink skeleton towers gave a practical context that was easy for pupils to explain and justify their algebraic models. It has also been used as a short task for GCSE coursework with linear models for foundation level pupils. This has produced some coursework of a high standard.

3 c POLYGONS AND STARS

The following worksheet is a summary of the task given to Year 10 pupils studying for the intermediate and higher tiers of GCSE.

POLYGONS-STARS

Figure 1 was created using parametric (Par), degree (Degree) and connected (Connected) mode and the following functions:

$$X_{1T}=5\cos T$$
$$Y_{1T}=5\sin T$$

with WINDOW

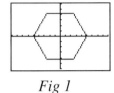

Fig 1

Tmin=0
Tmax=360
Tstep=60
Xmin=-9
Xmax=9
Xscl=1
Ymin=-6
Ymax=6
Yscl=1

Experiment with the values in WINDOW. Make a note of your observations and try to explain them. What effect does changing the number **5** in X_{1T} and Y_{1T} have on the appearance of the polygon?

Try $X_{1T}=5\cos (T+30)$, $Y_{1T}=5\sin (T+30)$

Sketch the result. Explore values other than **30**.

CHALLENGE – FIVE-POINTED STAR

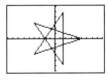

Fig 2

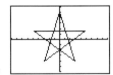

Fig 3

Figures 2 and 3 were produced by changing values in the WINDOW and small alterations to X_{1T} and Y_{1T}. Try to find out what these were.

Create your own pointed stars. How many different pointed stars can you make?

Background

This activity has been used with a wide range of pupils at both Key Stages 3 & 4 for different purposes. In one particular class it was used as a means of revising trigonometry and extending the trigonometric functions beyond the normal range of 0° to 90°. {**A4a**} It was also used to motivate pupils and help them see how mathematics can be used to model images and pictures. More able pupils extended their use of trigonometry to model and explore variations of the T-Cup ride (see part b).

The lesson(s)

I first showed the whole class octagonal and pentagonal ATM mats and asked them what other designs or logos they were familiar with. Some mentioned the logos used by car manufacturers and those of the different TV channels. I said we could use the graphic calculator to create pictures such as these using trig. functions. I drew a 30°, 60° right-angled triangle, with hypotenuse 5, on the blackboard and asked them how they could calculate the lengths of the other sides. The pupils had done some work on bearings and rectangular grid references and I then showed them how these calculations could also be used to calculate the co-ordinates of a point.

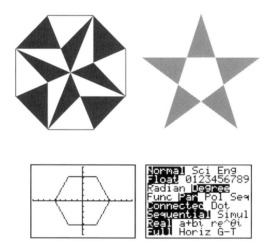

I showed them the picture of the hexagon using the viewscreen and OHP{**A4a**} and how I had created it using the Degree, Par mode. Also, the trig functions I had used and the WINDOW settings.

This was quite difficult for a large portion of the class but they were undaunted and I set them the task of trying to draw a pentagon. I challenged the more able pupils to draw the pentagonal star and gave out the Polygons–Stars worksheet{**A11a**} as a reminder for the calculator settings and to prompt their thinking about how they might reorientate their polygons/stars. Some pupils worked in pairs while others worked in threes and fours. By the second lesson, pupils were setting themselves their own challenges, some creating nested polygons in different orientations. {**A1c**}{**A13d**}

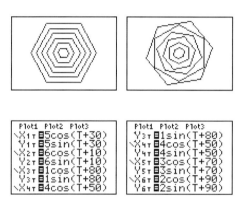

I asked the pupils, who produced the diagrams above, to tell me which hexagons matched which functions. They were able to explain quite clearly how they had arrived at their 'family' of hexagons, which numbers affected the size and which affected the orientation. A number of other pupils noticed that they could change the orientation by changing the value Tmin. We then discussed why this was so. Other groups of pupils generated circles (small step size) and families of ellipses. We discussed how the calculator draws 'approximate' circles. One particular group decided to produce a 'poster' of their work.

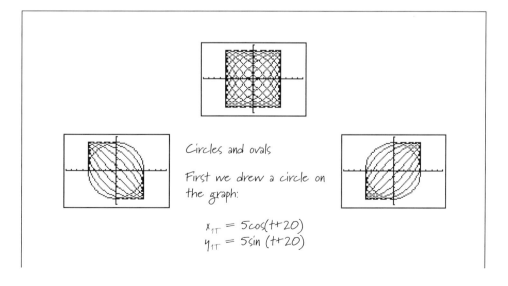

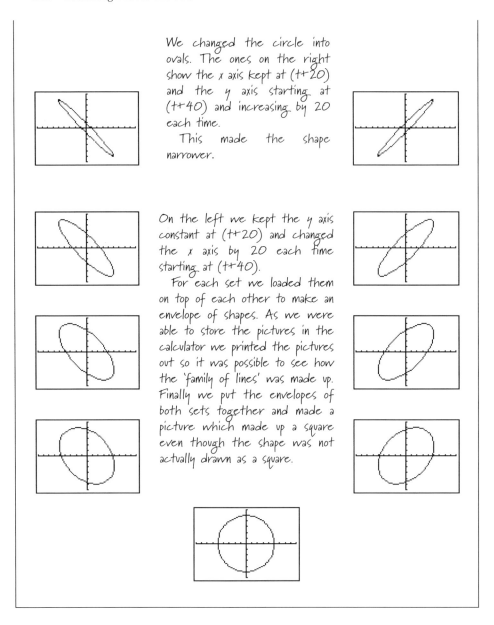

We changed the circle into ovals. The ones on the right show the x axis kept at (t+20) and the y axis starting at (t+40) and increasing by 20 each time.

This made the shape narrower.

On the left we kept the y axis constant at (t+20) and changed the x axis by 20 each time starting at (t+40).

For each set we loaded them on top of each other to make an envelope of shapes. As we were able to store the pictures in the calculator we printed the pictures out so it was possible to see how the 'family of lines' was made up. Finally we put the envelopes of both sets together and made a picture which made up a square even though the shape was not actually drawn as a square.

To ensure that pupils gained as much out of the activity as possible I got different groups to explain what they had been doing and how they had created their particular designs. {A2f} At different stages throughout the lesson I would ask the pupils to explain their designs in terms of the trig functions. {A2f}

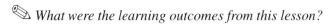

✎ *What were the learning outcomes from this lesson?*

3 d   THE 'TEA-CUP' RIDE

The task

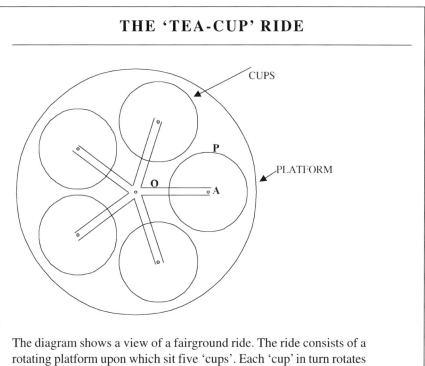

THE 'TEA-CUP' RIDE

CUPS

P

PLATFORM

O

A

The diagram shows a view of a fairground ride. The ride consists of a rotating platform upon which sit five 'cups'. Each 'cup' in turn rotates about its own axis. The platform rotates about the centre '**O**', while each cup rotates about the end of an arm (e.g. '**A**')

Explore the loci of a person sitting at the perimeter of a cup (e.g. '**P**') for different radii and rates of rotation.

This task has been used to develop pupils' visualization and ideas of locus. More able pupils have been set the task for their GCSE coursework. It has also been used to teach sixth form students kinematics (see extension task at the end of this case study).

The lesson(s)

I introduced this task by asking pupils how many had been to the local theme park and which rides they had been on. Several of them knew the 'tea-cup' ride and I asked one of them to describe it to the others. I showed them a plan view of the ride (prepared using a wordprocessing and dynamic geometry package) {**A11a**} on the OHP. I then asked them to imagine looking down on the ride and to visualize the path (locus) of a person sitting in one of the cups as both the platform and cup rotated. I told them that for a single revolution of the platform (about *O*) the cup travelled through two revolutions (about *A*). Also, that the radius of the cup (*AP*) was half the length of the arm (*OA*). I asked them to sketch their ideas in their exercise books and compare them with their neighbour's drawings. There was a great deal of discussion about the number of loops and whether they would be inside or outside a larger 'circle', whether the starting position of the person (*P*) made any difference. I asked them how they could check. Several said that they could make some accurate drawings. I said that in addition to their compasses, protractors and rules they could use geo-strips, paper fasteners and card. I also made available some A3 paper. {**A13d**} Some of the pupils decided to construct part of the ride, i.e. a single arm with an attached circle, marked every ten degrees. They were then able to produce quite a rapid locus.

This took most of the lesson, but as pupils arrived at their solutions to the particular problem I told them that for the remainder of the lesson and the next, I now wanted them to explore the ride for different radii and rates of rotation. They had to decide on the particular values. I said it would be sensible for them to divide up the tasks in their groups.

There is a small group of very able pupils in this class and I set them the task of trying to model the ride using trig. functions. They could then use 'Omnigraph' or the graphic calculator to produce several different loci quickly. {**A13d**}{**A14a**} They had coped well with the 'Polygons and Stars' using the graphic calculator and this was a natural extension to see if they could apply their knowledge of trig functions to this new problem. To start with they modelled the first problem, with the cup revolving twice about *A* for every revolution of the platform about *O*, incorrectly with the co-ordinates of *P* being:

$$X = 2\cos(T) + \cos(2T)$$
$$Y = 2\sin(T) + \sin(2T)$$

 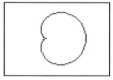

They had actually produced a cardioid instead of the figure which they had produced from their compass and ruler drawings.

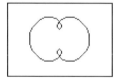

They soon realized their mistake{**A8a**}. They had forgotten to take into account that the cup was rotating *relative* to the platform and therefore at three times the rate, not two, from the observer's point of view.

They were then able to produce a wide range of loci to model and explain the effect of different starting points for *P*. For example, the following locus was produced with *P* starting at 90 degrees to the arm.

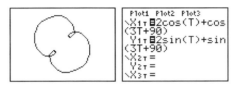

They also explored what would happen if the cup rotated in the opposite direction, e.g.

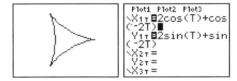

and the impact this would have on a person sitting in the ride.

A number of these pupils continued to work on this activity and submitted it for their GCSE coursework. **{A3c}.** They also generalized their formula to increase the efficiency and speed of producing loci:

$$X = A\cos(T) + B\cos(RT)$$
$$Y = A\sin(T) + B\sin(RT)$$

where *A* and *B* are the radii of the platform and cup respectively, and *R* depends on the comparative rates of revolution of cup and platform. Other pupils, although unable to model the locus using trig functions, were able to insert values into the given model to check their own loci. **{A8b}** I also set the class the task of finding out the names of the curves that they produced. This introduced them to new words to describe curves that crossed and touched (double points and cusps) and ways in which they might classify their loci.

Extensions in the sixth form

I have used this and other fairground rides to add interest and context to the mechanics section of the 'A' level course. I added the following extension task:

> The central point can be driven up to about 20 r.p.m. and it is recommended that 'a force of no more than 2g be exerted on the human frame' (NASA).
>
> Design a suitable ride

 You might like to tackle this problem yourself.

3 e   DISTANCE – TIME MATCH

Background

The following classroom studies are taken from a cross-curricular research project supported by the Teacher Training Agency (TTA) and the project report *Data-capture and Modelling in Mathematics and Science*, editors Oldknow and Taylor, referred to earlier in Chapter 2e. It was written for the Mathematics Curriculum IT Support group, which was funded by the Department for Education and Employment to help promote the use of ICT to enhance the teaching and learning of mathematics.

Each school used the CBR motion detector, in both science and maths lessons, attached to a teacher's TI-82 or 83 graphing calculator, projecting via the 'Viewscreen' LCD pad on top of a standard OHP. The CBR contains a program in its own memory called 'Ranger' which can be easily downloaded to any compatible graphing calculator. This enables easy control of the CBR and allows a variety of styles of use. In the first *'classroom study'*, a mathematics teacher from one of the Portsmouth schools (a girls' school) describes some of the approaches he has used. They illustrate nicely how he managed his lessons around a minimum provision of technology, and also how he built progression into the different activities he planned. We have also included summary reports from other schools in *'other studies'* to indicate the different approaches and methods of organization that can be used with this technology.

Classroom study

At my school, distance–time graphs are introduced in Years 8/9 depending on the abilities of the groups and so the following work was developed mainly for use at KS3. My main aims for the CBR activities were to try and address some of the issues concerning understanding of graphical interpretation using activities that promoted discussion and provided time for reflection. {A2a, c} Brian Hudson (*Micromath* **13**(2) 1997) describes this as a 'cycle' of: '...observation, reflection, recording, discussion feedback (test)'. The first set of activities are using the 'Distance Match' option from the 'Applications Menu'. I found that this was suitable for intermediate and higher groups in Year 8. With a higher Year 9 group the second set of activities are using the distance–time graphs from the plot menu and the third set involved using the functions of the graphical calculator to fit equations of lines to parts of the distance–time graphs. {A2a, c}{B14b}

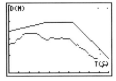

An example of a Distance Match graph – the third screen shows the target graph with straight lines – and a pupil's attempt to match it. **{A1b}**

The lesson(s)

This activity was started by showing on the OHP one of the graphs from the 'Ranger' program that fitted the constraints of the room. There was then classroom discussion about what the graph could mean and what it represents. We examined the axes and looked to see if we could work out the co-ordinates of what were considered by the pupils to be the key points of the graph. The class was then split up into groups and given fifteen minutes to try and work out a journey that would correspond to the graph shown. They were each given an A3 piece of squared paper so that they could, if they wished, sketch the graph. They put a diagram of the journey onto a piece of sugar paper. At the end of the fifteen minutes, one of the groups volunteered to show their conclusions and to map out the journey in the classroom. The CBR was then used so that one of the members of the group could walk through the journey to see how close their match was. There was then a class discussion about how successful the attempt had been and how the journey could be changed in order to more closely match the graph on the OHP. **{A1b}** The class was then given another five or so minutes to review their ideas in the light of what they had seen and then another group volunteered. After two or three attempts quite a successful match was made. **{B11b}** The pupils were then encouraged to write about their experiences and how their ideas had changed throughout the lesson and how they had changed their initial ideas to get a closer match.

For the second set of activities the 'Plot' menu was used. Working in groups of five, the pupils started by devising a journey which they mapped out on the floor of the classroom, taking measurements as necessary. Then, on a piece of A3 graph paper using the same axes as in the 'Plot' menu, they sketched as accurately as they could the graph of what the journey would look like on a distance–time graph. They needed to consider not only the distances involved but also the time needed to travel each part of the graph. When their graphs were ready, after about 30 minutes, the groups took it in turns to explain about their journeys show their graphs and then, after some rehearsal, to plot their journeys using the CBR. **{A1b}** There was then some classroom discussion about how close the OHP graph was to the sketch that the group had produced and the good points of the sketch were picked out by the pupils and ideas were offered about how the sketch could be improved. This activity ran over three lessons and during that time the groups were increasingly more able to recreate their journeys on the OHP.

The third activity again used the 'Dist Match' application. One of the graphs was chosen and shown on the OHP. Each pupil then wrote a report about the graph, describing it as a journey as accurately as they could. Meanwhile I copied the distance–time data stored in the two lists L1, L2 from the OHP calculator onto eight other graphical calculators using the cables and the transfer function. There followed a classroom discussion about the graph on the OHP and the key features were agreed on by the class. They were then split up into groups of four so that they could work on a copy of the graph that I had loaded into their calculators. I showed them on the OHP how to do a graph fit using the 'Y=' functions and set the pupils the task of finding the equation for the first part of the graph. They were given about five minutes to get as close as they could and then volunteers put their ideas onto the OHP. There was classroom discussion about how close each attempt was to the original graph and a consensus was reached about the 'correct' equation. **{B12b}{B13b}** Similarly the equations of the other parts of the graphs were worked out. During the next lesson, the activity was repeated using a different 'Dist Match' and the equations of the lines were compared. The pupils then set out to find out how they could set up a system so that they could describe lines, i.e. how steep they were, etc. Once the pupils had written a journey in the form of a set of equations, they were encouraged to devise a journey which they mapped out in the classroom and to work out the journey in the form of equations only. Each group then set the rest of the class the task of sketching the graphs from the equations that they gave them and then of translating the graphs into a journey. Whilst the rest of the class were engaged upon this task, the group setting the problem were using the 'Plot' menu to produce their own graph using the CBR and then were encouraged to see how closely their equations-based graph matched the one produced by the CBR.

Other studies

Other teachers preferred to prepare an OHP foil with examples of, say, five possible distance–time graphs and to get the students to try to match each one using a CBR and a graphing calculator in groups. Using say five CBRs and calculators, it was possible to organize groups of six to perform the movements on the playground or in the corridor.

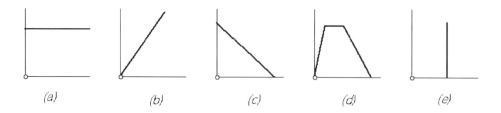

(a)   (b)   (c)   (d)   (e)

For example, in a Year 10 science lesson the pupils were given a variety of different shapes of (piecewise-) linear distance–time graph to try to reproduce: (a) horizontal, (b) diagonal upward, (c) diagonal downward, (d) vertical and (e) a mixture of diagonal upward, followed by horizontal, followed by diagonal downward. Groups of seven or eight shared a TI-82 and a CBR, and were let out into the playground to try to 'walk' appropriate journeys, and to keep notes. Subsequently they were asked to write up their observations back in the laboratory, and to describe the velocity at different points on each distance–time graph. The vertical line generated a great deal of discussion, and some very creative thinking! **{B14b}**

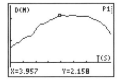 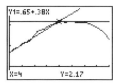

Meanwhile, in a Year 11 maths class, the students had also spent a lesson on data-collection and qualitative fitting. This was followed by a lesson on quantitative work in trying to decide suitable linear equations to 'fit' the distance–time graphs. Then they were asked to think of other shapes of mathematical curves they knew, and to try to 'walk' the appropriate trip. The second screen below shows one group's attempt to 'walk a parabola'. The noisy data points in the middle are due to the limitations on the CBR's operating range between a maximum of about 6 m and a minimum of about 0.5 m. With this data projected, the teacher then got the class to work at finding a quadratic function which gave a good fit to the data points. At first they tried fitting a quadratic in the form: $y = ax^2 + bx + c$, but then it was suggested that, since its minimum was around (4,0) a curve of the form $y = k(x - 4)^2$ might be easier to work with.

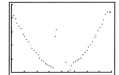 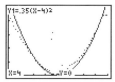

3 f   MODELLING A BOUNCING BALL

The CBR can also be used easily in other situations. For example, the 'Ball Bounce' application in the 'Ranger' program allows you to capture the distance from a bouncing ball to the ground against time as on p. 149. The CBR can be detached from the calculator while performing the experiment. Person A stands, perhaps on a chair, holding the CBR pointing towards the ground, while person B holds a ball (such as a basket ball) at least 0.5 m below the CBR. On the word 'go', A presses the CBR's trigger button and B releases the ball. It may take two or three attempts to get the ball bouncing more or less vertically. Then the CBR can be reconnected to the calculator for the captured data to be downloaded and displayed. The data have been transformed so that measurements are taken from the lowest point reached (i.e. the floor), rather than the distance from the CBR.

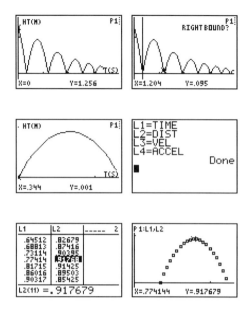

A cross-curricular project

The following account was written by a maths and a science teacher who were working together. They were keen to forge links between the two subjects and draw upon the relevant and *natural* opportunities in science lessons involving data handling to carry out mathematical analysis and modelling.

Although the language used in mathematics and science is similar, the words used can often have different meanings, for example the word 'modelling' can be used qualitatively or quantitatively. When the pressure of a gas is measured as it is compressed in a cylinder at various volumes, a phrase such as '*the smaller the volume, the greater the pressure*' expresses one model of the relationship between the volume V and the pressure P. The expression PV = constant is a stronger quantitative model which allows you to predict the pressure P at any volume V. In science lessons we tended to place greater emphasis on the less precise qualitative form of modelling. For the most part pupils are given scientific formulae such as $d = v \times t$ (distance = speed × time) and these are then rearranged and used to solve straight forward problems. We wanted our pupils to formulate their own models and be able to form links between the two subjects. We decided that a piece of coursework that able Year 10/11 pupils could use for both mathematics and science, would be an effective and efficient way of forging these links for both pupils and teachers. It would need to satisfy both the science and the mathematics criteria, and encourage an investigative approach using research, planning, collection of data, analysis of results and evaluation. We felt that exploring the bounce of a ball would satisfy this criteria. **{A2a, c, g}**

We decided that we should do the practical ourselves so that we not only had first-hand experience of it but we could also help the pupils identify and iron out any technical difficulties. We also wanted to explore the potential scientific and mathematical content. This is what we came up with:

- *Science:* we would expect the students to research the science behind the bounce. They could predict the height of bounce based on previous experience and identify the equation (research for level 8 planning). **{A3c}** Once they had identified the equation they would be able to apply it to their real data and explore the effect of different variables on the bounce of the ball. They could also look at energy changes that have taken place and try to explain them. **{A2g}**
- *Mathematics:* they would need to research the equation for the bounce of a ball and then establish how close this model fitted the real data they would collect in their experiments. [See the modelling section of chapter 2 for ways in which pupils tackled this problem.]

We were surprised at the ease with which data could be collected and the speed at which the pupils could analyse and fit different functions/models to this data. Our own scientific and mathematical knowledge was being stretched and we both felt that we were working *with* the pupils, doing real maths and science. The pupils suggested several lines of enquiry on how the size, temperature and material affected the path and height of the bounce. They also dealt well with the practicalities of how to get fair and consistent real data.

This is a list of hints and tips that we and the pupils found useful for carrying out this experiment:

- It is best to have the CBR clamped to a surface and to let the ball drop from a predetermined, labelled height.
- The surface that the ball bounces on should be smooth and hard. An upturned table can be used for carpeted areas.
- Large balls are better than small ones, with a smooth rather than rough surface. A tennis ball causes problems because the vibrations are absorbed and there is a fuzzy picture, similarly with a golf ball.
- The drop of the ball should be between 0.85 and 1.5 metres.
- Remember the ball must be at least 0.5 metres from the CBR

Evaluation: pupils' and teachers' reactions

Here are some pupils' comments from one school on how they found using the CBR for practical work in the classroom had helped their learning.

Sebastian Day   Maths Lesson   2.10.97

The main thing about the lesson wasn't what I learnt but what I will remember.

Because of the lesson I doubt that I will ever forget the equation for a line.

$y = mx + c$

Nor will I forget what each of the letters stand for.

Thinking about the lesson, having some one walk up and down the classroom made it easier to understand the graph and decode the information that was given to you.

But now because of this, whenever I see a complicated graph all I have to do is imagine myself walking the same as the graph lines and then I can understand exactly what's happening.

Another thing that I learnt that I'm sure I'll find useful is that the gradient for a line on a distance-time graph is the same as the speed.

Russell Labibi   Maths Homework   3.10.97

The lesson worked well and it was a good way of teaching something which otherwise could have been boring. I learnt a lot about distance-time graphs. I learnt about accelaration and velocity. The equation $y = mx + c$ is used to draw lines on graphs. y stands for the y axis, m for the gradient, and c for the intercept.

The intercept can easily be read off of the graph. To work out the gradient you do the distance travelled divided by the time travelled. The graphic calculators were also good, keeping the class interested. It was also a good way of teaching us how to find gradients and intercepts.

Terry Ward 10 HW

In maths between 29/9/97 and 30/9/97 we were doing work with a graphic calculator. In the first lesson we were using sensors to learn how a graphical calculator plots a distance-time graph. We had to move forward or backwards to try and match a graph on a wall. The sensors detected how far backwards or forwards we travelled and plotted it against the graph displayed on the white board, e.g.

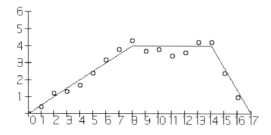

In the second lesson, sir displayed a graph on the white board and then handed out some graphical calculators. The graph was displayed on each calculator and our job was to enter the co-ordinates to match the graph. After a while we found out the equation by trial and improvement. Sir told us how to find the intercept without an intercept point and we also re-learned the equation for a straight line.

All the teachers in the project found the equipment extremely reliable and easy to use. Obviously the sensitivity of the CBR, and its range of 0.5–6m, restricted some of the ideas that they discussed for practical work. For example, it wasn't really possible to measure speeds of cars on a road, or easy to pick up a rolling object on the ground. But clearly a good range of practical activities were possible, which previously would have been impracticable to carry out, either in science or mathematics. The teachers were clearly encouraged by the way that the pupils responded to this kind of work.

The teacher from the Portsmouth Girls' School summed up his reactions:

> The use of the CBR and the graphical calculators was very popular with the girls. By monitoring the discussions and the interactions during the activities I observed many cycles of 'observation, reflection, recording, discussion feedback (test)'. The technology used in this way, supporting collaborative learning, empowered the girls to develop their levels of understanding as they tried to fulfil the aims of the activities. I believe that by developing more activities within the framework that I have set out above, using the CBR actively encourages pupils to make the very important links between graphs and algebraic relationships.

He went on to quote from Paul Ernest (1996):

> First of all there is the active construction of knowledge, typically concepts and hypotheses, on the basis of experience and previous knowledge. These provide a basis for understanding and serve the purpose of guiding future actions. Secondly there is the essential role played by experience and interaction with physical and social worlds, in both the physical action and speech modes. This experience constitutes the intended use of the knowledge, but it provides the conflicts between intended and perceived outcomes which lead to the restructuring of knowledge, to improve its fit with experience.

It is interesting to contrast the pupils' positive responses with those problems observed by Kath Hart:

> . . . several pupils found difficulty with travel graphs, even though they appeared to be able to give the correct answer. It was clear that several of those interviewed had incorrect perceptual interpretations of the graph. Some thought of the graph as a journey that was up and down hill, or as directional on the ground, and found it difficult to deal with the abstract notion of distance from the origin . . . Many had no idea what was intended, while others had very vague ideas about graphs . . . While many children will be able to read information from a graph or to plot given data, it seems only a few will be able to understand the connection between an equation and a graph.

Other teachers reported on the remarkable progress of less able pupils, such as a bottom set Year 9, in their understanding and interpretation of such graphs, even with access to a single CBR. {A5}

3 g   WRISTS AND NECKS – DESIGNING A LONG-SLEEVED SHIRT/BLOUSE

> How do manufacturers decide on the sizes of collars and cuffs? What advice can we give?

Background

This starting point has been used with GCSE mathematics and statistics classes as a means of introducing them to a range of statistical measures and forms of representation such as box and whisker plots, histograms, scatter graphs, etc. It is also a useful way of showing pupils how ICT can be used to support their statistical surveys in increasing the speed and efficiency of processing their data. In the study that follows, the teacher used the TI-83 graphic calculator because of its range of statistics features and the fact that it could be used in the normal mathematics classroom. She also used the opportunity to cover the topics of ratio and proportion, place value degrees of accuracy and rounding to two decimal places. The pupils were reasonably familiar with the graphics calculators, having used them for everyday calculations and for plotting graphs.

The lesson(s)

Clothes play an increasingly important part in pupils' lives and I thought this task would make an interesting starting point for the mathematics, in particular data handling skills, that I wanted to teach. I asked them if they were aware of the kind of decisions that clothes manufactures have to make when designing and making say shirts and blouses. How do manufacturers decide on the size of collars and cuffs? A number of pupils suggested that this would depend on the design of the shirt or blouse, whether it was loose or tight fitting. I agreed but asked them whether they thought there was a connection between wrist and neck measurements. Several said that they thought that there might be, and offered that the neck was probably about three times the wrist. I then said we would collect some measurements from them and that I would show them how to use the statistics functions on the calculator to find answers to this, as well as look at the diffrent ways we could display the data. Later they could use the graphic calculator to explore questions of their own.

I didn't have sufficient numbers of tape measures, so I handed out strips of A3 paper for them to take measurements. I said it would be interesting to see if there is a gender difference and said it would be useful to enter these separately. I entered their results directly into the 'teacher's' graphic calculator using the viewscreen and OHP for the whole class to see. I inserted four headings: FW, FN, MW, MN (female wrist size, female neck size, etc.).

The full set of results is as follows:

FW	15	17	20	15.5	17.5	16	15	15	15	17	17	16	15.5	16
FN	32	35	41	35	36	33	35	34	34	37	35	35	36	34
MW	16	20	19	19	17	18	17	15.8	17.6	16.5	17.8	19.5	17.5	
MN	36	39	42	41	38	38	39	38	40.1	37	37	40	36	

Some of the pupils wanted to enter the data into their calculators while others wrote them down in their exercise books. At this stage I did not want them to be distracted by questions about 'which keys to press'.

I then asked them how we could check out their conjecture that the neck was 3 times the wrist. Some suggested that we just divided **FN** by **FW** and **MN** by **MW** and compare several answers, others suggested finding the average size neck and wrist. I asked them to do this in any way they chose. Most pupils used the graphic calculators in the normal home screen mode. I showed them how we could calculate the ratio, male wrist : male neck,very quickly using the list commands (much like a spreadsheet).

I then showed them how we could calculate the average ratio for boys in two ways:

I said they could choose whichever they found easier. We discussed the 'funny' symbols on the third screen above, including standard deviation, and I said that this was a way of measuring the variation. We also discussed what would be a suitable degree of accuracy.

I then asked the pupils to look at the female data and compare those with the boys. I encourage pupils to help each other and most worked in pairs or threes. This makes it a lot easier when working on new skills with computers or graphic calculators. As a memory aid I also have a large display of the calculator pinned to the notice board at the front of the class with some of the key menus such as WINDOW, STAT and MATH highlighted.

I asked them what else they could do to check the relationship and several suggested a scattergraph. I said they could plot the data (boys and girls) onto graph paper or use the calculator. They would need to think about scales and staring points on the axes. I showed them how to plot the points on the GC and for them to find a line of best fit. They could plot the data (boys and girls) separately and/or together.

I asked them for suitable sets of values for the axes. Wrist is on the *x* axis and Neck the *y* axis. We superimposed both sets of data, squares for females and crosses for males .

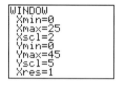 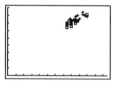

They were familiar with plotting functions so I asked them to select better values in the WINDOW and experiment with lines of best fit for both sets of data. One group produced the following for the combined data sets:

  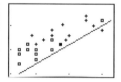

Later, pupils established that $Y = 2X + 3$ gives a better fit (by eye).

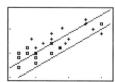

In the following lessons we discussed how we might try more 'mathematical' ways of getting a line to fit, through, for example, finding the 'average' wrist, neck point on the graph and looking at the lines that passed through this point. I also suggested that they could split the data in half (say, sorting on wrists) and find two averages, or use the line that passed through the lower and upper quartiles. (They noticed that they could get the quartiles, along with the mean, in the 1-Var Stats option.)

I told them that the graphic calculator will work out a 'best fit' and showed them how this was done for the female data.

  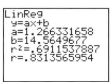 

I then asked them to round the 'calculator equation' to a suitable degree of accuracy and compare this with their own. Some were curious to know how the calculator did this and I said that 'basically it minimizes the distance between the line and the points'. The plot below shows the female data.

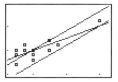

Later on with the more able pupils I showed them how they could manipulate the lists to look at the difference between their observed data (O) and the expected data (E) predicted by their model. We found the 'average difference' in two ways; using ABS(O-E) and (O-E)^2.

By the second and third lessons they were quite familiar with plotting scatter graphs manipulating the lists, including transferring data between calculators. I also showed them how to use the box and whisker plots and histogram options. The box and whisker plots are a really useful and accessible way of comparing data sets.

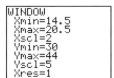  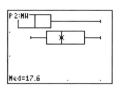

I highlighted different parts of the box and whisker and asked them to interpret the diagram for the female and male wrist measurements.

After showing them how to plot a histogram for the female neck sizes, I asked them to experiment with the scales (group size) and to compare male and female results.

In the third lesson I asked them to think of other data, and relationships, that might be important to manufactures in the clothing industry. Some pupils continued this topic and presented it for their coursework. One pupil found a reference to Leonardo da Vinci's 'Vitruvian' man and the Golden section/ratio on the Microsoft Encarta™ CD-ROM and explored relationships between different sections of the body.

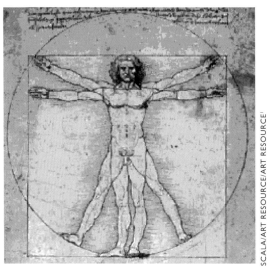

This drawing from the notebooks of Leonardo da Vinci, known as 'Vitruvian Man' after the architect Vitruvius, demonstrates the proportions of the Golden Section: the sections of the body from head to waist and from waist to feet are to each other what the section from waist to feet is to the length of the whole body. The fact that the 'divine proportion' was to be found in the human body was seen as highly significant in the Renaissance, the age of humanism.

He also got a great deal of satisfaction in understanding the following explanation (provided by Microsoft Encarta™).

Golden Section, in art and mathematics, a geometric proportion based on a specific ratio in which the greater part is to the lesser what the whole is to the greater. It is most clearly expressed as a line intersected in such a way (see diagram below) that the ratio of AC to CB is the same as that of AB to AC.

This ratio has the numerical value 0.618 . . ., which can be derived as follows: If AB = 1, and the length of AC = x, then AC/CB = AB/AC becomes $x/(1 - x) = 1/x$. Multiplying both sides of this equation by $x(1 - x)$ gives $x^2 = 1 - x$; therefore, $x^2 + x - 1 = 0$. This equation can be solved by using the quadratic formula, which yields the equation $x = (- 1 + \neq)/2 = 0.6180339 \ldots$ Recognized as an aesthetically pleasing ratio, the Golden Section has been used as the basis on which the elements in a painting, or in an architectural scheme, are arranged.

Plato is generally credited with establishing the study of the Golden Section, and the Greek mathematician Euclid, writing in the 4th century BC, defined this proportion in his chief work, *Elements*. The Golden Section was of great interest to artists and mathematicians of the Renaissance, when it was known as the Divine Proportion and was regarded as the almost mystical key to harmony in art and science. *Divina Proportione,* a treatise on the subject written by the great Renaissance mathematician Luca Pacioli and illustrated with 60 drawings by Leonardo da Vinci, was published in 1509, and influenced artists and architects of the age, among them Leonardo, Piero Della Francesca, and Leon Battista Alberti.

The Golden Section has also been used by later artists. Experiments suggest that human perception exhibits an innate preference for proportions that accord with the Golden Section. This in turn implies that artists may almost subconsciously arrange the elements of a picture according to those ratios.

3h   A GARAGE DOOR

A Problematic Garage Door

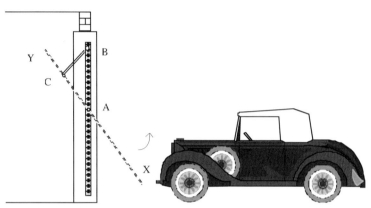

In the up and over garage door above, the door XY is 2 m high and AC = CY = BC = 0.5 m.

The door is opened from the outside by pulling X outwards and upwards.

A projecting pin in the door at A, slides in a vertical channel in the door post (shaded section on the diagram), while C is made to rotate about B by rod BC.

When the garage door is 30° to the horizontal how high will X be?

How far from the garage door should the driver stop the car to be able to open the garage door?

Explain why the locus of C is part of a circle.

What is the locus of Y and why?

What is the locus of X?

What implications does this have for:

- the length of the drive in front of the garage;
- the shape of the front/rear of the car?

Background

This activity has been and can be used for pupils from Key Stage 3 to post-16 years. It has been adapted from an activity described in *Mathematics Meets Technology* by Brian Bolt. In the following study we will attempt to indicate how this task might be developed with pupils of different age and ability. I hope this will also illustrate the rich source of mathematics that can be found in the study of everyday objects, especially mechanisms of the type described in Brian Bolt's book. The brief reports below give a flavour of the kind of mathematical activity that can derive from this starting point.

 We leave it to you to flesh out the details using your own choice of ICT tool.

The lessons

Key Stage 3
The whole of this task can be done practically using geo-strips, drawing pins and/or paper fasteners. The loci of C and Y could be drawn practically which will help pupils in their explanations and reasons for their loci. The locus of X can be constructed using the above practical resources but a proof is probably beyond pupils at this key stage.

Key Stage 4 (higher) and post-16
The problem can be modelled using co-ordinates and parametric equations involving trigonometric functions. Graphs can be drawn using ICT. Additionally, or alternatively, the problem can be modelled using dynamic geometry software.

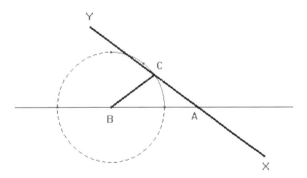

This concludes the case study aspect of this chapter. We have already shown the use of a completed activity review sheet on pp. 194–5. We have also prepared a simple planning tool which we include on the following page with a list of the activity review questions.

PLANNING A LESSON

Some points to consider when planning a lesson incorporating ICT:

- The main learning objectives/intentions for the lesson
- How will you cater for pupils of differing ability?

    This might be through, e.g.
    - a common starting point accessible to all, with differentiation through questioning, extension tasks;
    - differentiated tasks.

- To what extent the use of ICT will enhance teaching and learning:
  ICT may support pupils' learning through, for example, enabling them to explore many cases rapidly (increased efficiency) and learning from feedback (see NCET's Pupil Entitlement, p. 189).

- Classroom organization and resources
  The kind of task(s) you will use, adapt or design yourself including ICT support/prompt sheets, prepared files (e.g. spreadsheet template, data file etc.), extension tasks.
  Will the class be working together, in collaborative groups or in pairs? Encouraging pupils to help each other is particularly important when pupils are using a particular ICT tool for the first time.

- How will you address the extent to which learning objectives have been addressed?

- Review and evaluation
  You might also include an evaluation of the task itself, whether it was appropriate for the learning objectives, any adaptations you might make in future etc. In addition you should evaluate the contribution that ICT made to pupils' knowledge and understanding. The activity review sheet should help here.

Activity Review

The purpose of this sheet is to provide you with some prompts to guide your analysis of the activity and help you prepare back to the rest of the group.

1. What did you expect from the task, i.e. purpose and learning intentions?

2. What additional knowledge and skills did you need:
   about the technology
   about the mathematics
   about teaching strategies and approaches?

3. What additional knowledge and skills did the pupils need:

about the technology
about the mathematics
about learning strategies and approaches?

4. What was the focus of your teaching on developing skills or understanding?

5. Did the pupils focus on understanding or pressing buttons?

6. In what ways were your answers to questions 4 and 5 affected by the use of the technology for the topic?

7. Would the use of the technology for this topic change the order in which concepts were taught?

8. What were the benefits/disadvantages of using the technology?

9. What would you do differently next time?

At this point we hope you have read, and tried, enough to feel enthused to want to try using some ICT for real in your classroom (if you haven't done so already!). As with almost every other aspect of teaching, you should find it gets easier as you practise more. If possible it is best to have someone else you can compare notes with, seek advice from, plan jointly with, talk through your successes and disasters (yes – we have all had them!), etc.

 You should now re-read the TTA's Expected Outcomes to see just how far you think you match up to them at this point.

It would be a miracle if you could say that you have already met them all! But you should be able to see just how much progress you have made towards them already. Before leaving this practical section of the book you should now start to draw up a personal action plan for your intended development over the next three or four years, say. Think which activities and ICT tools you are going to concentrate on to begin with, and plan to get confident and competent in their use. Prioritize your 'gaps', and plan to meet some of them next year, some the year after and so on. Keep an eye on what forms of further Continued Professional Development may be open to you. Look out particularly for activities mounted via subject professional associations, such as the ATM and MA in the UK. There is also a worldwide training organization called T-cubed, for Teachers Teaching with Technology, which exists in most countries round the world to support teachers using hand-held, and other, technology particularly in mathematics and science.

Obviously we hope that you will enjoy reading the rest of this book, but we will take the opportunity to wish you 'bon route' in applying ICT in making your teaching, and your pupils' learning, of mathematics more effective. Good luck.

Chapter 4

Why integrate ICT into mathematics teaching?

This chapter looks outwards to what others have said, done and researched, about the links between mathematics, ICT and education. It is intended to help you answer for yourself the question: 'why should we aim to integrate ICT into mathematics teaching?' The range of references at the end of this chapter should be particularly helpful if you intend to undertake any further academic work, such as an MA module, as part of your CPD.

Three possible reasons

We are in an era of increased educational accountability, and one in which a certain scepticism has grown about accepting the judgement of professionals. In many aspects schools are being asked to produce policies and development plans 'in the light of research and inspection evidence'. We have recently seen a huge change in the organization and methodology of the teaching of mathematics in primary schools in England through the National Numeracy Strategy. This strategy claims to be based on just such research and inspection evidence. However, in her plenary address to the British Congress on Mathematics Education in Northampton, July 1999, Professor Margaret Brown analysed these claims, point by point, to show that in each case there is conflicting research evidence. In essence, then, it is rare in education that one can point to genuinely persuasive evidence that treatment X will have a beneficial effect in terms of characteristic Y. Because of the rapid pace of change of technology, and the political issues surrounding mathematics education, it is hardly surprising, then, that we cannot identify overwhelming research evidence to support the claim that using ICT in teaching mathematics significantly improves students' learning of mathematics. In fact we should probably be rather sceptical of any research which made such a claim. This is not to say that some important and interesting research has been conducted, nor to say that the converse case has been demonstrated! In this chapter we will point to some interesting pieces of research, to surveys of research and to calls for research. We will also look at some official reports that have impacted on ICT and mathematics in the last twenty years, as well as pointing to some work suggesting future directions in mathematics education.

In addressing the title of this chapter we can identify at least three reasons for promoting the integration of ICT in mathematics teaching in schools:

1. Desirability
2. Inevitability
3. Public policy.

Desirability

In order to show that ICT use is desirable we need to say in which ways it is desirable. There may be many of these. In terms of students, the use of ICT may:

- engage their attention and motivate them;
- stimulate their curiosity;
- encourage them to develop their problem-solving strategies;
- provide models and images which aid them in concept formation;
- improve their test and examination results, etc.

In terms of teachers, the use of ICT may:

- improve their efficiency;
- reduce their administrative burden;
- release more time to address students individually;
- provide better records of students' progress;
- be a stimulus to re-thinking their approach to mathematics teaching;
- be a stimulus to re-thinking their understanding of mathematics;
- be a means to communicate with other teachers sharing common problems etc.

In terms of schools, the ICT may:

- improve efficiency and reduce teaching costs;
- improve examination results and the school's position in 'league tables';
- reduce truancy, social disruption, etc.;
- improve provision for students who are not learning in their native tongue, etc.

For example, a lot of attention has been given in the media to the comparative results in mathematics of the Third International Mathematics and Science Study (TIMSS). So it might be thought nationally desirable for a country, such as England, to take steps to improve its performance. However there are inevitable questions about comparing like with like. For example, in some countries the teaching of the use of electronic calculators is a compulsory part of the curriculum, whereas in others it is not. So it is not surprising, then, that when questions are chosen for such international comparisons they are taken as far as possible from the intersection of the various countries' curricula. However, a particular skill, such as the addition of fractions, may represent a considerably larger proportion of one country's curriculum than another's. So imbalances are inevitably built into the system. It may also appear that a number of countries that discourage the use of calculators, such as in SE Asia, may perform better in TIMSS tests than those in Europe and America, say, which encourage their use. But is it calculator use which is the critical factor, or would these countries achieve even better results if they promoted calculator use? A test case here is Singapore which is a country which achieved very highly overall, but within which students who were familiar with calculator use outperformed those who were not.

So establishing a case for desirability is still a question of values and judgement. It is also, inevitably, a political one, especially in regard to the funding of educational research, and to the credentials of the researchers, their brief and their methodology. The issue is clouded further by the involvement of commercial interests. In Europe we are seeing an increasing amount of so-called public–private partnerships between government and major companies. The amount of public money available to support educational research has been eroded, and increasingly researchers seek sponsorship from private firms. Not surprisingly, many such companies express preferences towards lines of enquiry more directly related to their own priorities. So it may well be that important, feasible research remains unconducted for want of essential support.

Inevitability

Technology becomes inevitable where the conventional alternatives no longer exist, become prohibitively expensive, or impose such obvious restrictions that their use cannot be rationally supported. For example many fields of publishing are moving from print to electronic form. This applies to conference proceedings, to reference works such as encyclopaedias, to small-circulation textbooks, to specialist journals, etc. So we can safely claim that it is technologically inevitable that a school reference library should provide access to materials on CD-ROM and the internet. Can we make a similar claim for the provision of ICT tools in mathematics? Well, certainly in England it has been common practice to teach the use of tables of logarithms and, in some cases, slide rules in secondary schools as aids to computation. So the move to making the teaching of calculator use compulsory for students ages 9–11 could be seen as acceptance of such a technological inevitability, especially as calculators are more powerful, more convenient, easier to use and cheaper than the alternatives. The year 2000 is UNESCO's international year of mathematics, and in the UK it is promoted by the Department for Education and Employment (DfEE) where it is called 'Maths Year 2000'. Interestingly one officially proposed aspect of that programme is a celebration of the power and use of the calculator, a far cry from the official line even two years previously.

The jury is still out on, for example, the educational inevitably of the use of graphing, statistical, geometric and algebraic ICT tools in addition to the numerical computational tool – the calculator. However their mathematical inevitability is beyond doubt. The political rationale behind UK Maths Year 2000 is the need for a technologically innovative industrial and commercial sector for the UK to sustain its world position economically. In short we do not have the raw materials or cheap labour to compete, so we must do it by being smarter. Similar analyses are affecting policy in other countries, such as France. So whether something becomes educationally inevitable depends upon the socio-economic evolution of the purposes of education.

Public policy – the UK 1979–2000

As far as public policy in the UK is concerned there has been a remarkably consistent acceptance of the educational benefits of ICT over the past twenty years, irrespective of which political party has been in power nationally or locally. When the first semiconductor-based integrated circuits (silicon chips) were produced it became clear that their application would have an enormous impact in nearly all aspects of life. Shirley Williams, then Minister of Education in James Callaghan's Labour government, announced the first Microelectronics Education Project (MEP) in April 1979, just before the general election, which Labour lost. Margaret Thatcher's Conservative government came to power on a platform which included less central government, fewer Quangos (Quasi-autonomous non-governmental organizations) and reduced public expenditure. So MEP was clearly for the chop. However it was because of pressure from industrialists, particularly from hi-tech companies in the electronics and communications fields, that MEP was re-born that December. Since that time there has been a branch of the civil service in the ministry of education specifically responsible for encouraging the development of ICT use in schools. At the time of writing, there is a government minister who has specific responsibility for ICT developments in schools.

Following the end of MEP, the government set up first its MESU (Microelectronics education support unit), which was succeeded by its NCET (National Council for Educational Technology) and, in 1998, by BECTa (British Educational and Communications Technology Agency). In 1988 the government commissioned a three-year evaluation study of the impact of IT on children's achievements in primary and secondary schools. The ImpacT Study report was published in 1993. In 1993–1994 the NCET funded a large number of small projects using portable computing technology across the curriculum and throughout the 5–16 age range which were evaluated by the National Foundation for Educational Research (NFER) (see Stradling *et al.* 1994). Also in 1993, following a review of IT policy for schools at Key Stage 4, the government set up a number of subject guidance committees called CITS (Curriculum IT Support Groups) with membership drawn from the principal teachers' subject associations.

The term ICT is itself fairly new. It was generally called IT (Information Technology) until Sir Ron Dearing, former chairman of British Telecom, was called in to undertake a review of the National Curriculum for schools in England, Wales and Northern Ireland in 1994. The 1999 review has recently taken place. A general stipulation for those undertaking this review from David Blunkett, the Secretary of State for Education and Employment, was that each subject (with the exception of physical education at Key Stages 1 and 2) should strengthen the mandatory use of ICT.

Independently of the advent of ICT use in education a major event in mathematics education also took place at the end of the 1970s, during James Callaghan's premiership. This was the establishment of a commission of enquiry into the state of mathematics teaching, chaired by Sir William Cockcroft. By the time the committee's report *Mathematics Counts* was published in 1982 the electronic calculator had become commonplace, but computers were far from firmly established in schools. The report, then, discusses more about the potential for ICT use in mathematics in schools, than on lessons to be drawn from its use. The senior inspector of schools in mathematics at the time was Trevor Fletcher HMI (Her Majesty's Inspector of Schools).

In 1983 the government published Trevor Fletcher's discussion paper *Micro-computers and Mathematics in Schools* based on a year-long survey he undertook on ICT use in schools. That year the government sponsored a number of subject conferences to develop policy for the MEP. Trevor Fletcher chaired the mathematics group, whose edited report appeared in Mathematics in Schools in 1985. In 1986, as MEP neared its end, the government sponsored another round of subject conferences. The mathematics review was conducted by MEP's National Mathematics and Statistics CBL (computer-based learning) Review Panel, chaired by Adrian Oldknow. Its report *Will Mathematics Count?* was published by CET (Council for Educational Technology) in 1987. In 1993 the government sponsored another round of subject conferences about ICT, this time with a wider membership mainly drawn from the professional associations. The mathematics conference was also chaired by Adrian Oldknow who wrote its report. The reports from these conferences were not published, but were used by the government in drawing up its policy for the delivery of IT in secondary schools as Key Stage 4 (14–16) through subjects such as mathematics, science, technology and geography.

The government's Mathematics Curriculum IT Support Group was set up in 1993 with membership from the mathematics teachers' professional associations: the Association of Teachers of Mathematics (ATM) and the Mathematical Association (MA) under the chairmanship of Adrian Oldknow. It also had representation from the government's Department for Education and Employment (DfEE), its National Council for Educational Technology (NCET) and from the Office for Standards in Education (Ofsted, formerly HMI). This group published a range of materials to support the use of ICT tools in mathematics teaching. These included:

- data-capture and modelling in mathematics and science;
- developing IT across the mathematics department;
- dynamic geometry;
- mathematics and IT at work;
- mathematics and IT – a pupil's entitlement (primary and secondary versions);
- the IT Maths Pack.

Independently the professional associations have been publishing their own reports and resource material on ICT use in mathematics education. For example the ATM has produced:

- *Algebra at A-level: How the Curriculum might Change with CAS*;
- *Micromaths*, a quarterly journal;
- *Teaching, Learning and Mathematics with IT*;

and the MA has produced:

- *Computers in the Mathematics Curriculum*;
- *Graphic Calculators in the Mathematics Classroom*;
- *Spreadsheets: Exploring their Potential in Secondary Mathematics*;
- *Symbolic Manipulation by Computers and Calculators*.

The MA has now set up its own standing subcommittee on ICT, chaired by Adrian Oldknow (see http://www.m-a.org.uk). The government has also recently announced plans to support subject professional associations in developing in their subjects content accessible via the National Grid for Learning's Virtual Teacher Centre.

As a matter of public policy the government has set challenging targets for the training of all teachers in the use of ICT to support teaching and learning in their subjects. This applies equally to trainees undergoing a course of Initial Teacher Training (ITT) and to those currently in post. Funding has been provided from the National Lottery via the government's New Opportunities Fund (NOF) to train all eligible serving teachers throughout the UK in 1999–2003. The government's Teacher Training Agency (TTA) has provided a variety of printed and CD-ROM materials to support this training by enabling teachers to identify their training needs. Continuing support for teachers' professional development is currently being discussed under the terms of the newly formed General Teaching Council. The government has already alerted the subject professional associations that they will play an increasingly central role in defining and developing such CPD.

References to research from home and abroad

Against that background, we now provide a selective set of references to the extensive literature about ICT tools and the mathematics curriculum.

Calculators

Fey, J. and Hirsch, C. (1992) *Calculators in Mathematics Education*. Reston, Virginia: National Council of Teachers of Mathematics.

Foxman, D. (1996) *A Comparative Review of Research on Calculator Availability and Use, Ages 5–14*. London: SCAA.

Jones, S. and Tanner, H. (1997) 'Do calculators count?' *Micromath*, **13** (3), 31–6.
http://www.swan.ac.uk/education/research/smeg/calc/html

Ruthven, K. (1997) *The Use of Calculators at Key Stages 1–3*. London: SCAA Discussion Paper no. 9, March.

SCAA (1997) *The Use of Calculators at Key Stages 1–3*. London: SCAA.

Shuard, H., Walsh A., Goodwin, J. and Worcester, V. (1991) *Calculators, Students and Mathematics*. London: Simon and Schuster.

Graphic calculators and other personal, portable technology

Ainley, J. and Pratt, D. (1995) 'Planning for portability', in L. Burton and B. Jaworski (eds) *Technology in Mathematics Teaching*. Sweden: Chartwell-Bratt, 435–48.

Bowell, B., France, S. and Redfern, S. (1994) *Portable Computers in Action*. Coventry: NCET.

Dunham, P. H. and Dick, T. P. (1994) 'Research on graphing calculators'. *The Mathematics Teacher*, **87** (6), 440–45.

Hennessy, S. (1997) *Portable Technologies and Graphing Investigations: Review of the Literature*. CITE technical report No. 175. Open University: Institute of Educational Technology.

Hennessy, S., Fung, P. and Scanlon, E. (1999) *Portable Information technologies for supporting Graphical Mathematics Investigations: Findings of the PIGMI Project*. CITE technical report No. 187. Open University: Institute of Educational Technology.

Oldknow, A. (1995) 'Personal technology and new horizons', in L. Burton and B. Jaworski (eds) *Technology in Mathematics Teaching*. Sweden: Chartwell-Bratt, 97–108.

Oldknow, A. (1998) 'Personal computing technology: use and possibilities', in D. Tinsley and D. Johnson (eds) *Information and Communication Technologies in School Mathematics*. London: Chapman and Hall.

Penglase, M. and Arnold, S. (1996) 'The graphics calculator in mathematics education: A critical review of recent research'. *Mathematics Education Research Journal*, **8** (1), 58–90.

Ruthven, K. (1990) 'The influence of graphic calculator use on translation from graphic to symbolic forms'. *Educational Studies in Mathematics*, **21** (5), 431–50.

Smart, T. (1995) 'Visualisation, confidence and magic', in L. Burton and B. Jaworski (eds) *Technology in Mathematics Teaching*. Sweden: Chartwell-Bratt, 195–212.

Stradling R., Sims, D. and Jamison, J. (1994) *Portable Computers Pilot Evaluation Report*. Coventry: NCET.

Geometry and visualization

Coxeter, H. (1969) *Introduction to Geometry*. London: Wiley.

Goldstein, R. *et al.* (eds) (1996) *Dynamic Geometry*. Coventry: NCET.

Hoyles, C. (1998) 'A culture of proving in school mathematics?' in D. Tinsley and D. Johnson (eds) *Information and Communication Technologies in School Mathematics*. London: Chapman and Hall.

Hoyles, C. and Healey, L. (1997) 'Unfolding meanings for reflective symmetry'. *International Journal of Computers for Mathematical Learning*, **2**, 27–59.

Nemirovsky, R. and Noble, T. (1997) 'On mathematical visualization and the place where we live'. *Educational Studies in Mathematics*, **33**, 99–131.

Royal Society (2000) *Teaching and Learning Geometry pre-19*, (report of a Working Group chaired by Prof. A. Oldknow), London: Royal Society/JMC, in press.

Schumann, H. and Green, D. (1994) *Discovering Geometry with a Computer: using Cabri Géomètre*, Cartwell-Bratt.

Wells, D. (1991) *The Penguin Dictionary of Curious and Interesting Geometry*. London: Penguin.

Algebra and CAS

Barzel, B. *et al.* (1999) *New Technologies – New Means of Mathematics Teaching*. Holabrunn: Pedagogical Institute of Lower Austria.

Goldstein, R. *et al.* (1995) *Algebra at A-level: how the Curriculum might Change with Computer Algebra*. Derby: ATM.

Hunter, M *et al.* (1995) 'Using a computer algebra system with 14–15 year old students', in L. Burton and B. Jaworski (eds) *Technology in Mathematics Teaching*. Sweden: Chartwell-Bratt, 307–24.

Oldknow, A. and Flower, J. (eds) (1996), *Symbolic Manipulation by Computers and Calculators*. Leicester: Mathematical Association.

Royal Society (1996) *Teaching and Learning Algebra pre-19*, (report of a Working Group chaired by Prof. R. Sutherland) London: Royal Society/JMC.

Sutherland, R. (1995) 'Algebraic thinking: the Role of the Computer', in L. Burton and B. Jaworski (eds) *Technology in Mathematics Teaching*. Sweden: Chartwell-Bratt, 275–880.

Taylor, M. (1995) 'Calculators and computer algebra systems – their use in mathematics education'. *The Mathematical Gazette*, **79** (484), 68–83.

Computers and the mathematics classroom/curriculum

Ball, D. *et al.* (eds) (1987) *Will Mathematics Count?*. Hatfield: AUCBE.

Bennett, P. (1991) 'Effectiveness of the computer in the teaching of secondary school mathematics: 15 years of reviews of research'. *Educational Technology*, **31**, 44–8.

Bloomfield, A. and Harries, A. (eds) (1996) *Teaching, Learning and Mathematics with IT*. Derby: ATM.

Fletcher, T. (1983) *Microcomputers and Mathematics in Schools*. London: DES.

Goldstein, R. (1997) 'Integrating computers'. *Micromath, 13* (1), 25–7.

Great Britain (1982) *Mathematics Counts* (Report of the Committee of Enquiry into the Teaching of Mathematics in Schools: chair Dr. W. H. Cockcroft). London: HMSO.

Green, D. and Oldknow, A. (1996) *Developing IT across the Mathematics Department*. Coventry: NCET.

Hoyles, C. (ed.) *Girls and Computers* (Bedford Way Paper 34). London: Institute of Education.

Johnson, D. (1995) 'Information technology – the virtual reality of the school mathematics classroom', in *Proceedings of the First Asian Technology Conference in Mathematics*. Singapore.

Kaput, J. (1992) 'Technology and mathematics education', in D. Grouws (ed.) *Handbook of Research on Mathematics Teaching and Learning*. New York: MacMillan.

Kaput, J. (1998) *Technology as a Transformative Force in Math Education: Transforming Notations, Curriculum Structures, Content and Technologies*. NCTM Standards 2000 Technology Meeting.

Kieren, T. (1998) 'Towards an embodied view of the mathematics curriculum in a world of technology', in D. Tinsley and D. Johnson (eds) *Information and Communication Technologies in School Mathematics*. London: Chapman and Hall.

NCET (1995) *The IT Maths Pack*, ATM, Derby and MA, Leicester.

NCET (1995) *Mathematics and IT: A Pupil's Entitlement*. Coventry: NCET.

Noss, R. and Hoyles, C. (1996) *Windows on Mathematical Meaning*. Dordrecht: Kluwer.

Oldknow, A. (1985) 'Mathematics and microcomputers: a Pendley Manor report'. *Mathematics in Schools*, **14** (2), 26–8.

Oldknow, A. (ed.) (1995) *Mathematics and IT at work*. Coventry: NCET.

Oldknow, A. and Taylor, R. (1999) *Engaging Mathematics*. London: Technology Colleges' Trust.

Sutherland, R. (1998) 'Teachers and technology: the case of mathematical learning', in D. Tinsley and D. Johnson (eds) *Information and Communication Technologies in School Mathematics*. London: Chapman and Hall.

Sutherland, J. and Mason, J. (eds) *Exploiting Mental Imagery with Computers in Mathematics Education*, NATO ASI Series F Vol 138, Berlin: Springer.

Watson, D. (ed.) (1993). *The ImpacT report: an Evaluation of the Impact of Information Technology on Children's Achievements in Primary and Secondary Schools*. London: King's College.

The mathematics of change

Kaput, J. (2000) 'Technology as a transformation in math education ...' in E. Galinde (ed.) *Technology and the NCTM Standards 2000*. Reston, Va: NCTM (in press).

McFarlane, A., Friedler, Y., Warwick, P. and Chaplain, R. C. (1995) 'Developing an understanding of the meaning of line graphs in primary science investigations using portable computers and data logging software'. *Journal of Computers in Mathematics and Science Education*, **14**(4), 461–80.

Oldknow, A. and Taylor, R. (1998) *Data-capture and Modelling in Mathematics and Science*. Coventry: BECTa.

Chapter 5

Where is it all going?

In this chapter we attempt to take a peek into the future, and to look at how ICT, mathematics and mathematical pedagogy may develop in the next generation. At least this should raise the question: 'where is it going?', even if does not actually provide any very reliable answers!

Even trying to foresee the future a year ahead is a very dangerous pastime. But we thought we would have a go at trying to look at some of the pointers from the past to suggest some possible educational futures for maybe 15–20 years from now. Education has become a far more reactive process as politicians, commercial interests and pressure groups have targeted the process and content of education, not just its organizational structure. The culture of 'leave it to the professionals, they know best' has long since been left behind! But those of us working in education do have a duty to stand up for things we hold to be important. So, for the future health of mathematics education, we need to be aware of ways in which our tenets may be threatened, and perhaps start to organize ourselves in ways which can help protect our integrity. On a lighter note, this kind of speculation can also be a fun activity for discussion with a group of students on a Friday afternoon!

Again we need to consider past developments, and future scenarios, for all three players in our little drama: ICT, Mathematics and Education.

ICT has, arguably, the shortest past, at least if we take the silicon chip as being its starting point. However mass communication, particularly in the form of radio, television and the press, has had a major impact on national and international politics this century.

Totalitarian regimes have increasingly found it difficult to hide facts from their populace when radio and TV sets in homes can receive uncensored reports and images from other countries. Clearly, too, information and communication have been major factors in military intelligence (and espionage), and maybe in averting major international conflicts since the 1950s. In the late 1970s, as silicon chip technology was getting established, and its range of applications beginning to take shape, BBC TV showed a series of futuristic programs called *The Mighty Micro*. These were written and presented by the late Chris Evans, who worked at the National Physical Laboratories. It is salutary now to return to Evans' book, also called *The Mighty Micro*, and see just how many of its apparently wild prophecies are now realized, such as home shopping, the cashless society, on-line newspapers, etc. For example, this week one of us has bought an airline ticket from Gatwick to Glasgow on the internet, exchanged drafts of a conference report with an editor in Australia by e-mail (including digital photographs of participants) and transferred funds from a savings account to a current account through on-line banking. So many aspects of the 'cashless' (and 'armchair') society are already established.

ICT, society and the world of work

One major social change that ICT has already brought is the destruction of many, many jobs in what we may call 'processing' industries. For example as recently as the 1970s many companies had large spaces, known as 'drawing offices', where many highly skilled and respected employees, called 'draughtsmen', worked at drawing-boards to produce accurate and detailed drawings. These were the means of taking ideas from designers and putting them in a conventional form from which others could make objects. Now designers can use commercial CAD (Computer Aided Design) packages on computers directly to produce such drawings without need for the human go-between. Similarly in the 1960s all commercial aircraft carried a 'navigator' as a member of the flight crew. These have all been made redundant by various refinements in electronic (now satellite controlled) navigational aids. Increasingly those who originate ideas, designs, strategies etc. can document and disseminate them directly using ICT tools without need for the large force of employees who previously were the human information processors. Furthermore the manufacturing process has also become far more highly automated. Our (first) industrial revolution can be seen as really just replacing farm-work with labour-intensive machine minding. Not until the introduction of full-scale robotics in the last twenty years or so have we really seen automation of the manufacturing process, with its consequent loss of jobs.

So, according to many economists, the future employment needs of industry are at the extreme ends of the intellectual, and social scale. To maintain competitiveness there is a strong need for very creative, versatile and highly skilled designers. There will always be a range of more physical, mundane tasks where human musculature is better adapted (and more cost-effective) than a robotic solution. But the job-displacing effects of ICT do not end in industry. We have already seen a large shift in employment from production to the so-called 'service industries'. But just at the present time we are seeing the loss of many 'processing' jobs in commercial firms such as banks and other financial institutions.

These trends mean that we will continue to see large changes in the world of employment opportunities for our students in the years to come. They also mean that society needs to be re-evaluating the purpose of education. But as teachers we cannot afford to be complacent. If teaching is seen just to be about spreading knowledge, filling empty vessels, training people to do new tricks etc., then surely ICT can do our jobs more effectively and economically? New multi-national conglomerates are being formed from mergers between conventional publishers (including those of educational books) and so-called 'media-moguls' (with interests in broadcasting and/or newspapers), often also involving collaboration with computer (software, hardware and internet) companies. The thesis is that we now have the ICT means to provide mass-access to information, and that the next commercial task is to ensure that sufficient 'content' for each school subject becomes available. So, if we are willing to take a Gradgrind view of education, at least in the so-called 'academic' subjects, then we are indeed on the road to redundancy.

By the way, Thomas Gradgrind was the mill-owner in Charles Dickens' *Hard Times* who, according to Collins' Dictionary 'regulated all human things by rule and compass and the mechanical application of statistics, allowing nothing for sentiment, emotion and individuality'. An oft-quoted example of which is when he teaches his own children that 'a cow is a quadruped ruminant', as if we would ever do anything like that in mathematics!

So far, then, we have pointed, perhaps rather gloomily, to the past, and potential future, impact of ICT on employment. More optimistically we can expect advances in ICT to mean continual increases in processing speed, transfer rates, storage capacity, picture definition etc. at decreasing prices. Current developments in both display and connection technology will mean that schools will not have to adapt to the physical constraints imposed by current technology such as the shape of desk-top computers, monitors and other external displays or the position of power-points, network cabling, etc. In the near future we can expect that we can select and position the ICT tool to suit both the educational context and the physical characteristics of its built environment. Of course this applies equally well outside the school, in homes, libraries, museums, cafés, etc.

Implications for education and the curriculum

In thinking about future directions in education we need to be prepared to challenge some of our long-held conventions. In doing so we are not subscribing to any particular point of view, but we feel that it would be unhelpful, maybe catastrophic, to adopt an ostrich-like position towards the potential for change. By considering carefully such issues, which you may at first find rather depressing, we hope that you will be in a stronger position to justify the retention and enhancement of those aspects you feel are the most important and fundamental to the process of education.

There is nothing really magic about choosing a number like 30 for a reasonable class size. This is about the number of young people who can fill a standard-size classroom without excessive discomfort. In some educational circumstances this can be far too many, in others we see duplication with parallel classes being taught in the same way. We already accept divergence in several situations, for example with respect to specially equipped rooms for science or technology. In mathematics many schools choose to set, or band, students by ability, and usually prefer to accept larger group sizes for the upper bands to allow more personal attention in the lower ones. In the last century in England a typical Victorian primary school might have, say, 100 pupils under the direction of a single school-master or -mistress. He or she was the manager of the learning, and was supported by a group of helpers who might be senior pupils ('prefects' or 'monitors') or apprentice-teachers. This is a model still to be found in many universities where the professor gives a lecture to a large class, who then attend workshops (or 'labs') in smaller groups under the supervision of a graduate student. The main difference being that the university students are learning voluntarily (at least in theory), so that the monitor does not need to resort to physical violence to keep them on task!

So here are a few interesting questions for the future of schools and teachers! How can we organize schools in particular (and learning, more generally) in flexible ways which use ICT to best advantage in catering for the needs of our students? Of course, wrapped up in that is the question: 'How do we need to (re-)define the needs of our students, in terms of the knowledge, skills, understanding, social interactions, moral education etc., for them to take a full part in society?' Of course this implies that teachers will be able to take full advantage of the available ICT, and that has implications for their (i.e. your) continued professional development (CPD). But another, very live issue, is one that affects other professions, such as medicine, too. Do (or should) all teachers need to be equal, or would it be more effective to have some 'super-teachers' who give inspirational lead 'lectures', and are the real 'subject-experts', who are supported by groups of, perhaps less well-qualified (and paid) support teachers? Given the current problems in many countries of recruiting sufficient new mathematics teachers with good subject qualifications it would not be surprising if politicians were seeking to apply ICT in this way to alleviate such problems. We need to be able to distinguish between policies based on sound educational arguments and those addressing issues pragmatically, such as supply and demand of teachers, financial restraints on the global salary bill, etc. Is subject expertise all that matters, or is education a qualitatively different process from, e.g. medicine? Do teachers possess and practise important skills other than just subject knowledge? If so, can these be effectively articulated and valued (or have they already been sufficiently defined), or is the throwing away of baby-rich bath-water inevitable?

When considering such questions in the context of a particular subject on the (current) school curriculum we again need to be prepared to re-assess the arguments for the inclusion of the subject, especially in the case of mathematics where it is a compulsory subject of study for all students. In the UK there are about 600 so-called 'specialist schools', many of which are given extra funding to develop specialisms in the educational applications of ICT. These are organized through a body called the Technology Colleges Trust (TCT). In the recent report *Engaging Mathematics* for the TCT (Oldknow & Taylor 1999) we did some research on why employers take on those with mathematical qualifications (particularly graduates), and what skills they were particularly looking for. The clear and consistent finding was that they sought mathematical processing skills (like making hypotheses, gathering data, testing and validating models, communicating using symbols, diagrams, etc.), rather than any particular content knowledge, coupled with what they called the 'soft skills' (and we now call the 'core skills') of problem-solving, working in groups, communicating with others, competence with ICT etc. While there must be more to mathematics education than just meeting employers' needs we would be very perverse (and suicidal?) if we did not ensure that we can accommodate them as far as possible.

As an extreme example let us consider the place of calculus. In England & Wales the tradition has been that this is a subject to be taught to students in the 16–19 age-range within an examination subject called 'Pure Mathematics'. It involves learning a set of basic techniques in differentiation (e.g. chain rule) and integration (e.g. integration by parts). The techniques are usually practised by working through a set of textbook examples without any context, and then by working at past examination questions. Some formalized 'applications' are usually introduced, such as using differentiation to find the maximum of a function which, e.g., models the volume of a box, or by using integration to find the volume of a container by rotating the area under a curve. Now this takes no account of the historical context of the development of calculus by Leibniz and Newton, who were trying to solve the differential equations resulting from predictive models in physical science. It certainly isn't approached at this stage as a rigorous branch of 'pure mathematics' in the current usage of that term. Computer Algebra Systems (CAS), such as *Derive*, are designed to perform such 'processing tasks' as symbolic differentiation and integration, and are extensively used in industry, commerce and research where such techniques need to be accurately and quickly applied. So, when designing mathematics curricula for the future, at any level, we must be much more explicit about the rationale for inclusion of aspects of content in terms of the needs its study will fulfil.

We also need to be more prepared to examine the rationale for teaching subjects in isolation. This varies between countries, but the UK position in schools has moved towards greater curricular isolation. However the students currently go to lessons in a range of subjects, many of which have features in common, such as their use of data. In a time of concentration on 'joined-up' politics perhaps we should be looking at providing more 'joined-up' education. To some extent the use of ICT can be a catalyst in this process. We are currently working with a group of teachers in mathematics, science, geography, design technology and physical education in the use of ICT across subjects, particularly hand-held devices such as graphing calculators, data-loggers and OHP displays used with computers, across subjects. Early aspects of that work were reported by Oldknow and Taylor (1998), and more recent aspects by Ransom (1999).

Mathematics is fundamental to technological development

So we have considered some possible developments in both ICT and education. But what of mathematics itself? There are some now well established links between mathematics and aspects of computing such as networks, digital logic, coding etc. Similarly a variety of mathematics courses have been established, with titles like 'Discrete Mathematics' or 'Decision Mathematics', specifically to complement studies in information technology or the like. Yet it is often the unexpected applications of the less obviously applicable branches of mathematics which are the most exciting. For example, geometry is a subject which is rapidly disappearing from the curriculum both in schools and in universities in the UK. Clearly computational geometry (the design of efficient algorithms for graphical displays) is very important for a whole range of computer graphics. However it is in this field that an unlikely application for fractal geometry has emerged. The English-born mathematician, Michael Barnsley, has pioneered the use of Iterated Function Systems (IFS) as a means of efficiently transmitting high resolution images for digital television. Consider the following image of a fern leaf. To transmit the set of 0's and 1's corresponding to the black and white dots (called 'pixels') of each such leaf takes a considerably greater amount of time than transmitting the algorithm (i.e. procedure) from which the image can be drawn using the computing facilities built-in to new digital TV sets.

Essentially the idea is to generate a random sequence of points $\mathbf{v}_r = (x_r, y_r)$ using a randomly chosen 'affine transformation' from a set of maybe four possible such transformations, each applied with different probabilities.

The algorithm is:

> **Choose a starting point v0 , set r = 0**
>
> **Repeatedly**
>
> > **Generate a random number p between 0 and 1**
> >
> > **Use this to pick the matrix A_k and vector b_k,**
> >
> > **Generate the next point by $v_{r+1} = A_k v_r + b_k$,**
> >
> > **Plot it**
> >
> > **Set r to $r+1$**

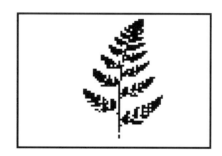

For example, the following data were used to plot the fractal fern with a TI-83:

$k = 1$ $0.00 \leq p < 0.02$ $A_1 = \begin{pmatrix} 0 & 0 \\ 0 & 0.27 \end{pmatrix}$ $b_1 = \begin{pmatrix} 0.5 \\ 0 \end{pmatrix}$

$k = 2$ $0.02 \leq p < 0.17$ $A_2 = \begin{pmatrix} -0.139 & 0.263 \\ 0.246 & 0.2224 \end{pmatrix}$ $b_2 = \begin{pmatrix} 0.57 \\ -0.036 \end{pmatrix}$

$k = 3$ $0.17 \leq p < 0.30$ $A3 = \begin{pmatrix} 0.17 & -0.215 \\ 0.222 & 0.176 \end{pmatrix}$ $b_3 = \begin{pmatrix} 0.408 \\ 0.0893 \end{pmatrix}$

$k = 4$ $0.30 \leq p < 1.00$ $A_4 = \begin{pmatrix} 0.781 & 0.034 \\ -0.032 & 0.739 \end{pmatrix}$ $b_4 = \begin{pmatrix} 0.1075 \\ 0.27 \end{pmatrix}$

The following program was used to produce the fractal:

```
Func:FnOff:PlotsOff: ClrDraw:0.13→I:0.13→J:0.5→V:0→W
0.1→Xmin:1.1→Xmax:0→Xscl:0.1→Ymin:1.1→Ymax:0→Yscl
[[0,0,0.5,0,0.27,0][-0.139,0.263,0.57,0.246,0.224, -0.036]
[0.17, -0.215,0.408,0.222,0.176,0.0893]
[0.781,0.034,0.1075, -0.032,0.739,0.27]]→[A]
While 2>1
Pt-On(V+I,W+J):rand→R:1→K
If R>0.02:2→K
If R>0.17:3→K
If R>0.30:4→K
V*[A](K,1)+W*[A](K,2)+[A](K,3) →Z:V*[A](K,4)+W*[A](K,5)+[A](K,6) →W
Z→V
End
```

Number Theory has seemed to be one of the least applicable aspects of mathematics, but now it underpins the data encryption algorithms essential for the secure transmission of information of all sorts, from bank transfers to calls on mobile phones. So 'blue sky' research in pure mathematics still has a strong claim for public support, even if there are no immediate prospects of applications. However it is also clear that the number of users of ICT tools far exceeds the number of researchers needed to develop new tools. So again we have another example where hard decisions may need to be made about the balance of resources to be devoted to training new researchers as opposed to the more general education required to support the needs of industry and commerce.

So it is clear that change is here to stay! It is also clear that mathematics will continue to play a vital part in both the development of ICT, and in its effective application in the world outside education. What is less clear is the ability of the mathematics education community, at all levels, to articulate just how vital mathematical skills are, and how their nurture and development in new generations of students is a creative and expert task quite distinct from training. If we can achieve this we can truly claim to be integrating ICT into teaching and learning, rather than preparing the ground for our replacement by it!

We very much hope you have enjoyed reading this book, and that it has given you the stimulus both to integrate ICT into your own teaching, and to face the challenges which the future will inevitably bring.

References

Oldknow, A. and Taylor, R. (1998) *Data-capture and Modelling in Mathematics and Science*. Coventry: BECTa.

Oldknow, A. and Taylor, R. (1999) *Engaging Mathematics*. London: Technology Colleges' Trust.

Ransom, P., (1999) *Collaborative Approaches to Teaching and Learning in Secondary Mathematics, Science and Related Subjects through the use of Low-cost Portable Technology*. London: TTA.

Appendix

Loading and running software

SOURCES OF SOFTWARE (AND GCs) USED IN THE BOOK

This book is accompanied by a CD-ROM for *MS Windows*™-based computers, produced by Texas Instruments. This contains 30-day trial copies of the full versions of *TI Interactive!* and *Derive for Windows V.5*. It also contains a demonstration version of *Cabri Géomètre* which has most of the functions of the full version. For information about ordering full copies of each of these see the TI website: `http://www.ti.com/calc/` . In the UK these can be obtained from educational suppliers such as:

Chartwell-Yorke 114 High Street, Belmont, Bolton, Lancs, BL7 8AL.
Tel: 01204 811001   Fax: 01204 811008   `Orders@ChartwellYorke.com`
`http://www.ChartwellYorke.com/`

Oxford Educational Supplies Unit 19, Weston Business Park, Weston on the Green, Bicester OX6 8SY.
Tel: 01869 343369   Fax: 01869 343654
`Sales@Oxford-Educational.co.uk`
`http://www.oxford-educational.co.uk/`

QED Books Pentagon Place, 195 Berkhamsted Road, Chesham, Bucks HP5 3AP.
Tel: 0345 402275   Fax: 01494 793951   `QED@talk21.com`

There are also files to support a variety of models of TI graphing calculators (GC), such as the TI-83 and TI-83 Plus used in this book. These include the GraphLink software to enable you to exchange programs and data between your PC or laptop and the GC using a suitable cable. There are also GC programs to support the use of the Calculator Based Ranger (CBR) and Calculator Based Laboratory (CBL) which can be transferred to your GC using the cable. Other useful sources of support can be found on the Vernier Inc website at `http://www.vernier.com/`. For information about obtaining TI graphing calculators, the GraphLink cable, the CBR and

CBL, as well as other related products, see the TI website. In the UK these can be obtained from educational suppliers such as:

Oxford Educational Supplies (see above).

Science Studio Systems Hanborough Park, Long Hanborough, Witney, OX8 8LH.
Tel: 01993 883598   Fax: 01993 883317
calculators@sciencestudio.co.uk
http://www.sciencestudio.co.uk/

For further information contact:

Texas Instruments UK Ltd (Guy Harris) 800 Pavilion Drive, Northampton Business Park, Northampton NN4 7YL.
Tel: 01604 663003   Fax: 01604 663004
gharris@ti.com http://www.ti.com/calc/uk/

TI loan programme (Sue Prestage) Tel: 020 8230 3184   Fax: 020 8230 3132
ticares@msn.com http://www.ti.com/calc/uk/loan.htm

T-cubed England & Wales (Ros Hyde)
http://www.t3ww.org/docs/england.htm

Nearly all *MS Windows*™-based educational computers, and many home computers, will have been supplied with a version of the *MS Excel*™ spreadsheet already loaded. There are also spreadsheet facilities in both *MS Works*™ and in *TI Interactive!*

The other software used in this book consists of the programming languages *MSW Logo*™ and *TrueBasic*™. *MSW Logo*™ is made available free of charge from Softronix: http://www.softronix.com/ . To download and install it there is a convenient link to "Free Software" on the Mathematical Association (MA) website at: http://www.m-a.org.uk/ .

The Mathematical Association 259 London Road, Leicester, LE2 3BE.
Tel: 0116 270 3877   Fax: 0116 244 8508   Offmanma@aol.com

TrueBasic™ is an up-to-date version of Basic for Windows. There is both a demonstration copy of this, and a free version for MS-DOS, which can be obtained from TrueBasic Inc. at http://www.truebasic.com/ or downloaded from the MA website above. In the UK, full copies can be obtained from:

Asher Research 16 Wellsworth Lane, Rowlands Castle, Hants PO9 6BY.
Tel: 023 9241 2668   Fax: 023 9241 3579   hbillam@asher.u-net.com

The MA website also gives links to demonstration and/or trial versions of many other useful pieces of educational software, such as the graph plotting software packages: *Autograph*, *Coypu* and *Omnigraph*.

Software to support the teaching of Number, and *Cabri* files to support the teaching of Shape, Space and Measures can be obtained from the ATM:

Association of Teachers of Mathematics 7, Shaftesbury Street, Derby, DE23 8YB. Tel: 01332 346599   Fax: 01332 204357   `http://www.atm.org.uk/`

FILES TO SUPPORT THE BOOK

For convenience, a large number of files supporting the illustrations used in the book are available from the Texas Instruments UK website: `http:/www.ti.com/calc/uk/` . These files are organized under the folder titles: Basic, Cabri, Derive, Excel, Exe, Logo, Pictures, TI-83, TII, Word.

The Basic, Cabri, Derive and Logo folders contain copies of the programs, worksheets and drawings used in the book. The Excel, TI-83 and TII folders contain copies of the data-sets, programs, spreadsheets etc. The Pictures folder contains a copy of the Sydney Harbour bridge photograph (p. 143). The Word folder contains examples of some of the forms, such as worksheets and review sheets, as well as a catalogue of which files relate to which pages of the book.

In the Exe folder are the programs GLASS, BEARINGS and TRANSFORM (Chapter 1B, pp. 13–15). These have been written in TrueBasic, and compiled in such a way that they should run in any Windows PC or laptop, whether or not TrueBasic is installed. That means they are 'executable' files, and are stored as, e.g., GLASS.EXE . So when you download any of these files and store them on your computer they can be run just by double-clicking on their name from whichever folder you have stored them in.

Index

DH